Electronic Projects for Musicians.

by Craig Anderton.

To access companion recorded audio online, visit:
www.halleonard.com/mylibrary

"Enter Code"
2810-2073-4375-2015

ISBN 978-0-8256-9502-5

HAL•LEONARD®

Visit Hal Leonard Online at
www.halleonard.com

Contact us:
Hal Leonard
7777 West Bluemound Road
Milwaukee, WI 53213
Email: info@halleonard.com

In Europe, contact:
Hal Leonard Europe Limited
42 Wigmore Street
Marylebone, London, W1U 2RN
Email: info@halleonardeurope.com

In Australia, contact:
Hal Leonard Australia Pty. Ltd.
4 Lentara Court
Cheltenham, Victoria, 3192 Australia
Email: info@halleonard.com.au

Cover design and art direction by Pearce Marchbank
Cover photography by George Taylor
Book design by Dudley Thomas
Schematic drafting by Craig Anderton
Illustrations by Vespa Copestakes
Soundsheet production by Craig Anderton
Edited by Janice Insola and Henry Rasof

Foreword

This book is long overdue. Many times I've heard musicians say: "I don't know a thing about the insides, but . . . " And I must admit I've been frustrated enough to smash a few things myself. If I'd had an organized reference to start with, countless hours would have been saved.

Electronics is scary at first; it appears to be a maze only a logarithm expert can get through. But not so, and this book proves it. In fact, you don't ever have to know what you're doing to learn, although it sure helps. Start at the beginning, be thorough, and apply what you learn. Don't get discouraged and don't worry. You never reach a stage where you know it all. "Gadgetry" is a very cumulative study. Some things refuse to work for pretty silly reasons, and it's not always the gadget's fault (you forgot to plug it in!).

Lastly, any level of becoming familiar with the electronics of your instrument can only make you a better player and can even save a gig.

So, fellow tinkerers, good luck, and I couldn't think of a better place to begin than right where you are.

JOE WALSH

Contents

Preface

As of this date, tens of thousands of musicians—many with no prior experience in electronics—have taken control of their sound, by building electronic modifiers from the first edition of this book. Beginners should be happy to know that the instructional material from the first edition has been left intact, and in some cases has been expanded. Those who have thoroughly absorbed the information in the first edition will be pleased to find a number of new and improved projects, as well as additional information on creating pedalboards and multiple effects systems, explanations on the theory of operation of the various projects, and ways to modify them for customized performance. So, while this new edition was still expressly written with beginners in mind, I believe there is enough additional material to hold the musician's interest even after he or she has passed the introductory stage of learning about this art.

One of the questions I consistently hear is, "But can I *really* build this stuff, even though I know nothing about electronics?" The answer is yes. My files are filled with letters from people who express amazement and delight at having built a high-technology device, by themselves, without any problems. If they can do it, if I can do it (remember I was once a beginner too!), then you can do it.

Why do it yourself? Perhaps a better question is why *not* do it yourself. While you generally save money compared with buying a commercially available device, you also have the satisfaction of creating something with your own two hands, and you learn enough about the project in the process of building it so that you can modify it to suit your exact needs. A less tangible, but perhaps more important, advantage is the increase in self-confidence that comes from knowing that you can make sense out of all those wires and parts, and turn them into a useful, working project. I've known numerous people who thought they'd *never* understand this stuff; but when they do, they feel a little better about themselves and their abilities because of it.

It took longer to rewrite this book than it did to write it in the first place, mostly because I wanted the projects to be equal to—and, if possible, superior to—other, comparable devices available on the market. This has meant that generally, the projects are somewhat more complex than those presented in the first book; however, over the years I've found that anybody who can successfully build a project with one IC and ten other parts can also successfully build a project with two ICs and twenty other parts. There are still a number of introductory projects, essentially unchanged from the first edition, for those who prefer to start off with something *really* simple.

In closing, I'd like to thank several people who otherwise might not get the recognition they deserve. First is Vesta Copestakes, a constant source of inspiration and a very fine illustrator/photographer; Jim Crockett, publisher of *Guitar Player* magazine, who first recognized the need for a book like this; Bill Godbout, for his technical assistance; Bruce Mycroft, for laying out the circuit boards so I could spend all my time writing; and the people at Music Sales (my publisher), who didn't hassle me or try to speed me up when I kept asking for more time to make this manuscript as good as I could possibly make it. Finally (save the best until last), thanks to all the people who enjoyed the first edition of this book—your support and your comments are the reason why this revised edition exists. May your projects always keep working!

Chapter One

If you don't know what a resistor is, don't know how to read a schematic, and wouldn't know a $10\mu F$ capacitor if you collided with one, Chapter 1 is for you.

A Little Theory

If you really want to get into theory, libraries, book stores, and electronic stores all have books about basic electronics. But for now, let's simply take a quick look at four important concepts: *voltage, current, resistance,* and *capacitance.* You don't really have to understand it all just yet; the important thing is to get a feel for the language.

Electricity is all about the motion of electrons. Electrons are all over the place as component parts of atoms, but when they're located inside the atoms of certain materials known as *conductors* (like wire, or other metals), you can play games with them. Actually, the motion of electrons in a conductor is a lot like traffic flow down a freeway. Wire is sort of a freeway for electrons; electrons are like little cars. If a bunch of cars are sitting in the middle of a highway out of gas, not much is happening. But give them a little energy, direct them (i.e., stay to the right, pass on the left, stop at red lights), and you've got an active freeway. Same with electrons: give them some energy, tell them what to do, and you've got an active conductor, which is the first step toward an active circuit. The opposite of a conductor is called an *insulator;* rather than encouraging the flow of electrons, it inhibits the flow, much as removing a section of highway guarantees that no cars are going to be traveling over that particular section.

Current is analogous to the number of cars going down the road. Just as bumper-to-bumper cars mean heavy traffic, bumper-to-bumper electron flow is considered heavy current. The measurement unit for current is the *ampere* (*amp* or *A* for short), named after the French scientist André Marie Ampère.

Voltage is a somewhat more elusive phenomenon to explain. It relates to the *intensity* of electron flow, rather than just dealing with the number of electrons going down a conductor. With our automobile analogy, voltage would be equivalent to the speed of the car in mph. A condition in a circuit where there is no voltage present is referred to as *ground*, or minimum possible intensity (zero volts—the *volt*, abbreviated *V*, measures voltage). There are still just as many electrons hanging around; but they have no intensity, and don't do anything. A more intense level of activity translates into higher voltage.

What provides this intensity? Well, in electrical circuits you need an area that lacks electrons and wants to acquire some, and an area that has a surplus of electrons. (The best example of this is a battery: one terminal is loaded with electrons just waiting to get out and do their number, whereas the other terminal is begging to have electrons come in.) The intensity with which the electrons want to get from one end to the other is the voltage. The medium through which the electrons make their journey from one area to another is the conductor.

This brings us to *resistance.* The reason for resistance is that when the electrons try to get from one area to the other through the conductor, they are always trying to move as quickly as they can, and you have to control them in some way. All conductors represent a certain amount of resistance, since no conductor is 100 percent efficient. To control electron flow in a predictable manner, you use *resistors*; these are electrical parts similar to conductors, but which resist to a greater or lesser extent the flow of current. Putting one in line with a conductor is like putting up a 50-mph zone in the middle of a highway: the energy level decreases, yielding a more controlled flow. The resisting ability of a resistor is expressed in *ohms* (named after Georg Simon Ohm, a German physicist of the 1800s and abbreviated by the Greek letter omega, Ω), and can cover a wide range. Ten million ohms will turn an electrical stream into a trickle, whereas 4 Ω won't slow things down much at all (that's why speakers have a low resistance value; you want as many electrons as possible to go through the speaker and move the paper cone back and forth to make things loud).

A close relative of resistance is *impedance*. Impedance is a measurement that's useful in analyzing the performance of audio circuits; just as resistance tells you something about how electrical current flows through a circuit, impedance tells you how audio signals flow through a circuit. To completely understand impedance takes some doing, since we're dealing with a pretty complex subject; so, aside from some additional information on impedance in the section, "Understanding Specifications: Glossary of Terms" at the end of this book, we won't delve into this any further.

There's one other word that needs examination while we're talking about theory: *capacitance*. Capacitors store energy as their primary talent; they are made of two metal plates, separated by a thin insulator. Connecting a voltage source to these plates creates an electric field between them. Storing energy in this field is called charging a capacitor, whereas drawing the energy out (say, through a conductor or resistor) is called discharging. This charge-discharge action allows a current to flow, even though the plates are insulated. Due to this property of a capacitor to react to alternating (charging and discharging) current, or AC, capacitors are frequently used to block direct current (DC, the kind that stays steady, like from a battery) but let alternating audio-type signals through. More capacitance indicates more energy storage capability.

Resistors

By far, the most common resistor you'll encounter is the carbon-composition type (so called because it's mostly made up of carbon materials), shown in Figure 1-1. They are small [6-12 mm (1/4 -1/2") long, by 3.6 mm (1/8 -1/4") wide], brown or tan cylinders with colored bands going around them. If you take a look inside any electronic equipment, you'll see a whole bunch of resistors. In some cases, you'll see metal-film resistors as opposed to the standard carbon composition type. These are usually somewhat smaller than carbon types, and are lighter in color.

The most striking feature of a resistor is the four color bands. These bands form a code which indicates the approximate value of the resistor. The reason I say "approximate value" is because precise resistance values are generally not that critical in electronic circuits (remember the speed zone analogy given earlier: very rarely do you see a 33.7-mph speed limit, since 35 mph is close enough). One of the bands will be either gold or silver; this one, called the *fourth band,* indicates the *tolerance*

(or, how much it can vary from its stated value) of the resistor. A silver band indicates 10% accuracy; a gold band, 5%. The other three bands represent the value, in ohms, of the resistor.

Figure 1-1

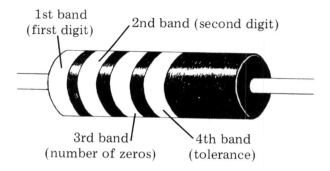

1st band (first digit) 2nd band (second digit) 3rd band (number of zeros) 4th band (tolerance)

Each number from zero to nine is assigned a color: 0 = black, 1 = brown, 2 = red, 3 = orange, 4 = yellow, 5 = green, 6 = blue, 7 = violet, 8 = gray, 9 = white. Now, the first band is the first digit of the resistor value, the second band is the second digit of the resistor value, and the third band is the *number of zeros* that follow the first two digits.

So, if you have a resistor that reads "blue-gray-red-silver," that means the first digit is blue, or 6; the second digit is gray, or 8; and the red band means that two zeros follow the first two digits. Putting it all together, you get 6-8-00, or 6800 Ω. The silver band indicates that the real-world value is within 10% of 6800 Ω.

Another example: brown-black-green-gold. This decodes to first digit 1, second digit 0, and five zeros. So you have 1-0-00000, or 1,000,000Ω. The gold band indicates that the real value is within 5% of 1,000,000 Ω.

To simplify matters, there are certain standard resistor values. The first *two digits* of any 10% tolerance resistor will be one of the following combinations: 10, 12, 15, 18, 22, 27, 33, 39, 47, 56, 68, 82. For example, you won't run across a 19,000 Ω, 10% resistor, nor will you see a 350 Ω one, because the first two digits are not standard 10% values.

So that electronics people don't spend a large portion of their time drawing zeros in resistor values, there are two commonly used abbreviations: k and *M*. k stands for a thousand, and *M* a million—a 22,000 Ω resistor, for example, is commonly called a 22k resistor. A 1,000,000 Ω resistor is called a 1M resistor, a 2,200,000 Ω resistor is called a 2.2M resistor. The abbreviation k was derived from the somewhat longer kilohm, which you'll sometimes see in print; you'll also sometimes see megohm or Meg instead of the simpler M.

Schematics from Europe, and most other parts of the world, abbreviate resistors values a little differently from

American schematics; when a resistor value includes a decimal point (i.e., 2.7k, 1.2M), the k or M is inserted where the decimal point would normally appear. Here are some examples of American nomenclature and the metric equivalents:

American	Metric
2.7k	2k7
4.7k	4k7
2.2M	2M2
5.6M	5M6

If there is no decimal point in the resistor value, then the metric and American designations are the same (Ω is used in both American and metric systems).

In addition to the stated value in ohms, another concern of resistors is how much heat they can handle. In the process of slowing down electrical energy, the dissipated energy has to go somewhere—it generally turns into heat. Resistors are rated in *watts* (abbreviated *W*), the unit of power, in regard to their ability to handle heat. For example, a 2W resistor can handle more power than a 1W type. However, the projects in this book aren't involved with heavy currents, so we'll mostly be using 1/4W resistors. These have the advantage of being physically smaller than 1/2W resistors, the other most popular type. You can always use a larger wattage resistor than the one specified if there's room, but never use a smaller resistor. An underrated resistor can overheat, thus changing its value and possibly damaging the circuit to which it connects.

Figure 1-2 shows some other types of resistors you may run across in electronic devices from time to time, such as power resistors (not just 1W — sometimes 10- or 20W in hefty power supplies); precision resistors (where you need an exact resistance value, and 5% tolerance isn't good enough); and metal film (low noise) resistors. Metal film resistors are great for audio projects, but they can cost plenty. Sometimes you can pick up metal film resistors surplus for a fraction of the original cost, which is worth it. Otherwise, stick to the common carbon composition type.

Potentiometers

Potentiometers (or *pots*, as they're commonly called) are members of the resistor family, except that they are variable resistors. As you can see in Figure 1-3, a potentiometer is just a circular resistance element with a sliding conductor called a *wiper* going across it. A pot serves the same function in electrical circuits that a faucet does in plumbing, namely, to regulate current flow. The most common example of a pot is the volume control on your amp or radio.

Figure 1-2

1/4W resistor

1/2W resistor

1W resistor

14.7K1%
metal film, precision resistor

800 OHM
10W power resistor

Figure 1-3

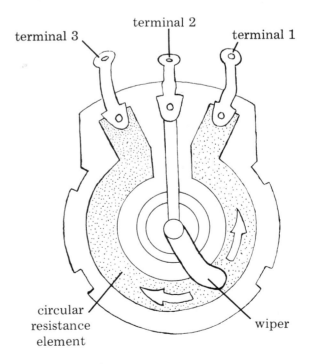
terminal 3   terminal 2   terminal 1

circular resistance element   wiper

You'll note that there are actually two variable resistors in a pot; as the resistance between terminals 1 and 2 gets smaller due to moving the sliding conductor toward terminal 1, the resistance between terminals 2 and 3 gets larger. Moving the wiper in the opposite direction produces opposite results. Sometimes you need to use both resistance elements, but many times you'll only use one. If you connect up terminals 2 and 3 or 1 and 2 only, you have what is called a *rheostat.* However, to simplify matters we'll refer to anything that's a variable resistance control as a pot.

One other characteristic of pots, *taper,* might cause some confusion. The taper of a pot is another word for the rate at which the resistance element changes. The most common taper is *linear,* which means that there is a linear change in resistance that occurs when you move the pot — turning it halfway gives half the resistance, a quarter of the way gives a quarter of the resistance, two-thirds of the way gives two-thirds the resistance, and so on. A *log* taper pot, however, has its resistance increase logarithmically from one end to the other. This means that turning the pot up halfway covers only about 10% of the pot's total resistance; turning the pot up two-thirds of the way covers about 40% of the total resistance; and as you get past this point, each degree of rotation of the control continues to cover a progressively greater amount of resistance. The reason for producing a control that follows a logarithmic characteristic is because the human ear itself responds to sounds in a logarithmic fashion; that is, for a sound to appear to steadily increase in volume, you have to actually increase the sound in progressively larger amounts—or logarithmically, in mathematical terms (see Figure 1-4). As a result, in volume controls it is frequently more desirable to have a logarithmic resistance change to compensate for the characteristics of human ears. Electrically speaking, however, a linear taper pot (which is easier to find) will do the job just as well as a log pot, although the action might not feel as good.

Figure 1-4
A volume change like this (a) sounds like this (b) to your ear.

Potentiometers come in a variety of styles (see Figure 1-5). The most common is the single rotary pot, although linear slide pots are gaining in popularity, especially in imported consumer elctronic equipment. Additionally,

sometimes one or more potentiometer elements are combined, producing a two-or-more-section ganged pot. Pots can also come with an on-off switch mounted on the back. Miniature pots for set-and-forget-type applications called *trimpots* also exist. These are electrically equivalent to regular pots, but are physically tiny and not designed for continuous handling. They usually mount with other components on a printed circuit board.

Good pots are unfortunately hard to obtain in small quantities at low cost. Adequate pots are fairly easy to find. Some pots are sealed from the outside air; this prevents dust and pollution from coating the resistance element and giving scratchy noises, as well as producing a more reliable device. Most common pots, however, are not hermetically sealed and are subject to long-term deterioration. Therefore, when you use pots in a project always make sure they are accessible and removable. You'll be glad you did a few years on down the road.

Figure 1-5
Clockwise from upper left-hand corner: a dual-section ganged pot, a single-section rotary pot, a rotary pot with an on-off switch mounted on the back, a miniature trimpot, and a linear slide pot.

Capacitors

There are three main characteristics that interest us as far as *capacitors* ("caps" for short) are concerned: the value (amount of capacitance), the working voltage (how much voltage the capacitor can withstand), and the size. Capacitors vary widely in size (unlike resistors, there is no "standard" capacitor package), and for some smaller projects it's a good idea to make sure that the capacitor you need can fit in the box that you've got.

A capacitor's value is expressed in *farads,* with one complication. A farad is a whole lot of capacitance—far too much to be usable in many electronic circuits. Therefore, capacitors are usually rated in microfarads (abbreviated μF; in older literature, the abbreviations *mfd* and *mf* are sometimes used), a microfarad being one-millionth of a farad (0.000001 farads). There are even some very low capacitance capacitors that are valued in micromicrofarads (a millionth of a millionth of a farad—pretty tiny!) Several years ago this was abbreviated as $\mu\mu F$, but nowadays the prefix *pico* usually replaces the prefix micromicro, and pico is certainly shorter and easier to deal with. A picofarad abbreviates as *pF*. Don't be confused—a pF is the same as a $\mu\mu F$, just a more modern name.

As in the case of resistors, schematics in most other parts of the world designate capacitor values in a different way from American schematics. First of all, in addition to the μF and pF, these schematics frequently use the term nanofarad (abbreviated *nF*). A nanofarad is equivalent to 0.000000001 farads. Here are some common capacitor values, expressed in μF, pF, and nF:

$$0.001\,\mu F = 1,000\,pF = 1nF$$
$$0.01\,\mu F = 10,000\,pF = 10nF$$
$$0.1\,\mu F = 100,000\,pF = 100nF$$

When a capacitor value includes a decimal point (i.e., 1.2 μF, 4.7 pF, 2.2 nF), the μ, p, or n is inserted where the decimal point would normally appear. Here are some examples of American nomenclature and the metric equivalents:

American	Metric
1500pF	1n5
4.7μF	4μ7
0.22μF	220nF
6.8pF	6p8

While the metric system of nomenclature may appear more complex at first, in actuality it is a more efficient, and less ambiguous, way to designate resistor and capacitor values. One advantage of the metric system is that

it's almost impossible to put a decimal point in the wrong place accidentally, as the metric nomenclature strives to avoid the use of decimal points altogether. Another advantage of the metric system is that you don't end up with big numbers—an otherwise clumsy 3900 pF becomes 3n9 in metric, which is much more concise.

Working voltage simply means the voltage up to which a capacitor will work reliably. If a capacitor is rated, at, say, 35V and you connect it to a point in the circuit with 40V, you will get a warm capacitor or a nonfunctioning one very shortly. Except for highly unusual cases, you can always use a capacitor with a working voltage higher than the one specified. It is not uncommon to have capacitors rated at 100V or more in a circuit powered by a 9V battery, simply because one rated at 100V may be easier to find or cheaper than one rated at 9V. In most any circuit, as long as the capacitors have a higher working voltage than the voltage of the power supply feeding the circuit, you're covered.

Size is inconsequential to proper electrical operation, but in terms of packaging it can get you into trouble. Capacitor size (as a rough rule of thumb) increases with either higher capacitance or more working voltage. If you're putting a circuit in a small box, a 1000μF capacitor rated at 10V might fit perfectly, but one rated at 100V may be bigger than the box itself. For this reason catalogs frequently specify capacitor dimensions right along with working voltage and capacitance.

There are two basic types of capacitors we'll be using: *disc* types and *electrolytics* (see Figure 1-6). Disc capacitors all look pretty much the same—a round, fairly flat ceramic blob of variable size with two wires coming out of it. They generally have fairly high working voltages

Figure 1-6

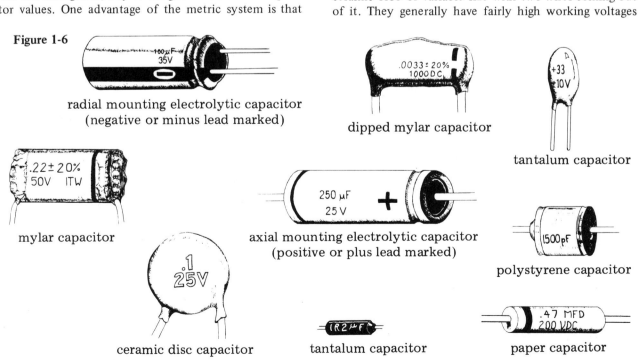

radial mounting electrolytic capacitor
(negative or minus lead marked)

dipped mylar capacitor

tantalum capacitor

mylar capacitor

axial mounting electrolytic capacitor
(positive or plus lead marked)

polystyrene capacitor

ceramic disc capacitor

tantalum capacitor

paper capacitor

(ratings of 500V are common on smaller values), but limited amounts of capacitance. Most discs can't get much more than .2μF packed into them; above that, they get impossibly big. Common disc capacitor values are 0.001, 0.005, 0.01, 0.05, 0.1, and 0.2μF. Disc capacitors can even give very small values like 10 pF. These are about 6.2 mm (1/4") in diameter, whereas sometimes like a 0.2μF disc can be about 2.5 cm (1") round.

Unlike the disc types, *electrolytic capacitors* are tubular, and have either *axial* or *radial* mounting. They also have one other quality: they are polarized. This means that electrolytic capacitors have a plus (+) and minus (-) end, just like a battery, and like a battery, if you hook up the plus and minus backwards it won't work right. On most capacitors, only one lead is marked for polarity—imported capacitors usually mark the minus end, American ones generally indicate the plus (why, I don't know). Although resistors and disc capacitors aren't polarized, many other electronic parts are, and it's important to hook the ends up correctly. One of the more common errors encountered in building electronic stuff is to miss the polarity of an electrolytic capacitor, a transistor, or what have you; so be careful.

A lot of capacitance can be squeezed into an electrolytic—they may go up to 40,000μF or more. For audio work requiring small amounts of power, though, you'll rarely use a capacitor larger than 1000μF.

One characteristic worth mentioning about electrolytics is that they age, because inside the body is a chemical that can eventually dry up. This takes anywhere from several years to many decades. Although this won't be a problem for most experimenters, if you expect to use a piece of equipment for many, many years, let the electrolytics be accessible for replacement should one deteriorate.

There are other types of capacitors you'll encounter. *Paper* capacitors are tubular, and fairly large; they have the same capacitance range as discs and are also nonpolarized. They are not much in vogue these days because they age and have been replaced by *mylar* types, which look similar to paper types, have many of the same characteristics, but last longer. For small and stable capacitance values (in the pF range), you'll encounter *polystyrene* types. These are tubular, very small, and usually plastic and silvery. The premium capacitors for large capacitance values are *tantalum* types; these are quite expensive unless purchased surplus. They are very reliable and perform well in critical circuits.

The final type of capacitor we'll cover is the *variable* kind. These are seldom used in audio circuits, because you can't make variable capacitors with lots of capacitance, and audio circuits generally require large capacitance values. The variable capacitor is to caps as the pot is to resistors.

14

Semiconductors

In addition to conductors and insulators, there is a third class of material that exhibits properties of both. Under some conditions, it acts as an insulator, and under other conditions it's a conductor. This phenomenon is called *semiconducting*—hence the name *semiconductor*—and allows a variable control over electron flow, forming the cornerstone of modern electronics. Semiconductors are called *active* components. Unlike resistors, capacitors, and other *passive* components, active components can (under the right conditions) put out more than is put in. This is called *gain*. All the projects in this book rely on some kind of *amplifier*, which is the term used for a circuit that gives gain.

You can consider semiconductors the heart of any circuit; like a human heart, they can work for a long time if handled properly, but they can also fail if abused. Appropriate cautions are included in particular projects, but certain precautions apply to all semiconductor devices. First, don't overheat them during soldering, as they can be damaged by excess heat. Anything reasonable is all right—they aren't as fragile as some people think—but you do need to take care. Most semiconductors may be put into matching sockets, completely eliminating the need for soldering. Second, be careful not to apply either excess voltage or voltage of the wrong polarity to a semiconductor. Wrong-polarity voltage, for example, means connecting the plus end of the battery to the minus terminal on the circuit rather than the plus (or positive) one. Although many of the circuits in this book are protected against improper polarity by two diodes, the problem still crops up in experimenting.

The simplest kind of semiconductor we'll be using is called the *diode* (Figure 1-7). A diode is really basic; it can't amplify, but its talent is being able to act as an electronic switch. If the diode points in one way, only positive voltages can pass through. If it's pointed the other way, only negative voltages can get through. If it's in a circuit which is AC (voltages in both positive and negative quadrants), one half of the AC will be lopped off. The protection circuit for improper polarity I just mentioned is shown in Figure 1-8. Pointing the diodes as shown effectively blocks a reverse-polarity voltage from entering into the circuit.

Diodes come in two basic types: *signal* diodes and *power* diodes. Signal diodes are usually small cylinders, sort of like resistors, but made out of glass and sporting only one band. This band is called the *cathode* and indicates polarity of the diode the way a (+) and (-) identify battery polarity.

Power diodes are somewhat larger, although you will find small ones (about the size of a 1/4W resistor) commonly available in 1- to 4A ratings. They will work just as well in the projects as signal diodes, but signal diodes

Figure 1-7

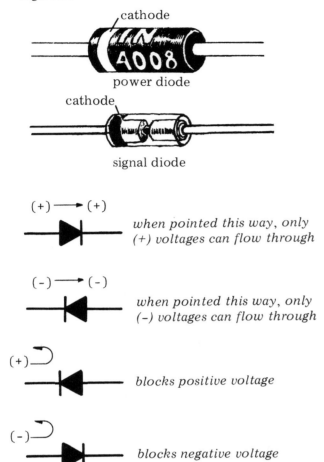

cathode

power diode

cathode

signal diode

(+) ➝ (+)

when pointed this way, only (+) voltages can flow through

(–) ➝ (–)

when pointed this way, only (–) voltages can flow through

(+)

blocks positive voltage

(–)

blocks negative voltage

Figure 1-8
Reverse-polarity protection circuit.

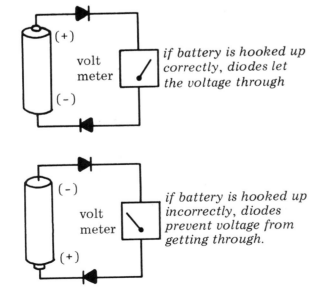

(+)

volt meter

(–)

if battery is hooked up correctly, diodes let the voltage through

(–)

volt meter

(+)

if battery is hooked up incorrectly, diodes prevent voltage from getting through.

can handle a moderate amount of power (certainly more than we need for the various projects), and cost less.

Diodes are rated according to two characteristics: voltage-handling and current-handling ability. It's common practice to use a diode that's considerably overrated, because the cost difference isn't that much and the reliability can be higher.

Figure 1-9 shows several examples of my favorite kind of diode, which is different from all the others; the *light-emitting* diode. This relatively recent addition to the diode family emits light when you feed it a couple of volts (how about that). Right now, the most commonly available color is red, but you can also get green, yellow, orange, and two-color types for a somewhat higher price. Light-emitting diodes (or *LEDs* for short) never burn out, for all practical purposes, under normal use; it's estimated that in 100 years, the only change you would detect would be a slight loss of brilliance. Additionally, because LEDs don't have a skinny little filament like a regular light bulb, they're immune to vibration and shock. However, they can be destroyed if too much current goes through them. Also, because (like any other diode) they are polarized, if hooked up backwards they won't light.

Figure 1-9
LEDs in several different case styles.

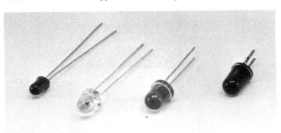

LEDs generally have a flat spot on the case or dot of paint to indicate the cathode; however, this is not always consistent from manufacturer to manufacturer. To check polarity, I generally use a little tester, as show in Figure 1-10, comprising a 9V battery and resistor. Hook up the LED; if it lights, the terminal connecting to the battery (+) is the anode, and the wire connecting to the resistor is the cathode. If it doesn't light, switch the LED leads around. If switching around the leads doesn't produce some light, you have either a dead battery or a dead LED.

A more complex semiconductor device is the *transistor*. A transistor has three terminals: one is the collector, one the base, and one the emitter. Electrons are *emitted* via one terminal and *collected* on another terminal. while the third terminal acts as a control element. Transistors come in a variety of case types, from small, epoxy-plastic types (see Figure 1-11) to large, metal-cased models (power transistors).

Figure 1-10
LED tester.

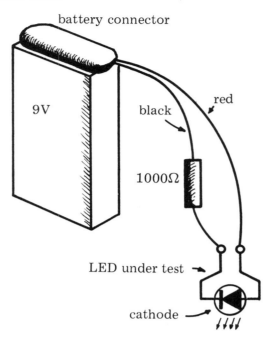

battery connector

9V

black

red

1000Ω

LED under test →

cathode →

Figure 1-11
The transistor on the left is in a metal case; the one on the right is in an epoxy-plastic case.

We won't be using many transistors, however, because technology has made the single transistor obsolete in many applications. Instead, a bunch of transistors, diodes, and other materials that mimic the functions of resistors and capacitors are deposited on a single crystalline base called a *substrate* to perform a complete function, such as amplify. These sophisticated semiconductor devices are called *integrated circuits* (ICs). You can find almost any electronic function in an IC, from computer memory cells to a dual low-noise audio preamplifier to tone generators—even medium-power hi-fi amplifiers, electronic gain controls, octave dividers . . . all kinds of things. ICs are commonly packaged in three types of cases: flatpack, DIP (dual in-line package), and, for lack of a better term, round. I advise passing up flatpack ICs,

as they are a hassle to work with, are more expensive (except in surplus), and are used mostly by people like NASA where the things have to work on the dark side of the moon. For those of us still on earth, however, DIPs will do just fine (refer to Figure 1-12 for illustrations of the different packages).

Figure 1-12
The leftmost IC is mounted in an 8-pin minidip package, the center IC in a TO-5 round package, and the rightmost IC in a 14-pin dip package.

Other IC packages are in use, but we will only be using either DIP or round types in the projects.

There are two major families of ICs, *linear* and *digital.* Digital ICs are used in computers, calculators, digital clocks, and other decision-making or number-counting circuits. The tuning standard (Project No. 16), which is a variation on a counting circuit, uses digital ICs; so does the electronic footswitch (Project No. 15), which has to make decisions (should I switch the effect in or out?)

However, most of the projects feature linear ICs. Linear ICs amplify, oscillate, filter, and do other interesting things. All audio equipment is based on linear circuitry, and the audio modifiers in this book are no exception.

By far the most popular linear IC is the operational amplifier, popularly called an *op amp.* This is simply a high-quality amplifier, capable of large amounts of gain, predictable behavior, low noise, and good frequency response. Since it's very difficult to get all desirable characteristics packed into one op amp, there are many different op amps to choose from. Some specialize in low noise at the expense of other characteristics, some have really good frequency response but lots of noise, some are designed solely to be blow-out proof, some are designed for low-budget applications, and so on. We'll mostly be using either low-noise- or extended-frequency-response units.

Some people get confused over the numbering system for ICs. ICs typically have 8 to 28 terminals, each of which is assigned a number for identification purposes. The numbers are assigned in the following manner: looking at the IC, you will see some kind of notch, dot, or other identifying mark at one end of the IC. With this notch pointing up, as in Figure 1-13, the pin in the extreme upper left-hand corners is pin 1. The pin below it is pin 2; continue counting until you reach the end of the row. At this point, jump over to the bottom of the next row and continue counting, but this time count up. The highest number pin is therefore in the upper right-hand corner.

Round ICs have some kind of tab, which indicates the highest-numbered pin. Looking at the IC from the bottom (or, the side where the leads come out), the pin to the immediate right of the tab is pin 1. Continue counting clockwise until you reach the tab, which is the highest-numbered pin.

People often become confused over IC nomenclature as well as the pin numbering scheme. When a company invents an IC, it assigns that part a certain number—say, 741—and then adds a prefix that stands for the name of the company. When other companies produce the same part, they in turn add their own prefix to the number;

for example, an LM741 is made by National Semiconductor, an MC741 by Motorola, a μA741 by Fairchild, an RC741 by Raytheon, and so on, An additional suffix may be added to indicate the type of packaging used for the IC, so that a 741 in a plastic case would be a 741P, and the same part in a ceramic case would be a 741C.

Finally, the prefix or suffix may be modified to indicate certain additional aspects of the IC's performance. An RC4739 is a Raytheon part designed for commercial use; an RM4739 is a Raytheon part designed for military use. Military parts are generally capable of operating over a wider temperature range, and meet certain high-reliability requirements set up by the government. However, they are considerably more expensive than consumer grade parts, and are not cost-effective for our applications.

By the way, many semiconductor vendors do not buy parts from just one manufacturer, since several manufacturers often make identical parts. So, rather than indicate that they have an RC741 or an LM741 in stock, they'll just say they have a 741 and drop the prefix and suffix. In this case, you can assume you're buying a plastic-packaged device intended for consumer applications.

A couple of people have asked me why other parts are necessary if ICs are a complete functional unit. The answer is twofold: certain parts are difficult to fabricate on an IC; and ICs are usually set up as general-purpose devices. Other parts do things like determine the amount of gain, current drain, and frequency response.

Figure 1-13
Identifying IC pins.

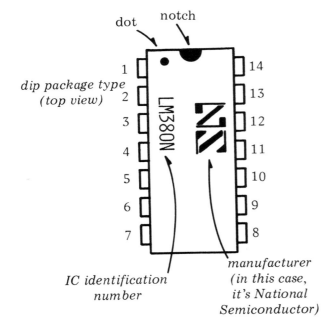

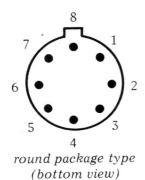

round package type
(bottom view)

Wire

You'd think the subject of wire (see Figure 1-14) would be simple—it is, but with some complications. The simplest kind of wire is bare wire—a solid, fairly thick piece of copper (or more likely these days, copper alloy), which can take electrons from one place to another. This kind of wire is popularly referred to as *buss* (or *bus*) wire.

The next step up in complexity is *insulated* wire—wire covered with a plastic sleeving or insulator which keeps it from shorting out to any other wires. Next is *stranded* wire—many thin bare wires covered with a plastic sleeving that insulates the entire bunch of wires and holds them together. Stranded wire has the advantage of being sturdier if the wire gets pushed around a lot; if you push solid wire around too much, it can bend and break.

These three types of wire are what you'll use for most point-to-point wiring in the projects. One handy feature of insulated wire is that the insulation comes in different colors to facilitate color-coding.

Gauge is the proper term for wire diameter; the best range for wire in these circuits is from #22 (largest practical) to #28 (smallest practical). The larger the gauge number, the *thinner* the wire.

Figure 1-14
Wire types.

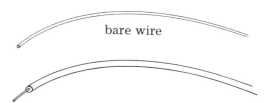

bare wire

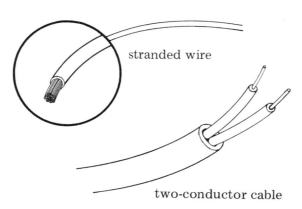

bare wire with insulation (or solid-core wire)

stranded wire

two-conductor cable

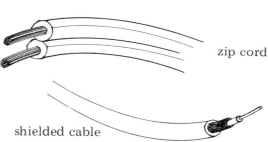

zip cord

shielded cable

The next part of the wire world worth looking into is *cable,* which we'll loosely define as more than one insulated wire inside a plastic sheath. Most musicians are familiar with *shielded cable,* the kind of wire used in guitar cords. Shielded cable has one (and sometimes more) insulated conductor, wrapped or covered by some form of conductive shield. This shield is usually some kind of conductive foil or crisscrossing pattern of very fine wires. By connecting the shield to a ground point, the wires which it wraps around are less susceptible to stray hum or radio signals. The wire inside the shield is referred to as *hot* compared to the shield, which is grounded (no volts—remember?). Sometimes shielding is not required, in which case the cable is simply referred to as *multiple-conductor* cable.

Low-capacitance shielded cable is a type of shielded cable designed specifically for audio applications. Without getting too technical, suffice it to say that all shielded cable exhibits a certain amount of capacitance. Under some conditions this capacitance reduces the treble response of an instrument such as guitar, especially if the cable is longer than a few meters (yards). For our projects, it certainly doesn't hurt to use low-capacitance cable, but it's not really necessary; regular shielded cable will do the job just fine, since most of the cable lengths will be under 15 cm (6") or so.

Twisted pair is similar to shielded cable; by using a pair of wires, twisting them, and connecting one to ground, the other one is somewhat shielded. Though not as effective as the wrapped type, it's still useful for many applications. A type of wire we won't be using, but you see a lot, is *magnet wire.* This is extremely thin copper wire, covered with a lacquer type of insulation, which is used for winding coils such as guitar pickups and speaker coils.

Coil cable I usually mistrust, unless it was made for Bell Telephone. The inexpensive imported coil cords commonly seen are shielded, but the shield is a flimsy kind of cloth with copper deposited on it in all the samples I've looked at.

The last type of wire we need to check out is *zip cord.* This is the brownish kind of wire found usually on toasters, lamps, radios, and other applicances that plug into the wall. Zip cord is two heavily insulated conductors designed to carry a reasonable amount of current. It's useful for speaker wires and power supply wires. One fact many people don't know: the two different conductors of zip cord are coded. Usually, one side of the conductor's insulation is ridged, while the insulation on the other side is smooth. While there is no real "standard" on the subject, most people using zip cord as speaker wire use the ridged conductor for the hot lead and the smooth conductor for the ground lead.

Mechanical Parts

Knobs. Everybody knows what a knob is. What you may not know is that there are different methods to hold knobs onto pot and switch shafts. Cheap knobs simply put grooves on the inside plastic wall which mate with matching grooves on the pot shaft. Types with a setscrew in the back are somewhat better, but the best are the kind with two setscrews, placed ninety degrees apart. This dual retaining action holds the knob on its shaft tightly and securely. Sometimes the setscrews use standard screwdriver slots, and sometimes hex nuts. To take off a knob with hex nuts requires a tool called an Allen wrench. Chances are, though, that you won't run into these too often, as hex nuts generally are indicative of a high-priced knob.

18

Switches. Switches generally complete or interrupt a circuit. Figure 1-15 shows a simple *toggle* switch schematically. With the switch closed, a conductor connects wires A and B; with the switch open, A and B are effectively insulated from each other. Most on-off switches are of this type. They are called single-pole, single-throw switches (or SPST) because one wire, the pole, can be switched to one other wire (the throw). A single-pole, double-throw type (SPDT) can switch a wire to two other wires (Figure 1-16). A double-pole, double-throw switch, (Figure 1-17) can switch each of two wires to two other wires. A toggle switch has each of the poles and throws brought out to a solder terminal, usually in a logical way, and comes in regular or miniature sizes.

Figure 1-15
SPST switch.

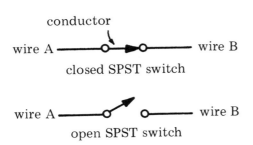

conductor

wire A ———————○—▶—○——————— wire B

closed SPST switch

wire A ———————○—↗ ○——————— wire B

open SPST switch

Figure 1-16
SPDT switch: wire C can connect to either wire A or wire B.

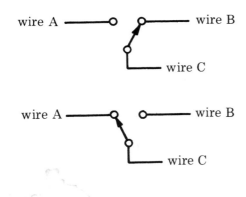

wire A ———————○   ○——————— wire B

wire C

wire A ———————○   ○——————— wire B

wire C

Figure 1-17
DPDT switch (schematicized): as 2 connects to 1, B connects to A; when 2 connects to 3, B connects to C.

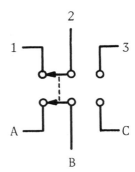

Figure 1-18 shows which terminals connect together when you push the switch toggle in different directions for a miniature toggle switch. Note that pushing the toggle *up* connects the middle and lower terminals together, while pushing the toggle *down* connects the middle and upper terminals together. Also, note that any DPDT switch can be used as an SPDT, DPST, or SPST switch by simply not using all the available terminals.

Figure 1-18
The terminals connecting together for the two toggle positions of a typical miniature SPDT switch.

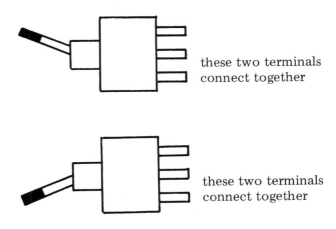

these two terminals connect together

these two terminals connect together

Figure 1-19 shows a number of switches. The *slide* switch is less expensive (but also somewhat flimsier) than toggle types. I tend to avoid them because they're hard to mount, and their non-airtight construction tends to pick up dust and dirt.

Pushbutton switches perform a switching function when you push down on a button. Sometimes these are available in a sturdy case (as shown in the photo) that's suitable for footswitching. Unlike ordinary pushbuttons,

Figure 1-19

Six different switch types. The one in the center is a DPDT miniature toggle switch; clockwise from the lower left-hand corner, we have a DPDT foot-switch, regular-size slide switch, regular-size toggle switch, rotary switch, and dipswitch.

footswitches do not have a *momentary* action, but a *sustained* action. This means that pushing the button once flips the switch one way, and pushing it again flips the switch the other way. There's more material on footswitches in Project No. 11, and Project No. 15 shows you how to replace the comparatively rare and expensive DPDT footswitch with a more common (available in hardware stores, for example), less expensive SPST type.

More complicated switching requires a *rotary* switch. This has phenolic or ceramic wafers with terminals brought out for the poles and throws. Usually the mechanism works similarly to the one detailed in Figure 1-20, with a detent mechanism hooked up so that the rotary switch clicks as you turn it around and the various conductors line up. Single-pole, 6-throw (SP6T), double-pole, 12-throw (2P12T), and other exotic switching combinations are possible.

With rotary switches and some other switch types, which terminals connect together in various switch positions may not be entirely obvious. To find out, use a continuity tester or ohmmeter (see Project No. 19) to check for continuity (a completed circuit, in other words) between the various switch terminals; make a note of which terminals connect together in various switch positions.

Our final switch type is the *dipswitch*. The one in the photo contains seven miniature on-off switches in a case not much bigger than a conventional 14-pin IC; in fact, dipswitches are size-compatible with standard IC sockets.

Dipswitches are not really intended as front panel switches; they have the same relationship to regular switches as trimpots have to regular potentiometers.

It's sometimes important to know the current rating of the switch, as well as the switching configuration. Most toggle switches can safely handle 2 or 3A of current at 125V, which means that they can control a fair amount of juice (about 250W). For us, any switch can handle the voltages we'll be dealing with; however, dipswitches are *not ever* suitable for switching 115V AC.

Figure 1-20
Single-pole, five-throw (SP5T) rotary switch.

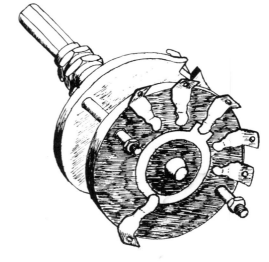

Figure 1-21

Four commonly used batteries. The little one in the front is an "AA" cell; the large one on the left is a "D" cell; the one standing up in the middle is a "C" cell; and the one on the right is a 9V transistor radio battery, suitable for use in many of our projects.

Batteries. Batteries come in different sizes, voltages, and current-producing capacities. Figure 1-21 shows four available types. The transistor radio battery is the kind most often used in accessories for the electronic musician; it combines small size with a fair number of volts, and a moderate amount of current-generating capability. "AA" cells, commonly called "penlite" cells, produce the least amount of ampere-hours (amount of current for a given amount of time). "D" cells are the most powerful. However, combining several batteries together in *series* (Figure 1-22) increases the current-generating capacity, as well as increasing the available voltage. Given that one "AA" battery will produce 1.5V, then two batteries will give 3V, six will give 9V and so on.

Figure 1-22

Combining three 1.5V batteries in series to yield 4.5V.

Batteries are also made from different chemical compounds, which give different power capacities. The simplest and shortest-lived type is the carbon-zinc battery. Alkaline cells give a longer life, although for circuits with low current drain there is little (if any) economic advantage to using them; alkaline batteries are most useful in circuits requiring a fair amount of juice. Another kind of battery is the mercury battery, although I wouldn't recommend it for most musical uses. It maintains a fairly constant output voltage until the end of its relatively long life, at which point the output voltage drops rapidly. For this feature, you have to pay a whole lot, and it just doesn't seem to be worth it (especially considering the ecological aspects of throwaway mercury batteries).

You will notice that there are devices on the market which claim to recharge carbon-zinc batteries. Actually, a lot of controversy surrounds charging batteries—does it really work and is it dangerous? The answer to both questions is yes. You can recharge carbon-zinc batteries (as long as they aren't too far gone) to close-to-new condition; however, if left to charge for an extended time, they can explode, sending battery acid out in various random directions. For this reason, most professional electronics people frown on recharging batteries. If you're liable to forget about charging a battery for a couple of days, I suggest not doing it.

Nickel-cadmium batteries, as opposed to carbon-zinc ones, are designed to be rechargeable. They require a special charging unit, which recharges them safely at a fixed, slow rate. It is possible to get nickel-cadmium-type "AA," "C," and "D" cells, but rechargeable nickel-cadmium transistor radio batteries are still quite rare.

For batteries, you've got to have battery *holders.* Electronics stores carry plastic or aluminum holders for "AA," "C," and "D" cells; some can hold up to six or even ten batteries of a kind. When holders are for more than one battery, they are always hooked up in series to increase the voltage. A useful hint to know (since 9V battery holders are difficult to find) is that a 9V battery will fit in a "C" cell holder.

Nine-volt batteries have a special connector which you've probably seen inside commercial modifiers or transistor radios. These snap onto the end of the battery and have two leads coming out, one black and one red. The black lead stands for minus (-) and the red for plus (+); more on them in Chapter 4.

A piece of slightly esoteric knowledge: by placing your tongue across the two terminals of a 9V battery, you can determine its freshness. A good 9V battery will give you a healthy, salty-tasting bite. The sharper the bite, the better the battery. With a little experience, you can taste just how good a battery is.

Something else to consider is that batteries age; this characteristic is called shelf life, meaning that should a battery have a shelf life of two years, even without use it will be dead after that time period. Therefore, avoid buying batteries at places that don't do a brisk trade in them. Many batteries are date-coded, so if you can figure out the code, buy as new a battery as possible.

Finally, remember that batteries just don't work if they're cold. If you bring in a battery from a vehicle parked outside in the cold, you'll have to wait until the battery warms up before it will give proper performance.

Grommets. Grommets (like the ones in Figure 1-23) are little rubber or plastic doughnuts. They are installed in pass-through holes for wires in metal panels, principally to keep the wire's insulation from scraping against the sharp metal that often surrounds a drilled hole. You'll see that most AC line cords pass through grommets on their way to the electronic innards of whatever they're powering.

Figure 1-23

Nuts and Bolts. The most popular sizes for electronic work are 4-40 and 6-32. It's a good idea to buy nuts and bolts in assortments, so that you always have hardware around. Screw lengths of interest will be 9.3 mm (3/8"), 6.2 mm (1/4"), and 21.8 mm (7/8"). The 6-32 types are a little heavier duty, and good for mounting stuff like transformers and panels. The 4-40 size is good for attaching solder lugs, mounting circuit boards, and holding down terminal strips.

Lockwashers. Lockwashers go between a nut and the surface being screwed through (see Figure 1-24). Lockwashers hold the screw tightly and keep it from becoming undone by vibration or other sinister forces.

Figure 1-24a and 1-24b
(a) Three different styles of lockwashers; (b) how a lockwasher mounts between the nut and chassis.

Solder Lugs. Solder lugs (shown in Figure 1-25) mount to a metal chassis with a screw through one end; the other hole is for attaching wires and making solder connections. Other types fit around the bushings of potentiometers, and have something to solder wires to at the other end (Figure 1-26). Actually, you can call anything that is metal and designed to have wires soldered to it a solder lug; for example, a potentiometer has three terminals which can be thought of as solder lugs.

Figure 1-25

Figure 1-26
This photo shows three standard lockwashers for potentiometers, as well as a lockwasher with a solder lug attached.

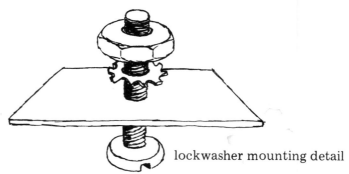

lockwasher mounting detail

The terminals coming out of switches can also be thought of as solder lugs. On some switches and other parts, you'll see screw terminals (Figure 1-27). Wrapping a wire around the screw and tightening it down is just not as reliable as soldering, so I generally either avoid these or remove the screws and solder anyway.

Figure 1-27
How to recognize screw terminals so that you can avoid them.

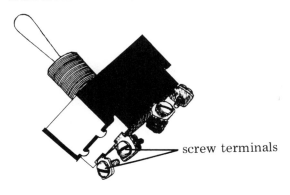

screw terminals

Terminal Strips. Pictured in Figure 1-28, these things are basically a bunch of insulated solder lugs to which you can connect wires; one of the terminals will have a screw hold for attaching to a metal chassis. This lug then becomes your chassis ground connection.

Figure 1-28

Quarter-Inch Telephone Plugs. Commonly called *phone plugs* (not to be confused with RCA *phono plugs,* the kind used on hi-fi equipment). Like switches, solder-terminal types are preferable to screw-terminal types. The mono plug has two connections, one for hot and one for ground—the hot is the tip, and the ground is the shield. The stereo kind has two hot conductors and a ground (see Figure 1-29). The body of the plug is usually made of plastic or metal—the metal ones last far longer, and I definitely recommend them.

Figure 1-29

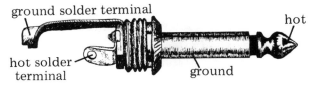

mono ¼" phone plug

ground solder terminal

hot

hot solder terminal

ground

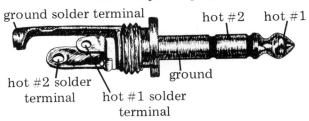

stereo ¼" phone plug

ground solder terminal

hot #2   hot #1

hot #2 solder terminal

hot #1 solder terminal

ground

Quarter-Inch Telephone Jacks. You'll find 1/4" telephone jacks (see Figure 1-30) on your guitar and at your amp inputs. These can be either stereo or mono. In the case of mono, there are two solder tabs; stereo jacks have three solder tabs, corresponding to the two hot terminals and ground. You can classify jacks as closed or open. An open jack is like the ones just described—jacks, plain and simple. A closed jack means that some kind of switching action is involved. A good example of this switching action is when you plug an earphone into a transistor radio and the speaker goes off—you're actually switching the speaker on and off with the jack.

Figure 1-30
The jack on the left is a stereo type; the one on the right is a mono open-circuit type.

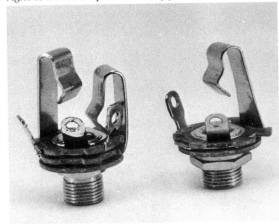

Figure 1-31 shows a mono closed-circuit jack both pictorially and schematically. Terminal A is the ground or shield terminal, C is the hot terminal, and B is the

23

Figure 1-31 mono closed-circuit jack

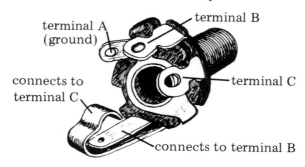

terminal A (ground)

terminal B

connects to terminal C

terminal C

connects to terminal B

with plug not inserted, terminals B and C short together

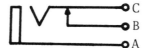

C
B
A

inserting a plug breaks the connection between B and C

C
B
A

switch. B normally presses against the hot terminal when no plug is present, but inserting a plug pushes the hot terminal away from the switch part. With stereo jacks, either one or both hot terminals can have a switching action built-in.

Whenever you use a closed-circuit jack, make sure you're soldering to the appropriate tabs. Mistaking the hot terminal for the switch will probably keep the device from working properly. There is a test to avoid this kind of mistake called a *continuity* test, described in Project No. 19.

Figure 1-32

The transformer on the left is a miniature audio type, which we use in Project No. 3. The one on the right is a power transformer suitable for stepping down 117V AC to 12V AC.

Transformers. Figure 1-32 shows a couple of transformers, one audio transformer and one power transformer. Power transformers convert the AC coming out of your wall to a lower voltage. Since 115V will often fry semiconductors, the transformer steps down that 115V to 6, 12, 15, or some other low voltage. Transformers can either be *center-tapped* or not; a non-center-tapped model can only work in certain power supply designs, whereas a center-tapped one will work in any kind of supply. Since we only use a power transformer in Project No. 13, we'll specify the proper kind to use at that time.

Cases. Most cases (or chassis) are made of metal for two reasons: one, metal is a conductor, so the case may be treated as a big ground area; two, metal is far stronger than plastic or phenolic, the other popular choices for cases. Your best bet is to stick to the aluminum type; steel eats through drill bits like crazy, requires more effort to drill, and has inferior shielding properties compared to aluminum.

Reading Schematic Diagrams

Now you know what kinds of parts we'll be working with, what they look like, and what their important characteristics are. Before we finish, we should talk about relating these parts to *schematic* diagrams.

Schematics are nothing more than shorthand wiring diagrams. Instead of drawing a wire, you draw a line. When connections go to ground, rather than drawing a line connecting all the ground points together, you simply attach a ground symbol to whatever needs to be grounded. Each part is identified by its own symbol, except for integrated circuits. Figure 1-33 shows the schematic equivalents for the parts and wiring connections we've talked about. You'll notice that there are sometimes two symbols given for a part—a preferred and an alternate. The preferred are what I use, but the alternates are common too, since schematics are not all standardized.

Integrated circuits have nearly as many schematic representations as there are ICs, but we'll use the two popular approaches shown in Figure 1-34. The first illustration shows the outline of a 741 IC, looking at it from the top (that is, the surface with the notch or dot). This method shows all the pins of the IC, along with their pin numbers. Frequently it is not necessary to show all the IC pins, since some pins are not of interest in many applications, and some aren't even connected to anything inside the IC. In fact, if you look through the projects and notice unconnected IC pins, don't worry; it's standard practice to use only the pins you need. One advantage to showing ICs in the "skeleton outline" form is that it's easy to visualize the actual wiring, since the schematic symbol looks like the IC itself.

Figure 1-33

resistor

potentiometer

ceramic, disc, or
mylar capacitor

electrolytic
capacitor

diode

light-emitting
diode (LED)

op amp

SPST switch

DPDT switch

seven-position
rotary switch

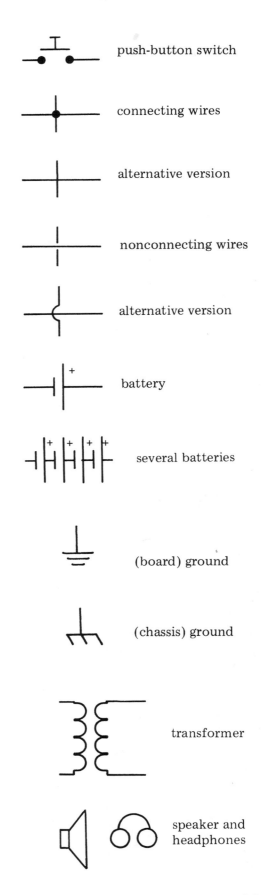

push-button switch

connecting wires

alternative version

nonconnecting wires

alternative version

battery

several batteries

(board) ground

(chassis) ground

transformer

speaker and
headphones

25

Figure 1-34

(a) Typical symbol for the 741, an integrated circuit containing an op amp (the little triangle). Pins 2 and 3 are inputs; 4 and 7 go to the power supply; 1 and 5 are necessary for applications which are not of interest to us currently; pin 8 doesn't connect to anything internally, and is considered an "nc" (no connection). (b) Here's another way to show a 741 op amp. For examples of both styles, see some of the project's schematics.

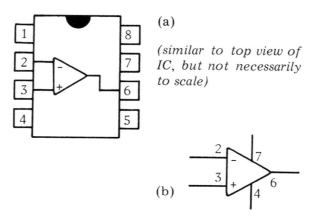

(a)

(similar to top view of IC, but not necessarily to scale)

(b)

The second illustration shows how to look at a 741 IC schematically. Since the 741 is an op amp, we use the symbol for an op amp as shown in Figure 1-33, and put pin numbers next to the leads coming out of the op amp. You'll notice that the power leads, pins 4 and 7, are shown coming out of the top and bottom of the op amp triangle. You'll also note that pins 1, 5, and 8, which are of no importance to us, are not shown in this method.

A lot of the ICs we use, however, are complex devices containing more than one op amp: an example of this is the 4136 IC, which contains four op amps in one package with fourteen pins. In this case, we can still draw a skeleton outline (Figure 1-35a) but it's frequently less cumbersome from a drafting standpoint to show a complex IC in the second method of Figure 1-35b. The power supply connection lines could come out of any of the op amps; or, one supply line could go into one op amp, and the other supply line into a different op amp, as shown. The reason why it doesn't matter which op amp shows the power connections is because with multiple op amp devices, the power lines are common to all op amps. Projects No. 10, No. 11, and No. 17 offer examples of how to show complex ICs schematically.

Digital ICs do not have their own symbol, so in the case of these ICs what we'll do is simply draw a box that represents the IC, and number the pin connections (see the Project No. 16 schematic for an example of this).

Any pins not indicated on the schematic may be ignored. The pins on digital ICs are numbered just like the numbering scheme for op amp ICs shown in Figure 1-34.

Since there is no standard way to show ICs schematically, both methods described above will be used to familiarize you with the various ways the electronics world draws them.

Figure 1-35

(a)

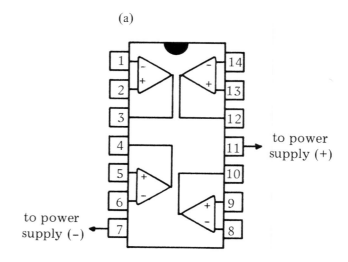

to power supply (+)

to power supply (−)

(b)

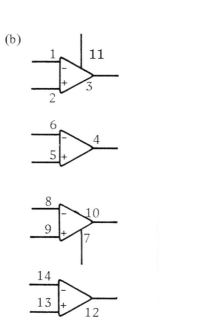

each op amp = ¼ 4136

Substituting Parts

Substituting ICs. A few people have had difficulty finding some of the op amps I like to use, particularly the 4739 dual op amp. Actually, there are many sources that carry the 4739, 4136, and other ICs used in the projects; thousands of people have found these parts without trouble, so hopefully you won't have any problems either. The reason why I've chosen these parts over more general-purpose op amps is because they are low in noise, virtually impossible to destroy, and inexpensive. However, in instances where you aren't too picky about noise, general-purpose op amps such as the 4558 dual op amp (a *very* common IC) can substitute for the 4739. Refer to Figure 1-36, which shows the pinout of the 4558 and 4739, and follow the directions below to substitute one op amp for the other.

Figure 1-36

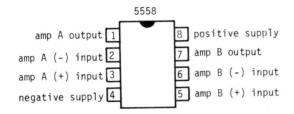

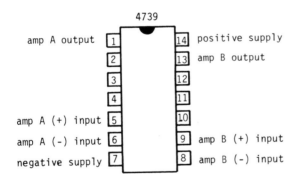

Wire the connections that normally go to pin 1 of the 4739 to pin 1 of the 4458.

Wire the connections that normally go to pin 5 of the 4739 to pin 3 of the 4558.

Wire the connections that normally go to pin 6 of the 4739 to pin 2 of the 4558.

Wire the connections that normally go to pin 7 of the 4739 to pin 4 of the 4558.

Wire the connections that normally go to pin 8 of the 4739 to pin 6 of the 4558.

Wire the connections that normally go to pin 9 of the 4739 to pin 5 of the 4558.

Wire the connections that normally go to pin 13 of the 4739 to pin 7 of the 4558.

Wire the connections that normally go to pin 14 of the 4739 to pin 8 of the 4558.

As you can see, what we've done is compared the pinouts of the two parts, and when something goes to, say, the (-) input of op amp A of the 4739, we instead wire it to the (-) input of op amp A of the 4558. . . and carry this procedure through until all pins (inputs, outputs, power supply, etc.) are accounted for and connected to the appropriate pins on the substitute op amp. Remember that pins 2, 3, 4, 10, 11, and 12 of the 4739 do not connect to anything internally.

Several years ago, a part called the 739 was manufactured, of which the 4739 is an improved version. However, the 739 is not suitable for use in our circuits because it requires several extra parts not included in the schematic or on the circuit board. Attempting to use this part will produce unsatisfactory results.

To substitute for the 4136, you can use either two 5558s or four 741s. The procedure for substituting for the 4136 is the same—look at the pinout, identify the terminals, and make the appropriate wiring changes to accommodate the different pinout of the substitute IC.

Substituting resistors and capacitors. Although these circuits work best with the parts values indicated, those experienced in electronics will no doubt be able to make changes to use their parts on hand without affecting the performance of the unit. It's often suitable to use parts that are close in value to the ones required. For example, if you want a $1.2\mu F$ capacitor and you only have a $1.0\mu F$ type, don't worry about the difference. Remember that capacitors are generally not that precise in value; so a $1.0\mu F$ capacitor could actually have a true value that's any where from $0.8\mu F$ to $1.2\mu F$ and still be within $\pm$ 20% tolerance. Likewise, if you need a 100k resistor and can only get 90k or 110k, don't worry about it; there will be little, if any, difference in overall performance. Frequently the most important property of resistors is how well they are matched, not whether they have precise values. So if two resistors of the same value are specified, don't change one without changing the other.

However, do keep in mind that the circuits in this book have been extensively tested over a period of years and are specifically optimized to work with the parts indicated. Unless you are aware of the consequences of what you are doing, try to use the specified parts whenever possible.

TABLE OF ELECTRONIC MEASUREMENTS

For your convenience, this table summarizes electronic units of measurement and their abbreviations.

Ampere (A) — unit of current measurement

MicroAmpere (μA) =   .000001 A
MilliAmpere (mA) =   .001 A

Farad (F) — unit of capacitance measurement

MicroFarad (μF) = .000001 F
NanoFarad (nF) = .000000001 F or .001 μF
PicoFarad (pF) = .000000000001 F or
                    .000001 μF or .001 nF

Hertz (Hz) — unit of frequency measurement

KiloHertz (kHz) = 1,000 Hz
MegaHertz (MHz) = 1,000,000 Hz

Ohm (Ω) — unit of resistance or impedance measurement

KilOhm (kΩ) = 1,000 Ω
MegOhm (MΩ) = 1,000,000 Ω

(In actual practice, the Greek letter Omega (Ω) is often omitted. Thus, 100kΩ becomes 100k.)

Volt (V) — unit of voltage measurement

MicroVolt (μA) = .000001 V
MilliVolt (mV) = .001 V

Watt (W) — unit of power measurement

MicroWatt (μW) = .000001 W
MilliWatt (mW) = .001 W
KiloWatt (kW) = 1,000 W

Chapter Two

A survey of how and where to find parts at reasonable prices.

One of the biggest stumbling blocks for electronic musicians and electronic hobbyists is finding the parts necessary to build a project. However, this need not be a difficult task; in fact, all the parts in this book are available from a number of sources. You can obtain parts by mail, or from retail electronics dealers (I generally use a mix of the two for my parts needs).

Finding Mail-Order Parts Sources

Go down to your library or newsstand and check out some of the magazines published expressly for electronics hobbyists (*Popular Electronics, Radio-Electronics, 73,* and *Science Electronics* are the most commonly available). Look in the back section of these magazines, and you'll see numerous ads for mail-order hobbyist supply houses. These ads generally include a partial listing of parts and prices, as well as giving instructions on how to obtain a catalogue. Many times this just involves circling a number on a reader service card bound into the magazine; a few weeks later, the catalogue will arrive at your door. In most cases, mail-order companies have lower prices and a wider selection of parts than local stores.

Finding and Buying from Local Parts Sources

In this case, your best tool is the Yellow Pages section of the phone directory. The subject headings you want are "Electronic Equipment and Supplies—Dealers" and "Electronic Equipment and Supplies—Wholesale."

Dealers are the retail stores, and they want your business, whether it's large or small. The prices are generally close to list prices because the volume they do is small in comparison with wholesale firms. Frequently they sell consumer equipment, such as stereos, calculators, and burglar alarms, as well as parts. Although a few stores have their own sources of supply for components, most dealers distribute "hobbyist" parts lines offered by various component manufacturers. While there are quite a few parts lines, probably the most comprehensive carried by local stores is the Calectro line, manufactured by GC Electronics, which includes resistors, potentiometers, semiconductors, transformers, speakers, knobs, and a bunch of other things, like preassembled modules. It also has printed circuit board kits, cases (both metal and plastic), and battery holders. Many stores will carry more than one line, so check out what's available.

A variation on the independent local retailer is the chain store. Probably the most familiar of these is Radio Shack, with stores all over the U.S.A. and other parts of the world. Radio Shack carries its own line of parts, which is roughly comparable to the Calectro line except that there is more emphasis on semiconductors. In recent years Radio Shack has started stocking some parts that are very useful to electronic musicians—maybe because of all the people who have this book and have stopped into their local Radio Shack to look for parts.

In addition to Radio Shack, there are chains of a more regional nature, such as Lafayette Electronics and Olson Electronics. Again, the Yellow Pages will let you know what's around.

One point to remember about retail stores is that you can usually ask questions about parts and electronics without getting funny looks. Frequently the person on the other side of the counter, and sometimes even the manager, will know less about electronics than you will after you've read this book, but they may be able to turn you on to either somebody in the store who knows what he's talking about, or to a regular customer who knows about electronic matters.

Wholesale stores are a different matter. They are set up to serve the industrial and/or TV repair market, and are used to catering to professionals. They don't like to be bothered with somebody who walks in and just wants one capacitor, although there are exceptions. If you can go into a wholesale place and specify exactly what you want and act like you know what you're doing, they'll be more inclined to deal with you. Remember, though, that these places are set up for the professional and that the employees have neither the time nor the inclination to do any thinking for you. If you're lucky, there will be a wholesale outlet in your community that also has an over-the-counter section for nonindustrial users. Here, the counter people are more likely to know about electronics, and if you are polite and look green enough, nine times out of ten they'll try to help you with any questions.

One way to be welcomed at wholesale stores is to obtain a resale number. Wholesalers interpret resale numbers as an indication of a sincere and professional interest in electronics, and some wholesale outlets won't even let you through the door unless you've got one. The state you live in issues resale numbers, which allows the professional manufacturer or distributor to avoid paying sales tax on the parts he buys, since the parts will be resold as part of a finished product and sales tax will be collected on that. If you intend to make anything for sale, a resale number is a valid permit to obtain. However, certain legal obligations *must* be complied with. First, some states will require a deposit; for small businesses, though, this deposit is nominal. Next, if you sell something to somebody you *must* collect the prevailing sales tax, and you are obligated to send to your state the sales taxes you've collected on a regular basis. Finally, if you buy parts for your own use and not for resale, you *must* declare them as taxable and pay the sales tax. Further information on resale numbers is obtainable from your county government (see Yellow Pages under "Government Offices—Sales Tax").

Another branch of the wholesale tree is the electronics distributor. These exist mostly to serve the industrial market; they expect orders that require hundreds or even thousands of parts, and carry products from specific companies. If you're lucky, there will be one in your area that has an over-the-counter section. Unfortunately this practice is on the decline, as over-the-counter volume is small compared to industrial volume and not worth the effort to the distributor.

Surplus electronics stores also deserve a look. Some surplus stores sell a wide selection of really high-quality parts at extremely good prices; others sell trash and rejects without giving you any real cash advantage. Remember that the reason why something is in a surplus store in the first place is because the original buyer didn't want it, due to any number of reasons (change

in styling, defects, business failure, and so on). So there is a definite "let the buyer beware" implied in dealing with surplus stores. This is not necessarily because of any dishonesty; rather, these stores don't have time to go through all their parts, and they leave it up to the customer to determine whether or not the part is suited for the intended application. Most of the time, surplus stores will cheerfully take back any part you find to be improper, but others don't, and you can't really blame them. People frequently will get an exotic part, blow it up through lack of knowledge, and blame the store.

Now that all these warnings are out of the way, let's examine the benefits of surplus outlets. First of all, the price is right, but most important, the parts are frequently difficult to obtain elsewhere and are of good quality. A part which may be obsolete for the space program may be perfect for the experimenter, and the saving is substantial. Also, companies will sometimes go out of business and sell their inventory for peanuts to surplus dealers to minimize their losses. This saving gets passed on to you. Additionally, the people at surplus stores are far more likely to know about electronics than the people at retail stores, since their very livelihood depends on being able to examine a batch of parts and determine whether it's something on which people would want to spend money.

An emergency parts source, although limited in scope, is your local TV repair shop (again, the Yellow Pages are a great help). Because they are not in business to sell parts, they don't have many on hand for experimenters, and if you do request something, it will sell for list price. This is only fair, because they have to make a living somehow and can't afford to deplete their parts stock unless they make something from it. But there have been many times when I needed a few feet of solder, or a resistor, and a TV repair place has had it. So although it's a last resort, it's still worth checking out, and you might meet some interesting and knowledgeable people that way (you may also meet a grouch or two).

Getting the Most out of Mail Order

Very few towns have enough electronics experimenters to support a large electronics retail store; you'll tend to find these only in larger metropolitan areas, and even then they may not be able to offer a wide selection of parts. As a result, many hobbyists have come to rely on mail-order shopping as an alternative to buying through retail outlets—particularly for locating ICs, which can be very difficult to find locally, even from distributors. Mail-order companies do not depend on walk-in trade, so anyone who lives near a mailbox is a prospective client.

People generally have two reservations about mail-order houses. The first is that you have to wait for the order to be processed and sent back to you, which can try your patience when you're hot to get started on a project. Second, there have been many cases of mail-order fraud (few involving electronics suppliers, however), and people are suspicious about sending off large amounts of money to some post office box halfway across the country. Luckily, though, these reservations are not really justified. Sometimes it *does* take time to get a part, but I have dealt with dozens of mail-order suppliers and the average turnaround time has been under a week. Many of these companies have toll-free or 24-hour answering services to take credit card or COD orders, and this can speed up the turnaround time to two or three days—not bad at all. There have been cases where it has taken two weeks to a month to fill a back order, but that can just as easily happen when dealing with a retail store if it doesn't have what you want in stock.

As far as fraud goes, I've certainly had companies mess up an order from time to time, but these problems are invariably due to human error rather than malevolence; a letter or phone call has always been sufficient to straighten out any problems. If a company has advertised in a magazine for more than six months or so, you can be pretty sure that it is a realiable operation. If I'm unsure of some new place, I'll send in a small order for a couple of parts; how well they process the order will tell me whether or not I want to order from them again.

To get the best results from mail-order companies, you should follow a few procedures. First, put your name and address on the order itself—simply including it on the envelope return address isn't good enough. Companies get really frustrated when they have a check, a list of parts, and no address. Second, keep any correspondence separate from orders if you want your order processed as quickly as possible. Third, avoid COD, as it costs you more money, and will also delay your order. Fourth, if you have trouble with a company, *write them.* Even the best mail-order houses cannot avoid an occasional goof; they have no way of knowing there's a problem unless you tell them. Last of all, if you're asking for advice, technical help, or something beyond a simple request for price lists or catalogues, include a self-addressed stamped envelope. This encourages a prompt (and often friendlier) response.

Getting the Best Prices: Stocking Your Lab

If you're only buying parts for a couple of projects, then retail stores are certainly the most convenient way to shop; but the lowest prices usually come from industrial distributors and mail-order houses (especially on large orders). One of the best ways to keep parts costs down is through quantity buying. If you can locate fellow enthusiasts in your area and pool orders, you can make substantial savings. For example, a single phone jack might cost 45¢, but the same part may go down to

37¢ if you buy 10, or 30¢ if you buy 100. Resistors can cost up to 15¢ each at the retail level; but if you buy 100 at a time, the price goes down to 1.5¢ each—one-tenth as much. If you buy just 10 resistors at retail prices, you've paid for 100 resistors at quantity prices . . . so you might as well get the 100, and have 90 "free" resistors left over for use in future projects. You'll note that certain parts crop up with regularity in the various projects (like 10k pots, $2\mu F$ capacitors, 1N4001 diodes, RC4739 ICs, and the like); this is done on purpose so that you can buy parts in quantity and save some bucks.

Another way to stock your lab is to scrutinize the ads in the back of electronics magazines. One company might make a great buy on capacitors, and offer them at a lower price than the competition for a period of a few months. Another company might have low prices on resistors, while another specializes in ICs. Keep your eyes open for bargains—once I ordered a "surprise package" of 10 rotary switches that cost me less than 1 switch normally does, and ended up getting 4 useful switches out of the assortment. You can definitely come out ahead on this kind of thing.

There is one caveat, though. Many companies offer semiconductors which are labelled "untested." These are sold at rock-bottom prices because most of the time they work marginally, if at all. Although experimenters can have fun with untested parts, it's best if you steer clear of anything marked "untested" unless you know how to test for functionality.

Table I shows some typical high and low prices on electronic components—but remember that component prices fluctuate radically. When economic conditions are good, semiconductor makers sell their stuff as fast as they can make it, and prices are high. But as soon as any kind of recession hits, prices end up being artificially low because there isn't enough customer demand. Of course, raw material costs, balance-of-trade situations, inflation, and a number of other factors ultimately influence the cost of the parts you use. When you buy this book, we may be in either feast or famine; look upon the prices given as guides, not maxims.

Parts Kits

As a convenience to the readers of this book, PAIA Electronics (see address in Table II) has agreed to stock complete parts kits for the majority of the book projects as well as circuit boards for these projects. Each parts kit includes a legended circuit board, resistors, capacitors, semiconductors, pots, and required sockets, and in some cases, switches and connectors. In case of difficulty, PAIA maintains a repair service. For further information and current pricing, write or call (405) 843-9626 to request the current catalog.

There are, of course, many other sources for purchasing individual components. Table II is a partial listing of prominent mail-order suppliers; while this list does not necessarily constitute endorsement, I've had no problems ordering from any of these companies in the past. When you have nothing to do some rainy day, write a batch of letters to the various companies and request their catalogues—you'll find out what's available and for how much.

TABLE I. Representative Prices ($U.S.)

component	high price (list)	low price (quantity price)
1/4W, 10% resistors, carbon comp type	.15	.015
1/4W, 5% resistors, carbon comp type	.20	.02
potentiometers (consumer grade)	2.00	.80
potentiometers (professional grade)	5.00	2.50
disc capacitors (under 0.01μF)	.25	.05
disc capacitors (over 0.01μF)	.35	.10
electrolytic capacitors (under 100μF)	.50	.20
electrolytic capacitors (over 100μF)	1.00-2.00	.50-1.00
LEDs	.35	.10
741 operational amplifier	.75	.30
small diodes	.30	.07
power diodes	.49	.10
knobs	.60	.15
switches (toggle, miniature)	2.95	1.10
switches (toggle, regular)	1.75	.75
switches (rotary)	2.00	1.20
jacks (mono, closed circuit)	.65	.30
jacks (stereo)	.75	.40

cases are difficult to locate; prices vary from $2 to $10 typically

TABLE II. Partial List of Mail-Order Houses

Allied Electronics—401 East 8th St., Fort Worth, **TX** 76102. Broad-line industrial distributor; not necessarily inexpensive. Parts can usually be ordered through local Radio Shack stores. Incidentally, Allied stocks the CLM 6000 opto-isolator used in some of these projects.

Ancrona Corporation—Box 2208, Culver City, **CA** 90230. Mostly semiconductor oriented; components, other items.

AP Products Inc.—Box 110, Painesville, **OH** 44077. Makers of experimenters' breadboards, which are fantastic little toys that make it easy to prototype projects without soldering. Check it out if you like to experiment.

Burstein-Applebee—3199 Mercier St., Kansas City, **MO** 64111. Broad-line distributor of components and electronic products.

Digital Research Parts—PO Box 401247, Garland, **TX** 75040. Carries some parts, modules, surplus, etc.

Delta Electronics—Box 1, Lynn, **MA** 01903. Parts, equipment, transformers, interesting surplus things.

Digi-Key—Box 667, Thief River Falls, **MN** 56701. Capacitors, semiconductors, resistors, diodes, other items.

Electronic Distributors, Inc.—4900 N. Elston Ave., Chicago, **IL** 60630. General electronics, parts, tools, test equipment.

GC Electronics—Rockford, **IL** 61101. Manufacturers the Calectro line of parts; write for info on nearby dealers carrying this line.

Integrated Circuits Unlimited—7889 Clairemont Mesa, San Diego, **CA** 92111. Semiconductors and some parts.

International Components Corporation—PO Box 1837, Columbia, **MO** 65201. Semiconductors and other components.

International Electronics Unlimited—225 Broadway, Jackson, **CA** 95642. Semiconductors and other parts.

Jameco Electronics—1355 Shoreway Road, Belmont, **CA** 94002. Many semiconductors, components, kits.

Meshna Electronics—Box 62, E. Lynn, **MA** 01904. Interesting surplus equipment, some components, things.

Mouser Electronics—11511 Woodside Avenue, Lakeside, **CA** 92040. Broad-line industrial distributor; mostly imported parts. Pots, resistors, capacitors, connectors. Fairly large minimum order required.

Newark Electronics—500 N. Pulaski Rd., Chicago, **IL** 60624. Broad-line industrial distributor; geared towards servicing industrial accounts.

Olson Electronics—260 S. Forge St., Arkron, **OH** 44327. General electronics, hi-fi, radio stuff, parts, and so on.

PAIA Electronics—1020 W. Wilshire Blvd., Oklahoma City, **OK** 73116. PAIA offers a broad line of musically oriented kits, and provides parts kits and circuit boards for the projects in this book.

Poly Paks—Box 942, Lynnfield, **MA** 01940. Semiconductors, surplus, readouts, hobby stuff, assortments.

Quest Electronics—PO Box 4430, Santa Clara, **CA** 95054. Semiconductors, components, kits.

Radio Shack—not mail order, but carries a line of electronic parts. Various locations; check the Yellow Pages.

Solid State Sales—Box 74, Somerville, **MA** 02143. Components, semiconductors, some surplus.

Chapter Three

Before you do any building, you need tools and a knowledge of how to care for them. This chapter covers drills, hacksaws, files, pliers, cutters, strippers, screwdrivers, soldering equipment, plexiglass tools, care of tools, and safety tips.

The parts cost of electronic projects isn't too high—in fact, once you learn the ropes of parts buying, you'll find that you can duplicate equipment that sells for hundreds of dollars with one-fifth the cash outlay. However, you will have to buy some tools; this is an initial investment which will pay for itself if you plan to get into music and electronics. Luckily, no really expensive or hard-to-find tools are necessary. A basic hand tool set can cost around $60, which isn't really too much when spread over a few projects. Besides, some of them (like a vise) you may already have lying around. Let's check out what's most useful, and some prices. Remember that prices given are approximate, and can vary widely depending upon the vendor and quality.

The biggest expenditure is a good drill. I recommend the kind that can take a 3/8" bit. Though slightly more expensive than the 1/4" kind, 3/8" is a common electronic dimension, and a 3/8" drill usually implies a heavy duty machine. Another needed feature is variable speed. Some variable speed drills can even reverse the drill bit direction or rotation at the flick of a switch. This feature isn't really necessary, but if you've got the bucks you might find it useful some time. Do make sure that your drill has a smooth variable speed action, though, from minimum to maximum speed. You can expect to pay anywhere from $25 to $45 for a drill.

To go along with your drill, you'll also need a set of bits. Typically you can get a set of average small bits (from 1/16" up to 1/4") for around $4. They won't last forever, but if you're only drilling aluminum and plastic they'll drill a lot of holes before they poop out. If you don't want a full set, you can get by with three bits: 1/16" (for drilling pilot holes —see Chapter 4); 1/8"; and 9/64" or 5/32". You'll also need the 3/8" bit mentioned earlier, and unless you're content to do a lot of filing, a 1/2" bit. Unfortunately these big bits are somewhat costly ($5 or so). If you're strapped for cash, just

get a 3/8" bit and enlarge the hole it makes with a file or tapered reamer if you need something bigger. Tapered reamers aren't too expensive and are useful for deburring or enlarging previously drilled holes (more about deburring shortly). A 1/2" diameter model is preferable to a 1" type.

Your final piece of drilling equipment is a center punch. The purpose of this device is to punch a small dimple (indentation) in metal or plastic by tapping it with a hammer on the nonpointed side. This dimple keeps the drill bit centered during its first few revolutions. You can get by with a nail in a pinch, but a real center punch is far more accurate.

You'll also need a hacksaw, principally for cutting potentiometer and rotary switch shafts to length. Almost any kind will do, but use a blade with fairly fine cutting teeth. While you're at it, get a spare blade—you'll need it at some unexpected later moment.

While we're still talking about metal-working equipment, you'll also want a few files. In addition to the hole-enlarging ability mentioned previously, when you drill holes in metal little burrs are left around the perimeter of the hole; you can use a file to get rid of these. You only really need two files: a rat's tail file, and a half-round type. Don't get big ones, since electronics work involves tight spaces most of the time.

For dealing with wire, bending components, and other light assembly work, you'll need needlenose pliers, diagonal cutters, and a wire-stripping tool for removing insulation. These run around $1 apiece for average quality units; check the jaws for accurate alignment and smooth action before buying anything, no matter how little or how much the item may cost. Fancy automatic wire strippers are available for about $8, but unless you're doing small-scale production you'll find they're more trouble than they're worth.

Next, your tool repertoire should include a medium-size screwdriver and a Phillips-head screwdriver, as well as a set of small jewelers' screwdrivers, Jewelers' screwdrivers are usually available (imported kind) for around $3 a set. These are handy for the set screws in knobs, but have many other talents in the fields of poking, prying, and scraping.

You'll also want a small crescent wrench for tightening nuts on pots and screws and, although it isn't really necessary, a pair of vise grips, which is a wonderful tool to have. To round out your selection of mechanical tools, get a small vise.

Now to soldering equipment. First item is a 25 to 40W soldering pencil (soldering "iron" may imply a big beastie that will probably burn out those little ICs) and some spare tips. Look around for something with a fairly small tip, as you'll save yourself a lot of hassle in tight places that way. And get some solder, too, but don't under any circumstances purchase acid-core solder! It won't work on electrical stuff, and can even damage it. The kind you want is 60/40 rosin-core solder (preferably the "multi-core" type). The "60/40" refers to the mixture of metals in the solder. Thinner solder is easiest to use, and costs about $15 a pound at industrial electronic outlets. My favorite type is Ersin Multi-Core. If you can't find thin solder, the standard kind at Radio Shack will do.

In addition to soldering, you might also want a desoldering tool. They come in all shapes, complexities, sizes, and costs, but the simplest kind is a squeeze bulb with a Teflon tip.

A lot of times I use plexiglass for panels, and you might want to work with it too. Plexiglass looks neat, as well as being fairly soft and easy to work, but there are a couple of special tools you will need. One is a plexiglass scorer for cutting the stuff. You can use a hacksaw, but the scorer zips through cutting big pieces and costs around $2, complete with instructions. Also, special

plexiglass drill bits are required. These are available from authorized plastics distributors (again, the Yellow Pages will tell you where to look), and are tapered to make drilling easy. Ordinary drill bits bigger than 1/8" or so will tend to tear the plexiglass, producing nasty looking holes that look like some vicious animal was at work. I use one 3/8" and one 1/2" plexiglass bit; for smaller size holes I use a 1/8" standard bit and enlarge it with a file or a tapered reamer.

Finally you need a tool for testing called a Volt-Ohm-Milliameter, or more simply, VOM (see Project No. 19 for instructions on how to use one). This little device has a meter which allows you to read amounts of resistance, amounts of volts, and current (not at the same time, though). You can pick up one for anywhere from $5 to $40; for most purposes the inexpensive type will do just fine, so you might as well opt for one under $20.

There are a few general rules for taking care of tools. First, if any of them come with instructions, *read them.* Your drill will come with instructions about lubrication, proper handling, and so on. These instructions should be followed, as should any directions that come with your soldering iron or VOM. Second, never use a tool for a purpose other than the one for which it was intended. Screwdrivers make lousy chisels, for example, and soldering irons are not available to little brothers or sisters for woodburning.

Drill bits respond well to sharpening at regular intervals, and you may want to pick up an oilstone to keep them happy. Also, *never* use plexiglass bits on any material other than plexiglass unless you have an urge to run out and buy a new bit.

Needlenose pliers are for fine work and wirebending. Don't use them on big klunky jobs where you should be using vise grips or the like, or you'll knock the jaws out of alignment and have to get a new set of pliers. The same goes for diagonal cutters; they're for cutting fine to

Figure 3-1

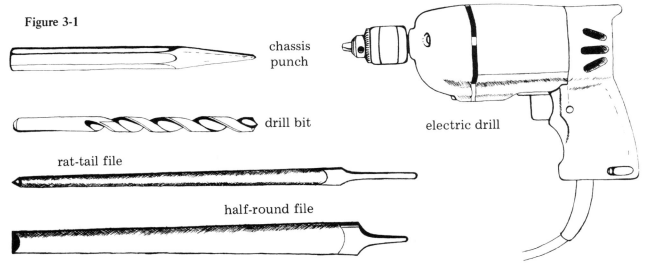

chassis punch

drill bit

rat-tail file

half-round file

electric drill

medium gauge wire. If somebody asks you to cut a piece of copper tubing with your cutters, politely decline and hacksaw through it instead.

Before moving on, a few words about safety are in order. The most dangerous tool you'll be using is the drill. Rule number one: *Keep your hair out of the way!* Tie it back or something, but be careful. Some people have gotten into real trouble by not remembering this rule. Rule number two is to use all three conductors of any-

Figure 3-2

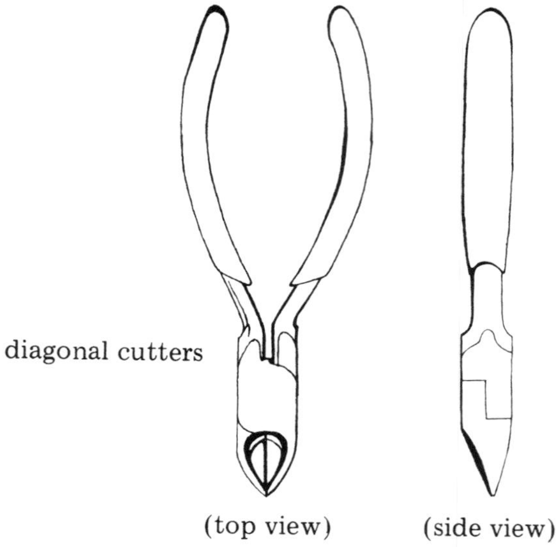

diagonal cutters

(top view)   (side view)

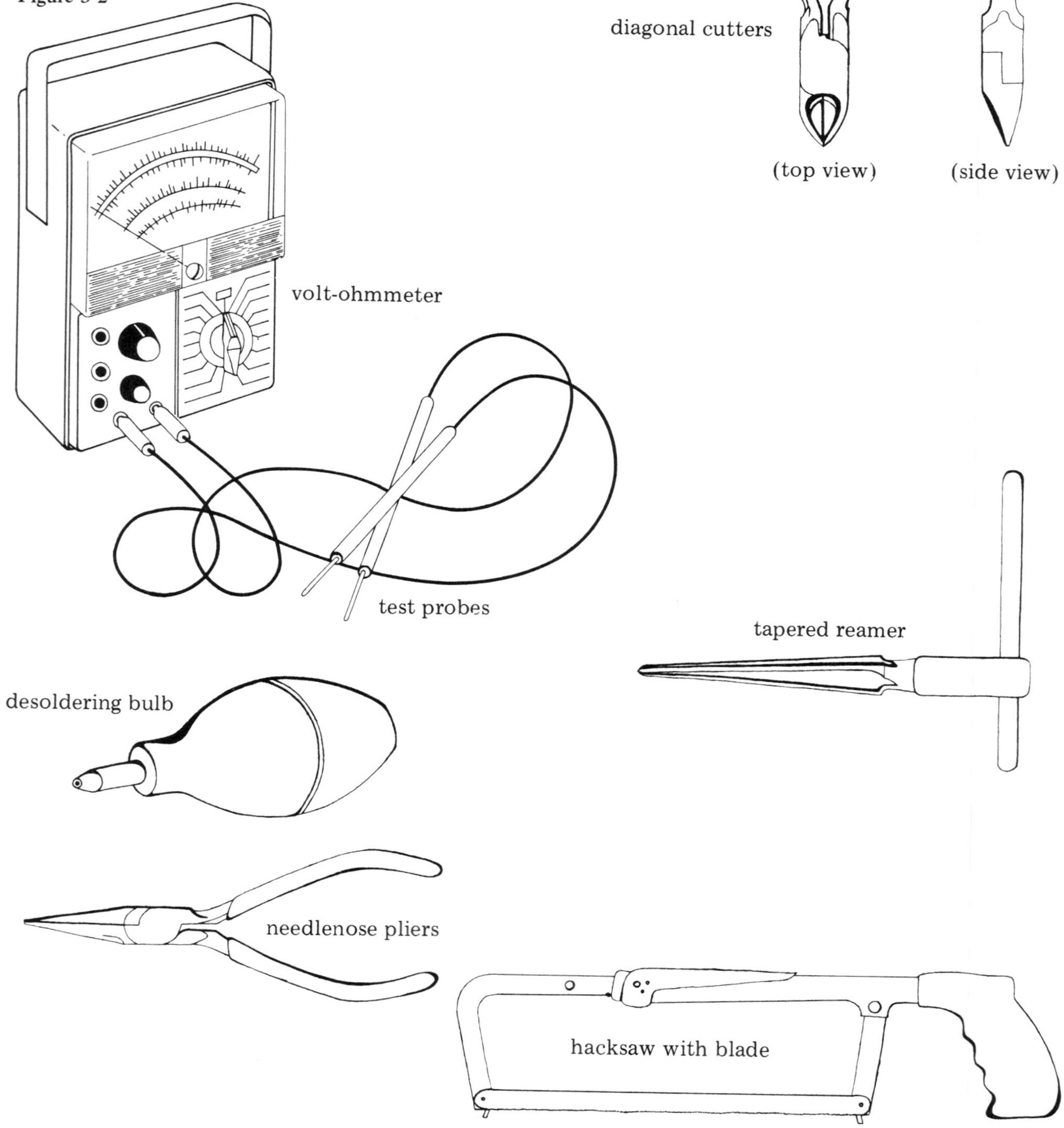

volt-ohmmeter

test probes

tapered reamer

desoldering bulb

needlenose pliers

hacksaw with blade

36

Figure 3-3

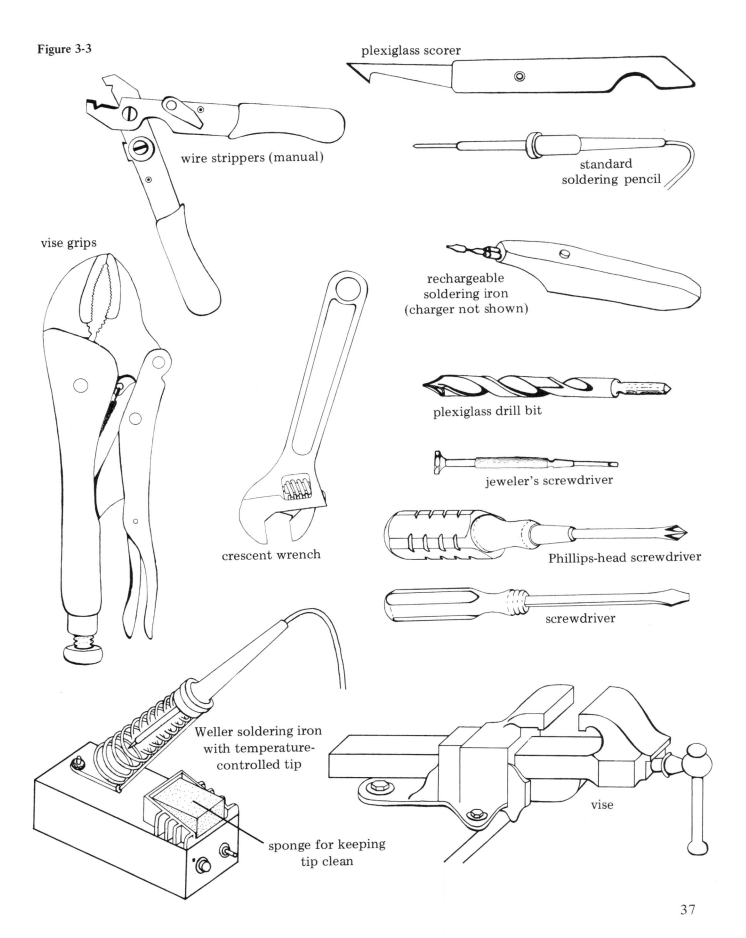

plexiglass scorer

wire strippers (manual)

vise grips

standard
soldering pencil

rechargeable
soldering iron
(charger not shown)

plexiglass drill bit

jeweler's screwdriver

crescent wrench

Phillips-head screwdriver

screwdriver

Weller soldering iron
with temperature-
controlled tip

sponge for keeping
tip clean

vise

thing requiring a three-wire cord. The one on the bottom is ground, and three-wire AC stuff is far safer than sticking on a three-to-two adapter and plugging that into your wall. If you don't have a three-wire outlet, use an adapter but take the wire coming out of the adapter and connect it to the screwplate on your AC outlet, as in Figure 3-4. The screw should go to ground and effectively does the same thing as the ground wire of a three-wire outlet. If you absolutely must use a two-wire setup, even though you shouldn't, don't stand on wet concrete barefoot, okay? You'll zap yourself unless the drill is properly insulated (most new ones are, but watch out for some older ones).

When you drill, don't hold the object you're drilling with your hands! Hold it with a vise, or vise grips, or anything suitable—should the drill bit slip or skid, you want it attacking the vise and not your hand.

Don't solder with shorts on if you're sitting down. Sometimes the rosin spits out and hits you on the leg; not really bad, but not fun either. Be careful where you lay down your soldering iron—don't put it where it can burn through its AC cord (this happens—don't laugh!). And watch for touching the wrong end of the iron. Be careful, these things are hot (around 600-700° Farenheit).

After this scary talk, I should probably mention that I have yet to do anything serious to myself, but a lot of that is because I listened to all the safety tips when I started. Be careful and use some common sense, and you won't have any trouble. Hands are precious to the musician, and even a small amount of care will keep them unscarred and unscathed.

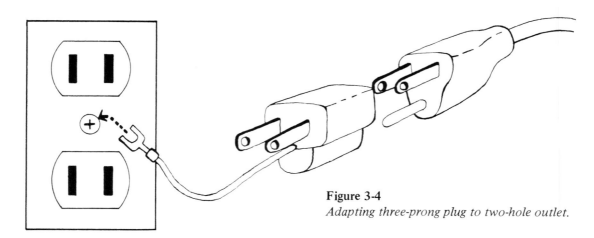

Figure 3-4
Adapting three-prong plug to two-hole outlet.

Chapter Four

If you have never built anything electronic before, Chapter 4 will help you out considerably. It tells you what you need to know to turn a pile of parts into an attractive, reliable, smoothly functioning unit.

Introduction

The process of building any electronic device can be broken down into several logical steps. Doing these steps in order saves a considerable amount of time, and promotes better results. One step of planning can save two in execution.

Step 1: Gather together any required parts, hardware, and tools.

Step 2: Fabricate a circuit board on which to mount the electronic components.

Step 3: Mount the various components on your circuit board and solder them in place.

Step 4: Select an enclosure capable of containing the circuit board, pots, jacks, switches, batteries, and the like. It's better to have too large an enclosure than too small an enclosure, as working in a cramped space can be frustrating.

Step 5: Drill holes in the enclosure and prepare parts for mounting in the chassis; for example, pot shafts may need to be cut, along with rotary-switch shafts.

Step 6: Wire the circuit board to the outboard parts.

Step 7: Securely mount the circuit board in the chassis. Sometimes it's best to plan for this (attaching angle brackets, drilling holes in the chassis where the angle brackets should mount) before completing step 6.

Step 8: Add knobs and label the various controls and jacks.

Step 9: Test the thing out for proper operation, then feel out its personality and operating characteristics.

We'll describe each of these steps in detail in this chapter; actually, we've already gone over step 1, so we're off to a good start. But before going any further, let's investigate the subject of soldering, as this is perhaps the most important part of putting together any electronic device.

Soldering Technique

Proper soldering is vital to the success of your projects; a great number, perhaps the majority, of problems with projects are due to poor soldering habits. Here are four important points to consider when soldering:

1. *Use the right tools.* Don't use irons over 60 watts, and don't use acid-core solder under any circumstances. The only acceptable solder is *rosin-core solder* that's expressly designed for electronic work. See Chapter 3 for additional information on choosing a soldering iron and solder.

2. *Keep your soldering iron tip in good condition.* The cardinal rule of tip care is to *not* let your iron sit in a warmed-up condition without having a thin layer of solder on the tip; otherwise, the tip will oxidize and work less efficiently. Here's how I recommend getting your iron ready for soldering:

—Wrap a turn of solder around the tip of your iron before plugging it in or turning it on. This way, when the tip comes up to temperature it will melt the solder and form the protective layer of solder we talked about earlier.

—Have a damp to slightly wet sponge sitting next to your iron (in a coffee can lid, ash tray, or the like). *Just before soldering, wipe the tip across the sponge to remove any excess solder from the tip; this produces a clean tip that creates better heat transfer for faster, more efficient soldering. When you're about to put the iron aside after soldering some connections, do *not* clean off the tip first; only clean the tip just before soldering a connection.

3. *Make sure the surfaces you'll be soldering together are clean.* For example, if you make your own circuit boards, you'll find that copper forms a layer of oxidation when exposed to the air; this layer makes it difficult

to make a good solder bond. The remedy in this case is to lightly rub the board with fine steel wool. Component leads can also become dirty or oxidized; use a rubber eraser, light sandpaper, or steel wool to clean off the dirt.

4. *Heat up the area to be soldered before feeding in the solder.* Don't just use the point of the iron's tip to solder; use the whole tip to heat the surfaces to be joined, as shown in Figure 4-1. After heating up the joint for a couple of seconds, feed in some solder and keep the iron

Figure 4-1

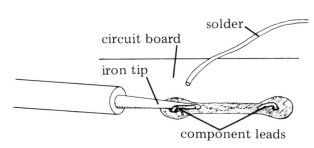

in position until the solder flows freely over the connection. The heating process can take differing amounts of time, depending on the type of connection. Circuit board connections usually require very little heat; all you have to heat up, after all, is a thin strip of copper and a component lead. Jacks, on the other hand, require a fair amount of heat; when they're mounted in a metal chassis, soldering to the ground tab requires substantial heat, as the chassis tends to draw heat away from the jack. Finally, do not disturb the connection as you remove the iron. Leave the iron on for an additional second or so after the solder is flowing freely, then remove the iron from the connection. Do not disturb the connection in the process, or the solidity of the joint will suffer as a result. Should this happen, reheat the connection while feeding in a bit more solder.

One of the main problems with solder joints is a *cold joint,* where not enough heat was applied to make the solder flow smoothly. Also, the rosin inside the solder (which smells a little like musk incense) cleans dirt and grease from the connections; if it isn't brought up to temperature, then the connection isn't going to get properly cleaned, which can also give a bad joint.

Figure 4-2 shows a variety of solder connections—what you should strive for and what you should avoid. Note that a good connection looks smooth, round, and shiny; poor solder connections look dull, tend to ball up, and are often grainy in appearance. One thing's for sure: If you can pull the lead out of its solder connection, the connection is no good. A good connection electrically is a good connection mechanically.

Now that you understand the basics of soldering, here's a simple project to extend the life of your tip considerably and save electricity at the same time. It is a soldering heat control, which can put your iron on stand-by so that it doesn't work at maximum juice all the time. It works on the same principle as those light dimmer switches that give a bright and low position; but note that this device is *not* designed to work with soldering irons that use a transformer or electronic controlling circuitry, and can damage them.

Figure 4-3 shows schematically how a soldering iron plugs into the wall. Figure 4-4 shows the solder heat control, which consists of a diode (a 1N4003 or any heavier-duty diode will work just fine) and a switch. Closing the switch applies full power to the iron; opening the switch diverts power through the diode, which cuts down the juice going to the iron and thus reduces the heat.

You'll find when experimenting that there are lots of times when you'll solder for several minutes straight, then quit for 10 to 15 minutes. That's when to use the reduced power. After you flick the switch to full juice, it takes only a few seconds for the iron to reach maximum heat again.

Desoldering

From time to time your problem will be not how to solder a component on to the board, but how to unsolder it. This could happen if you wished to convert an effect from low level to line level by changing a resistor, or needed to replace a defective (or incorrectly inserted) part. Before attempting to remove the part, remove as much solder as possible from the connection using one of the methods described below; then, remove the part by gently pulling on its leads with a pair of

Figure 4-2
Correct solder connection.

not enough heat; also dirty lead

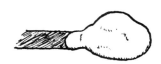
too much solder

. . . solder flows smoothly over area to be soldered

too little solder

Figure 4-3

How a soldering iron plugs into the wall schematically.

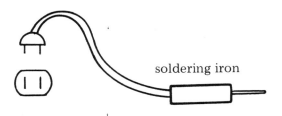

Figure 4-4

Using a soldering iron heat control. Observe good construction practices, since you're dealing with high voltages. Make all connections inside a metal case and make certain all connections are well insulated from each other and the case.

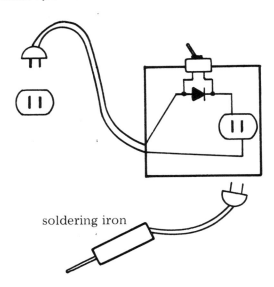

needlenose pliers. If the part still won't come out, remove some more solder; in extreme cases, pull out the part while applying heat to the connection to loosen the solder even more. Try to keep heat to a minimum to prevent damage to the part or the circuit board, and remember that desoldering takes more care than soldering; be patient. Here are two popular ways to remove unwanted solder:

1. *Desoldering squeeze bulb with Teflon tip.* It works like this: You squeeze the air out of the bulb first, heat up the solder that needs to be removed, hold the Teflon tip up against the solder blob, and let the air back in the bulb, pulling the molten solder with it. These are inexpensive and easy to use, but one drawback is that you must periodically clean out the bulb by unscrewing it from the tip, and clean out the tip itself with a solid piece of wire.

2. *Solder wicks.* These are pieces of braided wire that are especially designed to suck up solder. To use a solder wick, you heat the solder connection while holding the wick up against that connection; the wick removes virtually all of the solder by capillary action. You then cut off this section of the braid after the solder has cooled, thereby exposing more of the wick for desoldering your next connection.

The Care and Feeding of Printed Circuit Boards _____

About twenty years ago, printed circuit boards were a rarity; now, they are everywhere. Paradoxically, although they make assembly go much faster, they still require a time-consuming production process. For this reason, many giant electronic manufacturers have their circuit boards made by firms that specialize in PC board manufacture, rather than deal with the problem themselves.

The projects in this book are relatively simple, and as such require simple boards.* Those of you with a little electronic experience can probably wire the projects up on perf board without any trouble at all, saving yourself the trouble of making a circuit board. However, if you're so inclined, making circuit boards can be kind of fun, especially if you're new at the game. The basic process goes as follows: You start out with a piece of insulator that's flat, about 1.6 mm (1/16") thick, and has copper bonded to one side (sometimes both sides, but forget about that for this book). So, what you have is an insulator covered by a big copper conductor, and that's called a blank circuit board. Now, copper may be etched away and dissolved by a not-too-dangerous chemical called ferric chloride, which we'll call ferric for short. If you take a blank circuit board like the one mentioned above—insulator with copper on one side—and throw it into a tank of ferric, within about 45 minutes there won't be any copper left on the board. So by selectively etching away at the blank board, you can create areas of insulators (etched areas) and conductors (unetched areas). These conductors are called *traces*, and take the place of wires in a circuit. By drilling holes in the finished board, you can insert component leads through the board, having the leads come out on the *copper* side of the board; by soldering these leads to the traces, you've got a completed circuit, as shown in Figure 4-5. The catch to the whole process is how to avoid etching away the parts of the copper you want to keep.

_____

*The long dimension of each circuit board should be exactly 4.5 inches in order to fit in the Vector-Pak enclosure mentioned in a later chapter.

Figure 4-5

copper

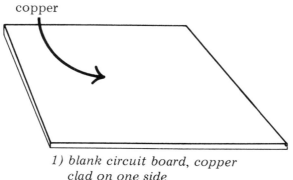

1) blank circuit board, copper clad on one side

2) lay down etch resist (tape, enamel paint, photoresist, etc)

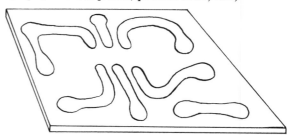

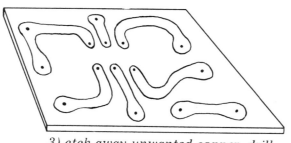

3) etch away unwanted copper, drill holes, strip away resist to expose copper underneath

4) insert parts through board at proper places

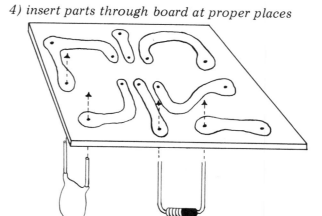

bend wires down

5) cut off excess lead length

7) side view of 6.

6) solder leads to circuit board for completed circuit

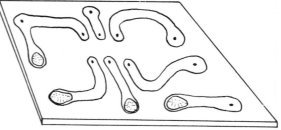

The least sophisticated way to deal with this problem is to just put little pieces of tape down directly on the copper, then dunk the board into a ferric bath. The tape prevents any solution from getting to the copper, but the drawback is a lack of ability to do fine work, which ICs require.

An easier way is to use a resist pen. These are like felt-tip markers; in fact, you can even use some stock felt-tip pens as resist pens. With this method, you lay ink down on the copper, let it dry, then toss the board in an etching bath. The dried ink keeps the etchant from the copper in those places where appropriate. But there's a problem here too, since the ink has to be on really thick to withstand sitting in the bath for twenty to thirty minutes; some of it can wear away and expose the copper underneath, which naturally starts to etch.

So, you switch to thicker ink . . . in this case, enamel paint seems to work well (you know, the kind for model airplanes that comes in little glass bottles). Get yourself a really fine brush, and paint on where you want the conductors to be. The enamel is very effective against etchant when you throw the board into the etch bath, although now you have the problem of getting the enamel paint off before you can solder to the copper. I've found that a variety of noxious and harmful chemicals do the job really fast, like ethyl acetate or toluene. You can also use paint thinner. Saturate a little steel wool with a chemical of your choice and strip off the paint. After the board dries, give a *light* final polish (you don't want to take off too much copper) with some clean steel wool and you're ready to go. I recommend wearing rubber gloves during the whole process; whatever strips off enamel paint also seems to have it in for rubber gloves, so work fast.

Should you use any of the first three methods, a few general tips. One, keep the copper clean. Sometimes a fingerprint will resist the ferric chloride and give uneven results. Two, keep dust and sticky surfaces away from the printed circuit board. One refinement I heartily recommend is using predrilled copperclad board. The kind of predrilled pattern you want is copperclad, single-sided *pattern P*; "P" means that there is a hole every 2.5 mm (0.1"), arranged in a grid fashion. Since IC pins are laid out with 2.5 mm (0.1") spacing between leads, pattern P is the easiest to work with.

Now for any perfectionists in the crowd, here's how professional circuit board manufacturers do theirs. The best circuit boards are made using photographic techniques. You make a negative of the circuit board pattern, then place that over a piece of copperclad board that has previously been sprayed with *photoresist.* Applying photoresist is almost like spraying a piece of photographic film on the circuit board. That way, when you place the negative over the board and expose it to light, an im-

pression of the negative pattern forms in the layer of photoresist. Then, you immediately throw the board into a developing bath, where developer combines with the photoresist to form a protective coating, thus protecting the desired copper traces. Finally, just like in all, the previous methods, you put the board in ferric chloride, watch the copper etch away, strip the photoresist that's left on the circuit board by using a stripping solution, and lightly scour with steel wool to keep the copper clean and free of grease for soldering. As a matter of common practice, it's a good idea to steel wool any printed circuit board (with exposed copper) lightly just before mounting and soldering parts.

If you want to do things photographically, the first step is to come up with a negative. Photocopy places, blueprint stores, and other photography-oriented shops can produce a negative for you if you take them the printed circuit pattern given for each of the projects in this book. This is another case for the Yellow Pages. The price is usually not too steep, but chances are a friend with a darkroom can do a satisfactory job for much less. The GC Electronics *Printed Circuit Handbook,* which you can find at stores that stock the Calectro line, gives further details on PC boards using photographic techniques. This little book turns you on to the most important things about PC boards, like making sure the developer is not put in a plastic tray, and so on.

No matter which method you choose to make PC boards, the etching process remains pretty much the same. Use plastic, rubber, or glass trays (dishwashing trays do just fine; so do small plastic garbage cans), as the ferric will eat away at a metal one. Next, ferric works best at higher temperatures, but don't over heat it or you'll get some nasty fumes. It's best to etch outside, because of the ventilation and the warming action of the sun. If you live in a cold part of the world, you might be better off doing your etching inside a basement or attic as long as it's reasonably well ventilated, and suspending a light bulb over the ferric to warm it up a bit.

While etching, it's a good idea to agitate the etch solution as much as possible. The idea is to put in just enough ferric to keep the board covered, then jostling the plastic tray (or what-have-you) so that fresh ferric continually washes over the copper. This hastens the etching process, and the board tends to etch more evenly.

Although ferric won't burn your skin if you come into contact with it, you will acquire a brown stain that's hard to get rid of. Ferric can also permanently stain clothes, as well as modify the color of small furry animals. Wear rubber gloves and an apron, and etch somewhere away from any activity.

After the etching process is all over and there's no more unwanted copper on the board, it's a good idea to put the board in a plastic bucket of cold water for at

Figure 4-6

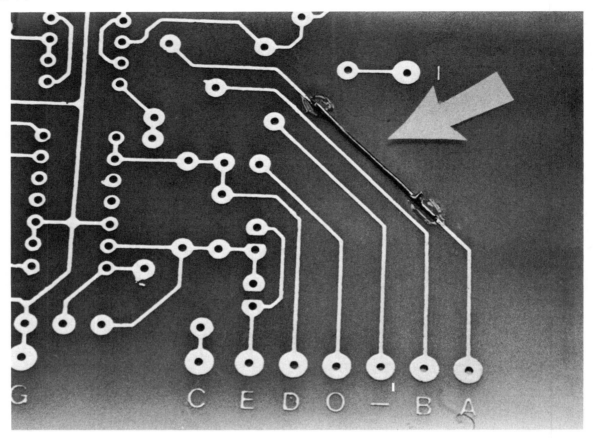

least a minute. This washes off any excess ferric, while the cold stops the etching action totally. After removing the board from the cold water, dry it off and check for any flaws or unetched areas before stripping the resist.

In some cases the etchant will etch away a piece of the trace. Should this happen, you can use a wire bridge to reconnect the trace as shown in Figure 4-6.

Many electronic stores carry little kits for making PC boards that come with detailed instructions. If you want to get into making circuit boards, I strongly suggest your getting one of these starter kits and getting your chops together with a few practice boards. Just remember to take your time, follow the directions, and resign yourself to the almost certain knowledge that your first board will be a total disaster. Your third, however, will probably be quite good—no missing resist, no incomplete etching, sharp edges on the traces, and all the other qualities that make a trouble-free and good-looking circuit board.

Perfboard Construction

There are alternatives to using conventional circuit boards; one of the most popular is to wire up circuits on a piece of *perfboard*. Perfboard is similar to predrilled copperclad board, except that there is no copper deposited on the board. The basic idea is to mount the parts on one side of the board, stick the leads through the holes, and run wires on the noncomponent side of the board to connect the various leads together. In fact, often you can simply use the leads coming out of the parts to connect over to other parts. Figure 4-7 shows the back side of a board (the tube fuzz, Project No. 24) wired up on a piece of perfboard.

The little connectors called *micro flea clips* are a natural adjunct to perfboard wiring. These fit into the 1 mm (0.042") holes in pattern P boards, and are handy when you want to attach a wire from, say, a pot or jack to something fragile like an LED. Rather than risk the mechanical instability of simply wiring to a part that may have delicate leads, you solder the delicate lead to a somewhat less fragile flea clip and then connect a wire to that. Figures 4-8 should put this whole matter across.

It takes a while to get the hang of flea clip/perfboard construction, since this method requires some pretty detailed work and a nice thin soldering pencil. But if you're doing just one board at a time it's the fastest way to go—I've used perfboard wiring with great success over the years.

Figure 4-7

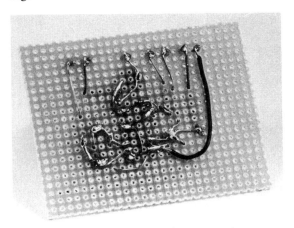

Figure 4-8

Closeup of vectorboard and micro flea clip. The distance between holes on the vectorboard is 2.5mm (0.1"), making it ideal for mounting integrated circuits, since their leads are 2.5mm apart. Leads from components can also go through the holes, which are 1.68mm (0.042") in diamater.

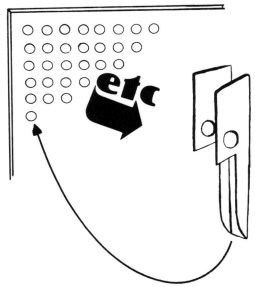

Another way to speed up perfboard wiring is through the use of a wiring pencil. This tool, made by a couple of different manufacturers, is generally available at electronic supply houses; it dispenses extremely thin wire through a pencil-like tip. You wrap a few turns of this wire around a component lead, then feed out some more wire and run this wire over to the next component lead. You wrap a few turns around this lead, and then proceed to the next connection. Because this is insulated wire, you can let it drape over other parts and leads without worrying about creating a short circuit. But what makes this insulation unique is that it is composed of a thin layer of some substance that melts when sufficient heat is applied. So, after you've wrapped a few turns around the component lead, you heat up the connection with a soldering iron and feed in some solder. The heat melts the insulation, and *voilà* –instant soldered connection. Luckily, the insulation melts only in the immediate vicinity of the connection.

In circuits where you need to connect a number of points together, the wiring pencil is a very efficient and timesaving technique. However, this method does require a bit of practice, mostly because you need to use a relatively hot soldering iron in order to melt the insulation. (I have a Weller soldering station where you can change the tip to vary the temperature; while I use the 600° tip for general circuit board wiring, I use a 700° tip when using the wire pencil.) The trick is to apply enough heat to adequately melt the insulation, but not apply so much that you damage any of the components. For further information on the use of the wiring pencil, refer to instructions included with each unit . . . or ask someone behind the counter of your local electronics emporium to tell you what it's all about.

You might have heard about a technique called *wire-wrapping*. While it may appear useful, in practice wire-wrapping is really most suitable for digital, high-density circuits that use lots of ICs and very few other components. So until you get into building your own computer, I doubt if you'll find wire-wrapping too valuable a technique to put together the projects presented in this book.

Loading the Circuit Board

If you've made your own circuit board, lightly steel wool the foil side of the board to prepare the copper for soldering. A bright, shiny board will be easier to solder and creates a better solder joint. If you're using circuit boards from the Godbout parts kits, these should *not* be steel wooled, as the copper has been covered with a thin layer of solder to facilitate soldering. Also, note that these boards are legended—this means that the component side of the board indicates which parts are supposed to go where.

Begin the loading process by mounting the resistors and diodes first. Bend the leads at right angles to make insertion into the holes of the PC board a little easier, and insert *all* components from the noncopper-clad (or nonfoil) side of the board. These parts should hug the board as closely as possible when loaded; for example, the resistors should mount flush against the board as shown in the upper drawing of Figure 4-9, and not be left "floating" as shown in the lower drawing. Next, bend the leads down against the copper side and solder them. Cut off any excess lead length so that it doesn't short against the other copper traces and pads; also, make sure your solder blob hasn't bridged across to any other traces. This is called a *solder bridge* and is a member of the short-circuit family! Avoid solder bridges if you want your project to work right.

Figure 4-9

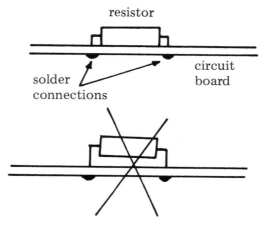

resistor

solder connections

circuit board

Next, put in your IC socket; note that the socket will have an indentation or mark to indicate the pin 1 corner of the socket. At this point a lot of people aren't going to want to spend the extra money for a socket, so I should mention an alternative: the Molex connector for ICs, which is a strip of little connector terminals (see Figure 4-10). You cut off two strips of seven pins each for a fourteen-pin IC, and put them in the appropriate holes on the board. (You may need to hold the strips temporarily in place from the top side with masking tape; that way, when you flip the board over to solder the pins they won't fall out). After you've soldered the pins to the board, break off the little connecting strips that hold the pins together, and you have a working socket. Although it's a little more difficult to insert IC pins into a Molex connector, the low cost makes this an attractive alternative. Do make sure you use a socket,

though. Not only does it make repairs and upgrading easier, but one of the prime causes of IC failure is excessive soldering heat, and a socket eliminates this possibility.

Mount the capacitors next after the resistors, diodes, and socket are on the board. Capacitors are not overly sensitive to heat, but solder them fairly rapidly with a good solder joint.

Since capacitors come in varying sizes, some circuit boards have extra holes drilled to accommodate different sized parts. For example, Figure 4-11 shows two ways of mounting a capacitor in its designated space. Figure 4-11a shows how a radial lead capacitor mounts in the board; figure 4-11b shows how to mount an axial lead type. In either case, make sure you get the polarity right.

Figure 4-11a

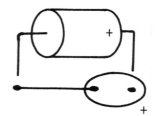

Figure 4-11b

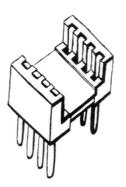

Figure 4-10

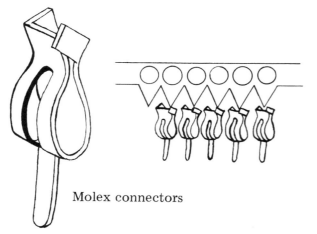

Molex connectors

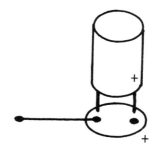

regular 8-pin socket

regular 14-pin socket

Figure 4-12a

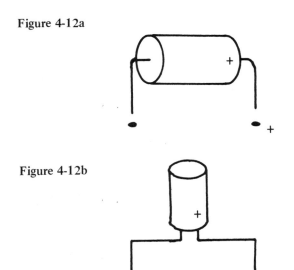

Figure 4-12b

There are several ways you can package your equipment so that it looks good and works well. For best results, choose a method that gives you adequate work room, yet isn't overly large. It's important to gather together all your parts before choosing a chassis—with the items in front of you, it's easier to estimate what size you'll need to contain the parts comfortably.

Many electronic outlets sell commercial boxes, finished and painted in different colors. The photos of various projects in Chapter 5 show some of the kinds you can expect to run into in stores. Some of the names to look for in finished metal boxes are LMB, Bud, Premier, Ten-Tech, and Radio Shack. These enclosures are easy to find and use, although they also tend to be expensive (especially for large enclosures).

An entirely different approach uses rack mounting. Rack mounting systems consist of rack panels and rack mounts (Figure 4-13). The panels have a standard width of 48.75 cm (19½"), but the height can vary from 4.4 cm (1.75") to many centimeters. With this type of approach, you have the advantage of *modularity*; for example, you can build a low-noise preamp on one panel, a phase shifter on another panel, and a reverb unit on yet a third panel, and mount them all in a rack mount. At a later date, you might wish to replace your preamp with a more sophisticated type that has tone controls—no sweat, just pop out the preamp panel, build your new preamp, and put it in where the old one used to be (leaving the others as they were). Rack mounting is

Figure 4-12a shows how to mount an axial lead part on a circuit board when only two holes are provided; Figure 4-12b shows how to mount a radial lead type in the same space. Note that the radial's leads are bent and formed to fit the available space.

Now that you've got the components mounted and soldered in place, check that all polarities are correct, that the solder joints are good, and that there aren't any solder bridges or board defects. If everything checks out, you're ready for the next step. By the way, don't plug the IC in its socket just yet; wait until all the outboard wiring is completed.

Figure 4-13

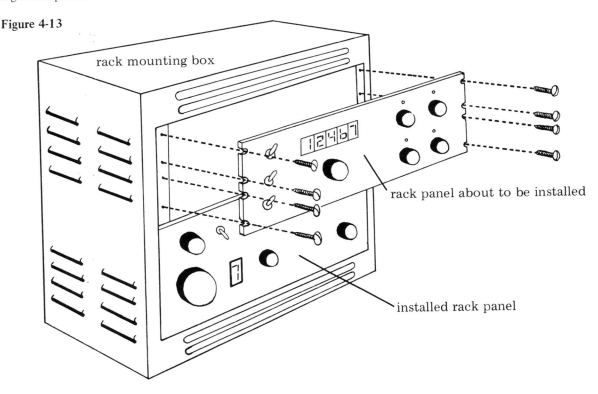

rack mounting box

rack panel about to be installed

installed rack panel

particularly useful if you plan to get really involved with electronics, but it certainly isn't the most portable system. Rack panels, incidentally, are available in a wide variety of colors, and a choice of either steel or aluminum. *Stick with aluminum!* Steel is really a hassle to work on.

One of my favorite packaging methods is to use a plain, unfinished chassis box as in Figure 4-14, and cut a plexiglass panel for the top. The chassis can be either spray painted or covered with some interesting contact paper. In case you haven't seen what's happening recently with contact paper, you may be surprised; there's shiny, glossy, and patterned stuff, not just the phony woodgrains and flowers I always remembered. Anyway, this method works best for mounting several little things in one box. That way, you have a compromise between

Figure 4-14

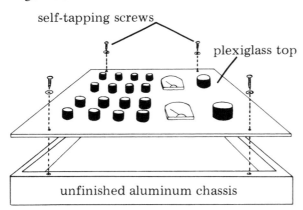

self-tapping screws

plexiglass top

unfinished aluminum chassis

Figure 4-15

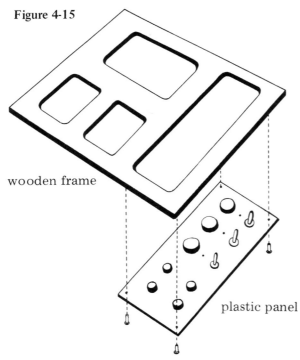

wooden frame

plastic panel

the previous two methods. You still have a portable box, but it contains a variety of functions that you might not be able to fit in one of the smaller, commercial boxes.

Another method is a cross between the last one and rack mounting. It involves making small plastic panels and mounting them on some kind of wooden or metal box (Figure 4-15). If different signal processors are put on different panels, you still have the advantage of modularity, but on a somewhat looser level than rack mounting. Also, you can make each panel a different color, and that's always fun to look at.

If you do decide to get into plexiglass techniques, there are a few hints you should know. When purchasing plexiglass from your distributor, ask if they have a scrap pile of odds and ends. Oftentimes when cutting plexiglass for customers there will be little strips and pieces left over—these get thrown into a scrap pile, where you can pick them up for a fraction of the regular cost (stores usually charge by the pound). You can find clear, colored, or translucent, but stick to plexiglass in 3.1 mm (1/8") thicknesses. The thicker stuff looks nice, but many times components won't mount through anything thicker than 3.1 mm; thinner stuff, on the other hand, isn't strong enough.

You may cut plexiglass with a hacksaw, but that's the hard way. An easier way is to use the plexiglass scorer mentioned in Chapter 3. You lay down the piece of plexiglass on a flat surface, get a straight edge (preferably metal), and run the scorer along the cut-line until you've made a significant groove in the plastic. Then, put the cut-line on top of a dowel (Figure 4-16) and apply pressure to both sides until the cut-line fractures with a snapping sound. You can't cut really small pieces this way, but in all other cases it's a timesaver.

The final packaging method we'll look at is the Vector-Pak module cage; for an idea of what this looks like, refer to the first photo in Chapter 6. Module cages are also made by Bud and some other companies, but chances are the Vector-type will be easier for you to order locally.

The backbone of the system is a large, rack-mountable structure called a *module cage.* It will typically hold eight to ten modules with identically sized front panels; more expensive versions allow you to use modules with differently sized front panels. Each module may be removed for easy servicing, is completely enclosed for shielding purposes, and has two panels (front and back) on which you can mount controls, switches, jacks, and the like. Figure 4-17 shows a photo of a completed module, but without the side panels in place so that you can see the circuit board contained within. The top and bottom of the module are a fixed distance apart and have grooves that hold the circuit board in place—which is why all the circuit boards in this book have a common

Figure 4-16

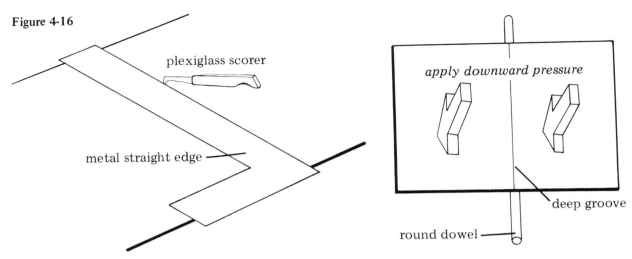

plexiglass scorer

metal straight edge

apply downward pressure

deep groove

round dowel

Figure 4-17

dimension for height. Figure 4-18 shows how a board fits in these grooves; notice the small card stop installed in the groove to keep the board from slipping around (these are provided with the Vector-Pak). Although the Vector company provides instructions on how to assemble these modules with each enclosure, the basic assembly order is as follows:

1. Open up the blister package for each module, and save the associated hardware in a *safe* place. Losing a screw on your workshop floor can be a real drag.

2. Drill the front panel to accommodate the various controls and switches, then drill the back panel to accom-

Figure 4-18

modate jacks and a power connector (see Figure 4-19). I installed a grommet in the rear panel through which the power wires exit. Be careful; pots need to be mounted quite precisely on the panel in order to avoid having the terminals short out against the metal walls of the module. In some cases, you may have to bend the pot lugs upward to prevent this from happening. Figure 4-20 shows a typical template, in this case for the ring modulator (Project No. 9). Note that the pots mount with their terminals facing to the *right* (viewed from the front) to prevent shorting problems.

3. Mount pots and jacks on the front panel (Figure 4-21).

Figure 4-20

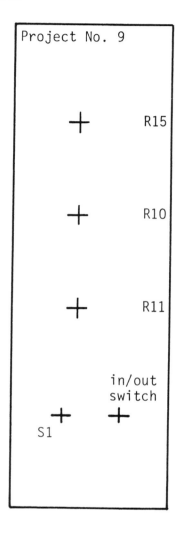

Figure 4-19

Figure 4-21

4. Center the loaded circuit board in the bottom plate groove, and use two of the card (circuit board) retainers provided to hold the board in place. I've found the best way to hold the card retainers in place is to tap them into the groove using a hammer and center punch.

5. Assemble the front and back panels, along with the top and bottom plates, using eight of the provided screws. The circuit board should now be held securely in place.

6. Wire the panel parts to the board. Leave about 0.5 cm (3/8") extra slack when wiring to the back panel.

7. When wiring is complete, temporarily remove the four screws holding the back panel in place. Slide the two side panels into place and screw the back panel

into place to complete the module structure. Note that these side panels have one end with a small indentation; this indentation butts up against the back panel to keep the panels from falling out should the unit be tilted backwards (say, during transportation). If the indentation isn't sufficiently pronounced, use a center punch and hammer to push it outwards a little further.

For those who want a truly professional, heavy-duty enclosure without having to actually machine it themselves, commercial module cages are an excellent way to go. Just think twice, and double-check everything, before you actually do any drilling to prevent an expensive mistake . . . and make sure you understand how the thing goes together before you even think about plugging in an electric drill or soldering iron.

Drilling

The drilling process uses a template to indicate where the holes are to be drilled, and a center punch to make a small indentation the drill bit can follow.

The easiest way to make a template is with graph paper, because that way you know that the holes are correctly lined up in terms of right angles and the like. After you've made the template, tape it to the chassis (use masking tape so you don't leave a residue and/or pull off the finish), support the back of the panel with a piece of wood, and use the center punch on each of the hole guides. When using the center punch on plexiglass, don't hit too hard or the plexiglass may crack. On metal, you can tap a little harder, but don't do it hard enough to deform the metal around it. All you want is a neat little space to center the drill bit during the first few turns of the drill.

You now have the holes punched. Take off the template, but keep it around. Some friend will see your gadget and want you to build one for him; if you've already got the template, you have a head start. Next, drill your holes. Metal is less critical than plexiglass, but still, if you're drilling a hole over 6.2 mm (1/4"), it pays to drill a 1.6 mm (1/16") pilot hole first, then use the big bit. Otherwise, the bit may "walk," even with the center-punched guide. Keeping the drill as vertical as possible, start it up at a fairly low speed (you do have a variable speed drill, right?) to make sure you're centered in the right place; when the drill starts to penetrate into the metal, speed up, but back off when you feel you're reaching the end. Oftentimes, the bit will start to grab when you reach the end. Keep on drilling, but remember the safety caution of earlier: *Don't hold the thing to be drilled with your hand!* It's hard to explain exactly why on paper, but if you ever end up with the drill grabbing onto a chassis and twirling it round and round at 2500 RPM, you'll see the logic of the statement. After you drill all your holes, use a file to clean off any burrs. Figure 4-22 shows a metal chassis

Figure 4-22

after drilling; eventually the tube sound fuzz was mounted in this box.

We mentioned drilling plexiglass in the last chapter. Here are some details. When drilling holes up to about 4.7 mm (3/16"), start with the smallest bit you've got and gradually enlarge the hole, using a larger bit each time until you get the right size. For holes between 4.7 mm (3/16") and 9.3 mm (3/8"), a tapered reamer works well for enlarging. For holes between 9.3 mm (3/8") and 12.5 mm (1/2"), drill a small pilot hole 3.1 mm (1/8") or so, then use the special plexiglass bits you get at plexiglass distributors. The reason for all these special cautions is that plexiglass is strong, but it is brittle; drill a couple of holes in a piece of scrap and get the feel before embarking on drilling an important panel.

Before we get off the subject of drilling, there's a fine point worth mentioning. On many rotary switches and pots you'll see a little tab (Figure 4-23). By drilling a hole for this little tab in the chassis next to the big (shaft) hole, you can lock the switch into place, giving

Figure 4-23

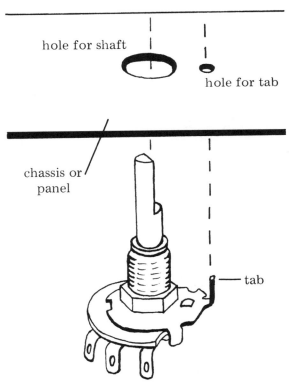

it a far more secure feel. This usually isn't necessary for pots because you're not putting much torque on a pot anyway (I just bend the tab off to one side), but for rotary switches the extra little hole is a must.

While you're in a metal-working frame of mind, it's a good time to cut pot and switch shafts to length, unless you were lucky enough to pick up some surplus pots that were already cut. Proper technique is to hold the shaft in a vise (Figure 4-24) and cut with a hacksaw. Never hold the body of the pot/switch! Be careful, also, to leave enough shaft length to fit comfortably into whatever knobs you've chosen.

Figure 4-24
Proper shaft-cutting technique.

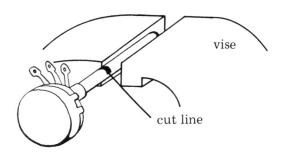

General Wiring

Wiring connects the circuit board, or guts of the project, to outer (or outboard) parts like pots, jacks, batteries, and switches. As such, much of your project's success depends on good wiring practice. I *strongly* suggest using stranded—not solid—wire, because it is more flexible. The thickness of the wire is assigned a number, called the *gauge* of the wire; for wiring up your projects, no. 24 to no. 26 gauge is just about optimum.

The first consideration when wiring with insulated wire is removing the insulation. Use a wire-stripping tool to remove about 6 mm (1/4") of insulation. Removing too much can lead to accidental shorts; removing too little can make for a poor connection, as excess insulation melts into the solder. When using wire strippers, be careful not to cut or nick the wire itself, or you'll end up with a weakened connection.

When wiring to a solder lug, you can either poke your wire through the terminal and solder, or wrap the wire around the lug and then solder. The former method is the easiest but not the strongest, since it depends on the strength of the solder to securely hold your wire in place. The latter method works best on terminals where you have many wires joining together; an extra-strong mechanical connection keeps the first wire firmly in place as other wires connect to the terminal (see Figure 4-25). This strong mechanical connection can be a hassle, though, if you need to remove the wire for some reason (like a wiring error or modification). In any event, remember to use good soldering techniques, take your time, and check your work as you go along to catch any possible errors.

Figure 4-25
Connecting wires to solder terminals.

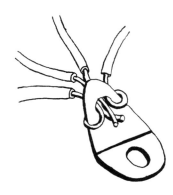

Figure 4-26
Connecting pad "G" to a ground lug.

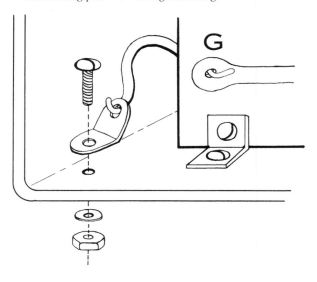

Figure 4-27

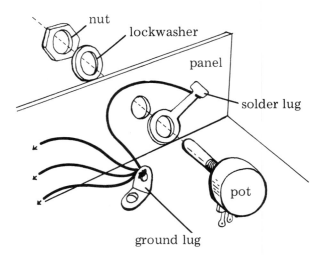

Grounding

Let's look at the schematic for Project No.1. There's a hitherto unmentioned schematic symbol, ⟂, which stands for *chassis ground,* and right now is a good time to examine its ramifications. There are many subtleties involved in proper grounding; the subject is really rather complex, but suffice it to say that some grounding techniques promote more stable circuits than others. The kind of method we're using is the *star* system of grounding. With this method, you mount a solder lug in your chassis or panel, and call this lug *chassis ground,* or the ground that connects to the chassis. (We'll talk about plexiglass, which is a special case, shortly.) Anyway, when you see the symbol for chassis ground, you run a wire from the point marked chassis ground to the chassis ground solder lug. You'll also notice that all project circuit boards have a point (technical name: *solder pad* or just *pad*) marked *G*; this stands for ground, and must also have a wire connecting it to chassis ground.

So what's the reason for the other ground symbol ($\perp$)? Many of the parts on a circuit board ground together at the circuit board. Since these points don't go directly to chassis ground, but rather to a ground point on the circuit board which *then* connects to chassis ground, we use a different symbol. We'll call this symbol *board ground,* even though no one else does. To sum up, when you see the board ground symbol ($\perp$), it means that that point connects to the ground trace on the board, which ultimately connects to a pad on the circuit board labeled *G*. When you see a chassis ground symbol (⟂), it means that that point wires directly to the chassis ground solder lug. Figure 4-26 shows a hypothetical circuit which gets the point across.

When dealing with metal cases, putting in a chassis ground lug grounds anything connected to that lug or touching the chassis. Therefore, any pot or switch cases that touch the chassis automatically become grounded, shielding the insides. You may notice that since the ground terminals of jacks also touch the chassis, it's technically unnecessary to run a ground wire from the jack ground to the chassis ground. *Do it anyway!* Frequently jacks come loose, and when they do, the ground contact may become intermittant. A wire prevents this problem.

Plexiglass is an insulator (except for some types of mirrored-back plexiglass), so you must run every chassis ground point to the chassis ground solder lug. With plexiglass the pot and switch cases no longer touch ground, so you have a light shielding problem. You can solve it by using some soldering lugs mentioned in Chapter 1 that fit over pot bushings. That way, when you mount the pot, you have a soldering lug in firm contact with the pot's case. Run a wire from this lug to the chassis ground

lug and the pot case will be shielded (Figure 4-27). If you run out of or can't locate these little lugs, a few turns of wire around the bushing will do the job.

Wiring the Circuit Board to Outboard Parts

There are two basic ways to do this kind of wiring. In some cases, you'll want to first attach wires to the board, then mount the board in the enclosure, and finally connect the wires to the outboard parts. In this instance, you'll want to make sure you have allowed enough lead length to actually reach the various outboard parts. The alternative method is to mount the circuit board in the enclosure, and *then* wire the board to the outboard parts. When you're building your project, it should be immediately obvious which approach is best for you. However, do leave a little slack in the wiring between the board and the outboard parts; otherwise, if you find you need to add a wire you forgot, or make a change on the circuit board, you'll have a hard time getting at the circuit board, since tight wires will tend to anchor it in position. One reason I like mounting projects in the Vector-Pak module is that both sides of the board are readily accessible, and easy to wire to the various pots, jacks, and switches.

Before you begin wiring, you need to mount all the outboard parts in the enclosure you're using as shown in Figure 4-28. Tighten all nuts as firmly as possible, so that jacks won't loosen from repeated plugging and unplugging, and pots don't come loose as you twiddle them. If

Figure 4-28

you do a lot of construction, you'll find it easier to invest in a socket wrench set instead of tightening all the nuts with a crescent wrench or pliers. I also advice using lock-washers on all pots, as this helps secure them in place.

Let's consider the actual process of wiring from the circuit board to the outboard parts.

You'll notice on the schematics that there are little letters that identify wires coming from outboard parts like battery connectors and jacks. These lettered terminals connect to like-lettered pads on the board via a length of wire. For example, if the positive supply line connects to the (+) point of the board, then you would connect that supply wire to the circuit board pad labeled (+). Another example: If a line on the schematic goes from a pot terminal to, say, a pad labeled B, then you would run a wire from that pot terminal to pad B on the circuit board. There are a few standard letters and symbols we'll use: G means the circuit board ground point, (+) stands for the positive supply voltage point, (-) stands for the negative supply voltage point, I means input, and O means output. Other than these, the selection of letters and symbols is more or less arbitrary. Figure 4-29A shows a piece of perfboard cut to fit in its enclosure; Figure 4-29B shows a wired tube sound fuzz.

Since it's annoying to wire up a pot the wrong way and have to shift wires around, I thought it might avoid some confusion to number the pot terminals. With the pot shaft pointing away from you as shown in Figure 4-30, looking at the *back* of the pot, the terminal on the left is 3, the middle one is 2, and the right hand one is 1. Sharp-eyed readers might note that this is the exact reverse of the numbering scheme used in the last edition of this book; there's a reason for that. At the time of writing the first edition, I didn't know that there was an industry standard way of numbering pot terminals, so I made up my own numbering scheme. The new pot terminal numbering presented here is now in step with the rest of the world.

Shielded Cable

To prevent pickup of spurious signals, we'll specify sheilded cable when connecting up some points on a board. Preparing shielded cable is difficult. First, cut through the outer insulation layer to get to the shield, usually a bunch of ultra-fine wires. Peel the shield back out of the way (a time-consuming process), to expose another insulated wire, which is the hot connector. Strip some of the insulation off this, and you're ready to go after you figure out how to fashion the shield into something suitable for soldering to a ground lug.

I've come up with a lazy way of dealing with shielded cable that I'll pass on to you, serialized in Figure 4-31. Be careful not to overheat the shield when soldering

Figure 4-29a

Figure 4-29b

Figure 4-30

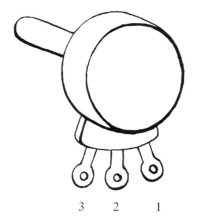

3   2   1

Figure 4-31a
Unstripped shielded cable.

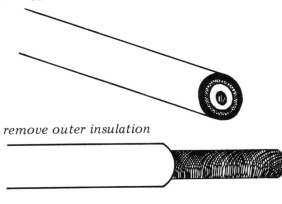

remove outer insulation

push back braid to expose inner conductor

strip ¼" of insulation from end of the inner conductor

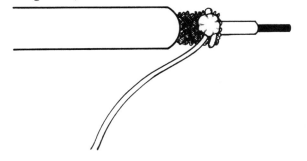

wrap bare wire around braid, then solder, being careful not to overheat

your ground wire to it, or you may short out to the inner connector by melting through its insulation.

Install the prepared shielded cable as follows. The shield never connects at both ends, which is just as well because that way you don't have to prepare a shield twice. The ground wire at one end connects to the ground terminal of the input (or output) jack; the hot wire from this same end connects to the hot of the input or output jack. The hot wire on the other end goes to point *I*, point *O*, or a footswitch, whichever is appropriate.

We'll indicate where to use shielded cable in the *construction tips* section of each project. However, it will be

understood that the shield only grounds at one end, usually to the ground lug on the nearest jack (or to the chassis ground).

Mounting the Circuit Board in the Enclosure

Let's examine three popular methods of PC board mounting, shown in Figure 4-32: vertical mounting method using L-brackets and screws; the horizontal spacers and long screws technique; and hot glue with insulators.

Figure 4-31b
Shielded wire soldered to monojack properly.

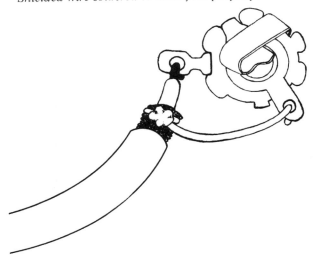

In method one, you can mount the board first, and then connect hookup wires to its pads—the other methods require connecting hookup wires to the pads before mounting the board itself, which requires extra lengths of wire. One way around the problem is to insert flea clips into the holes on the PC board that connect with the pads; that way, you can solder to the top side of the clip (Figure 4-33).

The advantage of method one is simplicity; the drawback is a lack of mechanical strength. Another problem might be finding small L-brackets, although many electronic stores carry them. Method two is sturdiest, but it takes more work, and you have to find spacers (although the barrel end of a Bic pen, when cut into spacer-size cylinders, does a good job of spacing when your supplier is out of stock).

Method three is quick and secure, but requires a hot glue gun. This is a tool that heats up little sticks of glue to liquify them. The hot, liquid glue then exits through a thin nozzle in the glue gun tip. When the glue cools (about a 30-second process), you're left with a strong bond. By the way, they *mean* hot glue—don't touch.

To use this method on a metal chassis, first glue a block of styrofoam, cardboard, or some other insulator

Figure 4-32

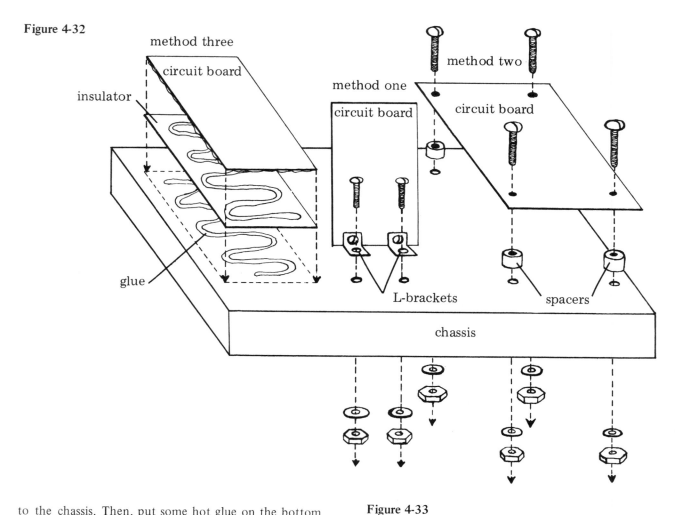

method three

circuit board

insulator

glue

method one

circuit board

L-brackets

method two

circuit board

spacers

chassis

to the chassis. Then, put some hot glue on the bottom of the circuit board and on the top of the insulator block, press together, and you have a mounted circuit board. When using plexiglass, the bottom insulator isn't needed, as you're already gluing to an insulator. While I don't think this is as good (or as neat) a method for mounting circuit boards as using angle brackets or spacers, for prototypes and similar applications it does the job. One hint, though: *test the module* before mounting it in this manner. Once the hot glue dries, removing the module will be a sticky and possibly difficult process.

Add the Knobs and Label the Functions _____

Putting the knobs on shouldn't require an explanation. One note of caution, though—use the correct-size screwdriver on setscrews (i.e., the biggest jeweler's screwdriver that fits). If the screwdriver is too small, there will be a tendency to bite and deform the screw, which nine times out of ten will not be made of the strongest metal in the world.

As far as labeling is concerned, you will have a tendency not to do any labeling, since it doesn't affect the

Figure 4-33

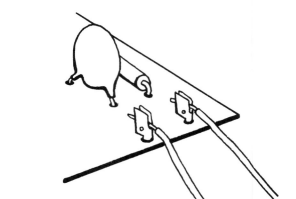

proper electrical operation of the circuit. *Do it anyway!* You'd be amazed how easy it is to forget which is the input jack and which is the output jack if you go away from your gadget for even a week. The fastest and cheapest way to label is with a Dymo labelmaker device. However, it doesn't look as good as some of the other methods you can use. A popular approach is to use dry transfer lettering and apply it directly on the chassis. Transfer lettering sheets are available at art supply stores; ask to see a dry transfer lettering catalog. The catalog will also explain how to put the stuff on in greater detail than I care to. After transferring the letters onto the chassis, spray a coat of clear acrylic over them for protection.

Although this is a popular way to letter, there are some problems. First, instant lettering doesn't like going on metal; it's designed to go on paper, or other slightly textured surfaces. Second, the acrylic spray doesn't really protect very well against deep scratches, which I guarantee you'll get.

To get around these problems, I've developed a somewhat different labeling process which still uses instant lettering. Figure 4-34 graphically shows the various steps. First, choose an appropriate color of adhesive-backed contact paper, and transfer your lettering to it. Then, get a piece of clear adhesive contact paper and cover over the letters you've just done. This gives excellent protection for the letters, and adds a subtle kind of matte finish. Next, cut out the contact paper sandwich you've just created, peel the backing off the sheet of contact on which you did the original lettering, and press the whole sandwich on your panel. If you don't get it centered quite right the first time, *carefully* peel it off and reposition. You can't do this too many times, though, as the adhesive will lose its sticking power.

Before we get into the construction projects themselves, I have a few words about the importance of aesthetics. You'll see a lot of electronic experimenters who throw together a bunch of parts in a chassis, label it with a commercial labelmaker, and forget about it. Many times it will work just as well as if it were carefully done, but the extra time spent on beautiful packaging is well worth it. Music, after all, is all about creativity and beauty—carry that into your electronics, too.

Aside from the inspirational value of playing with a beautiful piece of equipment, it's also worth more. Often the difference between a superior guitar and an ordinary model is workmanship, plated hardware, delicate inlays, and choice woods. Naturally, you'll play just as well on an axe that doesn't have beautiful inlays, but there is a great deal of satisfaction to be derived from playing a beautiful instrument . . . and even more satisfaction and confidence if you're the one who can point to it and say, "I made that."

Testing and Checking out Performance _____

It *takes time* to understand how to effectively use a special effects box; as a result, you shouldn't expect to immediately obtain the best results as soon as you plug in and turn on power. Instead, you should allow yourself a period of time to become familiar with the various controls to learn exactly what they can, and cannot, do.

For example, when I first prototyped Project No. 10, I was disappointed in the sound; however, that was before I had mounted the pots in an enclosure, added knobs, and put on labels. After doing these things, I started really getting into the various sonic possibilities that this unit could offer—and the more I used it, the more I liked it. You'd think I'd know better after all these years; after all, every musician should know that you have to practice your instrument in order to get good at playing it. When you put a special effects box in your signal path, you've just added more potential to your instrument, and it takes practice to realize that extra potential to the fullest . . . no exceptions.

Figure 4-34

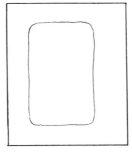

1) choose your piece of backing contact paper; outline the label, then transfer your lettering

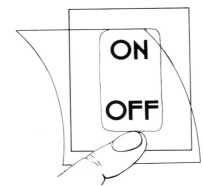

2) cover with clear contact paper

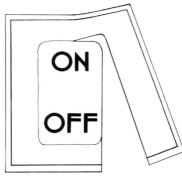

3) cut out label, take off adhesive backing, and affix to equipment

Chapter Five

We first discuss some important instructions common to all projects, and then give the complete story on building 27 projects.

Before we start building the projects, we need to discuss some additional information that pertains to the projects as a whole. Rather than repeat the same information over and over again in the text for each project, we'll simply group it together here for easy reference. It's a good idea to review these instructions, as well as the material presented in Chapter 4, before building any project.

Please note: Beginners should be aware that much of the information written about each device (particularly the sections on specifications and how the project works) is intended for the use of more advanced experimenters. It is not necessary for you to understand this material in order to successfully build and use these projects; rather than spend another 20 pages explaining such things as why a VAC RMS is different from a VAC pk-pk, we'll just assume that any beginners will be happy enough just to have a working unit—leave the technical stuff for another day. Those of you who have a basic "feel" for what specifications mean, but would like some additional information can refer to this glossary at the end of this book. Fair enough?

Format

Each project has a similar format, and generally groups information into the following sections:

Definition: Describes the function of the device as concisely as possible.

Background: Expands on the definition to provide additional information concerning the project.

Features: Describes what's neat about the project from a technical standpoint. Not necessarily intended for beginners.

Level of difficulty: Gives you a rough idea of which projects are more difficult than others; classifies them as beginner, intermediate, or advanced.

Construction tips: What to look out for when building the project.

Using the project: How to get the most out of your device.

Modifications: Tells how to customize the device for specific needs and applications.

In case of difficulty: Attempts to pinpoint the major sources of error particular to a given project in case it doesn't work. Use this section in conjunction with the chapter on trouble-shooting, which describes general trouble-shooting techniques.

Specifications: A description of the device in technical language; will no doubt confuse a beginner or two, but should be interesting to the aficionados. For more information on how these specs were derived, see chapter 9.

Line Level or Low Level

Many of the special effects devices in this book (fuzz, ring modulator, compressor, etc.) may be optimized for use with either *low-level* or *line-level* systems. The following should help you decide which is appropriate for your given application.

There are two major families of audio signals in the world, low-level and line-level. Line-level signals are strong, high-level signals; most professional audio equipment—mixing consoles, tape recorders, hi-fi power amps, etc.—is designed to work with line level signals.

There is one exception to the line level signal standard, though: guitars and guitar amplification systems. Since the signals coming out of guitars are low in level, guitar amps are designed specifically to work with these low-level signals.

If you intend to use these effects with a low-level instrument like guitar, and then expect to feed the output of the system into a guitar amp, follow the instructions on optimizing the unit for *low-level* operation. If you play an instrument with a high-level output (i.e., most synthesizers), or want to use these effects with professional audio systems, set the unit up for *line-level* operation. If the project gives no specific instructions on optimizing for different signal levels, then it will work equally well with either low-level or line-level signals.

If you can't decide which is proper for your application, go for line-level operation, as this is a more universal configuration these days (the only drawback to putting a low-level signal through a line-level device is increased noise).

If you want to use a low-level instrument, or high impedance output microphone to drive a line-level effects system, amplifier, or tape recorder, then simply run the instrument's signal through a device like the preamp (Project No. 1) or the compressor (Project No. 8). Either of these can convert low-level signals into line-level signals capable of interfacing with the professional audio world.

Connecting Power to the Projects

Except for a few projects, most of our devices need to have some kind of power source. Since power connections to the different projects are pretty similar, we'll go over the material here once rather than repeat it for each individual project.

Most of the projects that use power require two batteries. Those projects that require two batteries will have two power connection points, one marked (+) and the other (-). Figure 5-1 shows how you would hook up two batteries to these points, using two battery connectors. Battery connectors have two wires coming out of them; the red wire is from the battery (+) terminal, while the black one is from the battery (-) terminal. In the case of the tube fuzz the wiring is the same, except that you just ignore the battery that connect to the (-) point, since there is no (-) point for this project.

Using two batteries, one positive compared to ground and the other negative with respect to ground, creates what is called a *bipolar* power supply. By hooking the batteries up as shown, we've accomplished our goal of getting power to the project in question. But there's a problem: We haven't included any way to turn the batteries on and off . . . so let's look at that next.

Figure 5-1

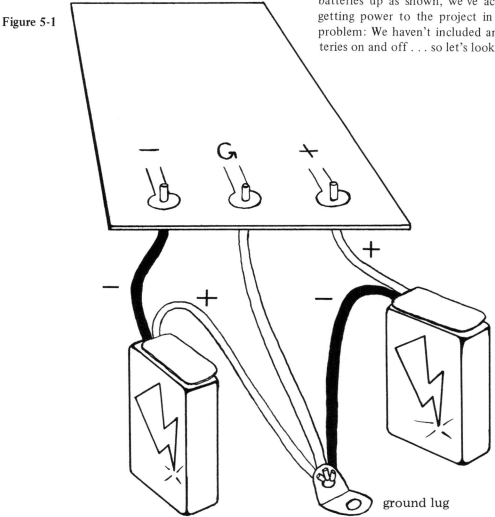

ground lug

Probably the easiest way to add an on-off switch is with a DPDT switch. We wire it up to interrupt both of the battery lines going to ground, as shown in Figure 5-2. Many people have asked whether they could wire up the on-off switching as shown in Figure 5-3, to avoid using a DPDT switch in favor of a less expensive SPST type. This will not work; even with the switch turned off, you're still drawing power from the batteries.

Notice that you could just as easily use a DPST switch, although these are less common than DPDT types. However, you will often run into pots that have DPST switches on the back; so, you might wish to wire up this switch so that turning a particular control fully counterclockwise turns off the power.

Either of these methods works fine, but there's another option that saves the cost of a switch and is sometimes more foolproof. I'm sure you've seen commercially available effects boxes where plugging a cord into the device turns it on, and unplugging the cord turns it off; here's how this type of switching circuit works.

In Chapter 1, we looked at stereo jacks that have a ground tab and two hot tabs. Figure 5-4 shows how a stereo plug inserts into a stereo jack; each of the hot leads of the plug matches up with corresponding hot terminals on the jack. But now let's look at Figure 5-5, which shows what happens when you plug a mono plug into a stereo jack. The tip of the plug connects to one hot jack terminal; the shield of the plug connects to the shield of the jack, and the other hot terminal of the jack connects to ground through the sleeve of the plug. So, by connecting the (-) end of a 9V battery to the solder tab that connects to the short contact arm of the jack, we have a primitive on-off switch. Plugging in shorts the battery (-) to ground, completing the circuit; removing the plug re-

Figure 5-2

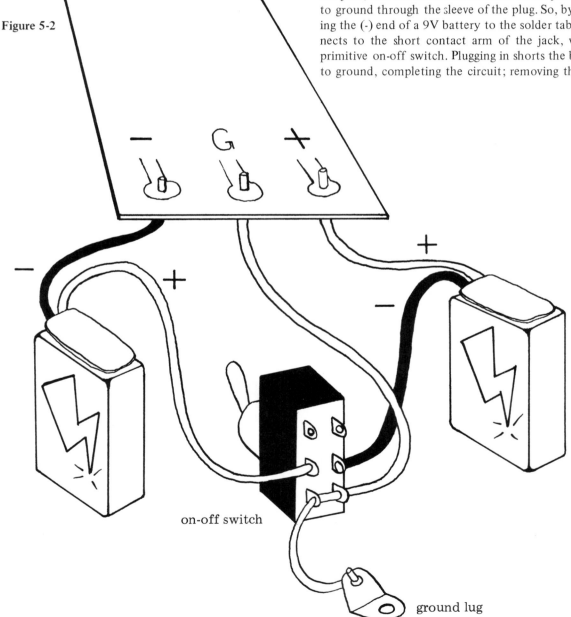

on-off switch

ground lug

Figure 5-3

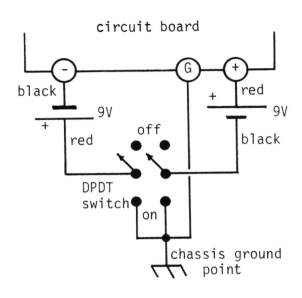

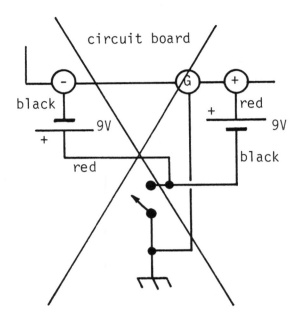

Figure 5-4

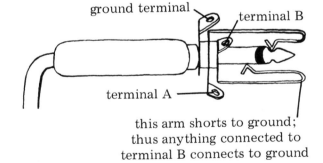

Figure 5-5

this arm shorts to ground;
thus anything connected to
terminal B connects to ground

sults in a disconnected battery. To simplify matters, we'll call the tab that connects to the short contact arm terminal B, and the tab that connects to the long contact arm, or tip, as terminal A.

For circuits requiring two batteries, it's a simple matter to use the stereo jack switching technique at both the input *and* output. That way, the input jack can turn on the positive supply, and the output jack can turn on the negative supply. Just remember to unplug your cords when you're finished playing, and the power will be turned off for longest battery life.

By the way, you don't necessarily have to use 9V transistor radio batteries, as these do have a somewhat limited current capability. If you want to get more time between battery changes, use six penlight cells to replace one battery and another six penlight cells to replace the other. The batteries (if only powering one or two projects) should last almost as long as their shelf life (i.e., how long they would last if just sitting on the shelf doing nothing). Figure 5-6 shows how to hook them up.

Figure 5-6

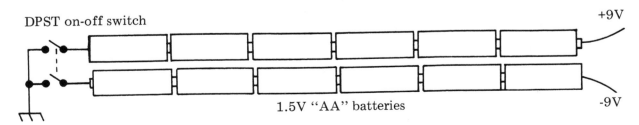

One final point about power connections: Most of the circuit boards not only have a pair of on-board polarity reversal diodes as discussed in Chapter 1, but also have a pair of electrolytic or tantalum capacitors connected from each supply line to ground. These are called *bypassing* capacitors, and accomplish several functions. With battery operation, these capacitors maintain a constant power supply impedance as the batteries age; they also prevent interaction between modules if you're powering many modules from the same supply, and if you're using an AC adapter that has ripple (hum), proper bypassing will minimize the problem.

Proper Care of the CLM6000

This part comprises an LED and wide-range photoresistor in a single, light-tight package. A photoresistor is like a resistor, except that its value depends upon how much light shines on it. With little light, it has a high resistance (10M and more); with lots of light, the resistance becomes small (less than 1,000Ω). The LED creates the different light changes in response to differing amounts of current flowing through it; so, you can think of the opto-isolator as being electrically equivalent to a variable resistor. By the way, note that opto-isolators designed for digital logic circuits (such as the MCT-2 and similar types) will not work in this application.

The CLM6000 has four leads, two for the LED and two for the photoresistor. The two photoresistor leads are long and skinny and come out of one end of the CLM6000, whereas the two LED leads are shorter and stubbier, and protrude from the opposite end of the part. The cathode lead of the LED is indicated by a little dot painted on the package next to the lead (see Figure 5-7a).

Figure 5-7a

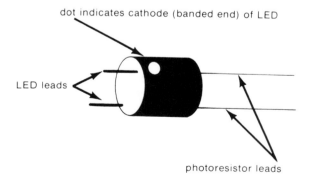

dot indicates cathode (banded end) of LED

LED leads

photoresistor leads

It's important to carefully note which lead is which, since a circuit with an improperly installed CLM6000 will not work.

Both the photoresistor and LED inside the CLM6000 are sensitive to heat, so solder quickly and leave about a minute between the time you solder the LED leads and the time you solder the photocell leads. In the projects, the LED leads mount directly into the board, while the photocell leads are bent over in order to fit into the other indicated holes on the board. Figure 5-7b shows how to match the CLM6000 leads up with the legend on the component side of the board.

Figure 5-7b

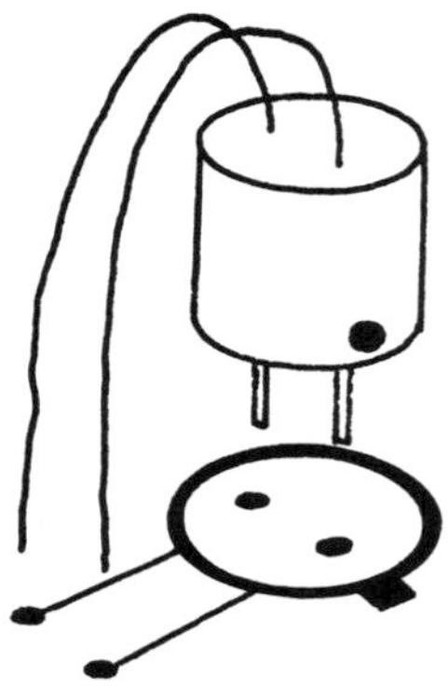

Jumper Wires

In some cases, it may be necessary to add a *jumper wire* to the circuit board. Although it is preferable to design circuit boards that don't need jumpers, sometimes it's just not possible to have one trace meet up with another trace; so, we cheat a bit and run a wire over the top (component side) of the board to connect the two traces together. Jumper wires are indicated on the component layout diagram with a line designated with the letter *J*. Use a piece of insulated wire to implement this jumper. Note that the circuit will not work if the jumper is not in place; so if a board doesn't work the first time you try it out, review the component layout and make sure you're not overlooking a needed jumper.

Transistor Orientation

Unfortunately, transistors are not always enclosed in standardized cases. On the various circuit board component layouts shown in Chapter 5, look carefully for the emitter, base, and collector lead designations (abbreviated e, b, and c) for each transistor used, and match these up with the e, b, and c designations embossed or printed on the transistor case. Even if these letters are not shown on the case, there should be an accompanying sheet with any transistor you buy that indicates which lead is which. Note that while the circuit board component layouts indicate a flat side and a round side for the transistor case, *this does not universally correlate to all transistors*. Without exception, match up the e, b, and c designations to insure that the transistor is correctly oriented. An improperly oriented transistor will sabotage your circuit, so be careful.

Project No. 1

PREAMP

Definition: A preamp increases the level of a signal. For example, a preamp with a gain of 10 can take a 1V input signal and turn it into a 10V output signal.

Figure 5-8

Here is the preamp, mounted in a Vector-Pak card module prior to installation in the pedalboard. The switch on the left is the clean/dirty switch; the one on the right is the in/out or bypass switch (see Project No. 23 for details on how to wire this into the preamp). The input jack is on the front, but all other connectors mount on the rear. In order to conserve panel space, the VU meter has been omitted from this module.

Background:

Some signals that emanate from devices are very low in level, such as the weak signals coming out of the guitar pickups or microphones. On the other hand, some devices (tape recorders, hi-fi power amps, studio consoles, and others) want to receive line-level, or high-level signals. A preamp can take a low-level signal and convert it into a high-level signal that is more suitable for interfacing with professional equipment. Advantages include a "fuller" sound and better noise performance compared to using a nonpreamped signal.

Features

- High-input impedance retains the fidelity of instruments with high-output impedances such as guitar
- Choice of "clean" (standard preamp) or "dirty" modes. The dirty mode simulates the sound of an overdriven amplifier

- Choice of three outputs: low-impedance unbalanced, inverting or noninverting, for use with guitar amps, some tape recorders, hi-fi power amps, etc.; and low-impedance balanced, for use with professional studio equipment
- Built-in VU meter amp
- Separate gain control and master volume control to optimize signal-to-noise ratio
- Low-noise and low-distortion characteristics
- Operates from +9 to +18V DC
- Drives long cables without signal loss or degraded frequency response
- Replaces hassle-prone studio direct boxes when recording direct into studio mixing boards
- Buffered, low-level output available at pad A

Level of Difficulty: Beginner to intermediate.

Constructions Tips

Because this circuit is capable of high gain, certain leads must be shielded, and all wiring should be kept as short and direct as possible. Input and output leads should be physically separated from each other by at least 1 cm (3/8") to prevent stray signal coupling.

Use shielded cable for the following connections: J1 to pad I; pad C to R6; S1 to pad E.

LEDs D1 and D2 should *not* light up. They are used only to create distortion in the *dirty* mode.

Using the Preamp

■ First, plug your instrument or microphone into J1. The preamp input accepts *unbalanced* output devices, which usually terminate in 1/4" phone plugs. To connect *balanced line* devices, which usually terminate in a three-wire XLR connector or more rarely in a 1/4" stereo phone plug, you will need to add an additional matching transformer. See Figure 5-9.

■ Second, determine which output jack to use for patching the preamp into your setup.

Use *J3* for feeding devices with *unbalanced, high-level inputs*. These include power amps such as BGW, Crown and McIntosh; most consumer and semipro tape recording equipment; budget PA mixers; line level studio effects; most synthesizer modules; and synthesizer "external input" jacks.

Use *J4* for feeding devices with *balanced, high-level inputs*. These include studio mic preamp inputs; most

Figure 5-9

How to adapt a balanced, low-impedance microphone to the preamp input using a matching transformer. The cord connecting the microphone to the adapter is usually a three-conductor type with XLR connectors at each end; the cord from adapter to preamp is a standard cord with 1/4" phone plugs at each end. The transformer is called a "high-impedance unbalanced to low-impedance balanced" type, and is available at many music stores and pro audio shops for around $15 to $20.

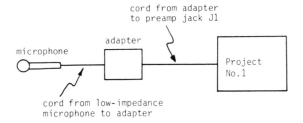

studio patch bay patching points; professional tape recorder inputs; some studio effect inputs; and professional-quality mixers.

Use *J2* for applications similar to J3, but where phase is unimportant. Using this output will give slightly better noise performance compared to J3.

■ Third, decide whether you want a *clean* or *dirty* sound. If clean, set S1 to clean. With the *master volume* about one-fourth of the way up, feed your loudest input signal into the preamp. Turn the *gain* control clockwise until you reach the maximum level that still gives a distortionless sound. Trim the master volume to the desired output level (usually 0 dB when feeding something like a tape recorder).

If dirty, set S1 to dirty. Adjust the gain control for the desired amount of distortion (clockwise=more distortion), then trim master volume for the desired output level.

Another way to obtain a dirty sound, even with S1 in the clean position, is to overload a low-level input (such as a typical guitar amp input) with the high-level preamp output. For this application, adjust the gain and master volume controls for whatever you feel gives the best sound quality.

Hooking up the VU meter amp: By monitoring the output of the preamp with the VU meter, you may adjust the master volume so that your output signal is consistently around the 0-dB point. For maximum versatility, the meter amplifier input is brought out separately to pad M so that you may monitor different points along the signal chain if desired.

To monitor the output of the preamp, connect pad M to pad P.

To monitor several effects, refer to Figure 5-10.

If you don't wish to use the meter, simply ignore terminals M and N. The meter does not need to be used for the preamp to work correctly.

The function of pad A: The output signal appearing at pad A is a buffered equivalent of the signal appearing at the input, and may be connected up to a jack in a fashion similar to J1. Use it for feeding effects that are designed to work only with low-level inputs. This option will not be required if you are using the preamp solely in conjunction with other projects presented in this book.

Figure 5-10

This diagram shows the preamp, compressor, and super tone control, with their inputs and outputs brought out to separate jacks. I've omitted other connections—power supplies, pots, etc.—for clarity. Pad M connects to a rotary switch which selects the part of the signal chain we wish to monitor. Position 1 monitors the preamp output, 2 the compressor output, and 3 the super tone control output.

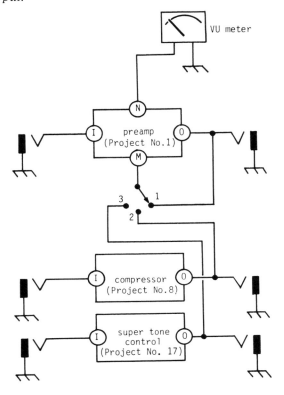

Modifications

■ The preamp response is ±1dB from 40Hz to 10kHz (1kHz = 1000Hz). You may remove C1 and C2 to extend the response to 20kHz *if* you've been careful with your wiring (no long, sloppy lead lengths, or inputs draped over outputs).

■ If the preamp has too much gain for your needs, change R10 to 220k. If too little gain, change R10 to 1M.

■ If you will only be using the preamp with guitar, and if that guitar does not include built-in electronics, you may replace C3 with a wire jumper for improved noise performance.

■ There may be instances where you don't need all the versatility of the present design. Let's say you're a guitarist, and all you want is a preamp to overload your guitar amp input—and that's all. In this case, simply plug your guitar into J1, your amp into J2, and you're ready to go. You don't need J3, J4, R3-R5, R8, R11, C4, C7, or C8; these may be removed from the board, or designed out altogether. The clean/dirty switch as well as R6 and R7 will still be completely functional.

In Case of Difficulty

■ Distortion, even in clean mode: Turn down *gain* control until distortion goes away, and turn up *master volume* to compensate.

■ Internal feedback, squeals, or other oscillations: Check lead layout. Use shielded wires where indicated. Make sure C1 and C2 are in place.

■ "Uneven" sounding distortion in *dirty* mode: Verify that D1 and D2 haven't been overheated or damaged during the soldering process.

Specifications

Current consumption: ±8 mA* @ ±9V DC supply voltage
Frequency response (clean mode, C1 & C2 = 5pF):

±1dB, 40Hz - 10kHz
±2dB, 40Hz - 20kHz

Frequency response (clean mode, C1 & C2 omitted):

±1dB, 40Hz - 20kHz

Output headroom, clean mode: greater than 10V pk-pk
Maximum input before clipping, clean mode, R6 fully clockwise: 100mV pk-pk
Output headroom, dirty mode: 3V pk-pk
Maximum input before clipping, dirty mode, R6 fully clockwise: 15mV[†] pk-pk

*mA = millamperes; 1mA = 0.001A.

[†]mV = millivolts; 1mV = 0.001V.

m = one thousandth.

Figure 5-11
*Artwork for the foil side of the circuit board, shown
1 to 1.*

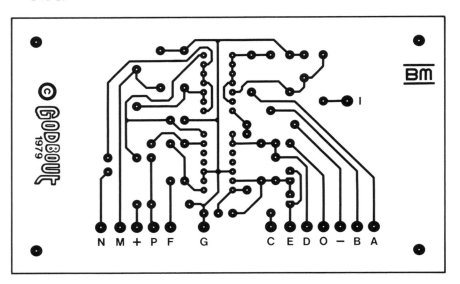

Figure 5-12
Component layout for the preamp.

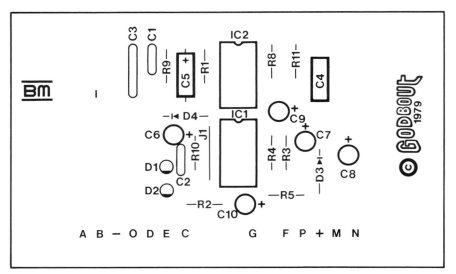

Figure 5-13
Preamp schematic.

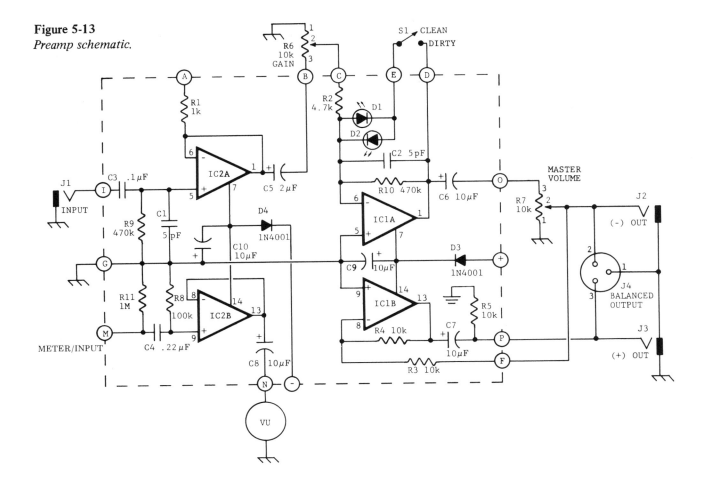

How it Works

IC2A is a buffer stage that loads the input signal down as little as possible; capacitor C1 promotes stability and helps minimize radio frequency interference. From here, the signal couples through C5 into the gain control. This varies the amount of signal that goes to IC1A, which is set up as a high-gain stage. With R6 up full and S1 in the *clean* position, the signal is amplified 100 times (plenty of gain, even for low-level signals). With S1 in the *dirty* position, LEDs D1 and D2 shunt across this high-gain stage to clip the signal and create distortion. Under these conditions, turning up R6 doesn't make the signal louder, but instead makes it more distorted.

The next step along the signal path is through C6 to R7, the *master volume* control. This signal goes directly to J2, the inverting output. The output of IC1A also goes into IC1B, which simply inverts the signal again to produce a noninverting output, and feeds this signal into J3. Since a balanced output requires both inverting and noninverting signals, the inverting output of IC1A and the noninverting output of IC1B feed the balanced output connector.

IC2B is the meter amp. It basically presents a minimum of loading to whatever signal connects to pad M, and then couples into the VU meter through C8.

Project No. 1 PARTS LIST

Resistors (all are 1/4W, 10% tolerance, except as noted)

R1	1k
R2	4.7k
R3 - R5	10k
R6	10k audio taper pot—controls *gain*
R7	10k audio taper pot—controls *master volume*
R8	100k
R9, R10	470k
R11	1M

Capacitors (rated at more than 10V for +9V, more than 15V for +15V)

C1, C2	5pF ceramic disc
C3	0.1μF (mylar preferred, disc acceptable)
C4	0.22μF (mylar preferred, disc acceptable)
C5	2μF, electrolytic or tantalum
C6 - C10	10μF, electrolytic or tantalum

Semiconductors

IC1, IC2	RC4739 or XR4739 dual low-noise op amp
D1, D2	Red LED
D3, D4	1N4001 or equivalent silicon diode

Mechanical Parts

J1 - J3	Open circuit 1/4" mono phone jack
J4	Optional XLR connector
S1	SPST switch—selects *clean/dirty* mode
VU	VU meter
Misc.	Case, knobs, two 14-pin IC sockets, circuit board, solder, wire, etc.

Project No. 2
METRONOME

Definition: A metronome is a device that marks time for musicians who wish to practice against a stable tempo. It emits a series of rhythmic clicks; the tempo of these clicks is adjustable.

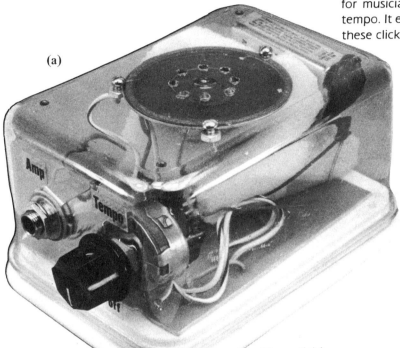

(a)

(b)

Figure 5-14
(a) I don't recommend you build your projects like this. But in this instance, I needed a metronome on 24-hour notice and built it in a refrigerator dish. (b) A closeup of the metronome circuit board.

Background:

Traditionally, metronomes are mechanical devices, powered by a wound spring. Eventually the spring winds down, which means the metronome requires periodic rewinding. This electronic equivalent will run for as long as the battery lasts, if desired.

Features

- Can go faster than mechanical metronomes
- Timing is virtually independent of supply voltage
- Includes optional amplifier feed for high-volume applications
- Low cost
- Runs from single 9V transistor radio battery

Level of Difficulty: Beginner

Construction Tips

This is a simple, noncritical circuit with few interconnections, and no special precautions are required.

For power, use a separate 9V battery or 9V AC adapter. As a general rule, projects using a speaker should have their own power supply. Figure 5-15 shows how to add a power on-off switch.

Using the Metronome

Turn on the power and adjust the *tempo* control for the desired tempo.

Figure 5-15

Adding an on-off switch to the metronome. An SPST toggle switch is satisfactory; better yet, use a pot for R3 that has an on-off switch mounted on its back.

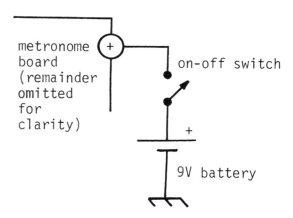

Suggested applications include providing a steady beat for jamming with friends when there is no drummer, and providing a *click track* for recording work. In this application, the metronome is recorded on one track of a multitrack recorder, and all subsequent parts are laid down to the tempo set by the metronome. After all the other tracks are filled, the metronome track may be erased to make room for one more overdub.

Modifications

■ For the loudest possible click, use a large and efficient speaker for SPKR. Smaller speakers give a more subdued click.

■ If you need a really loud signal, add the amp feed circuitry shown in Figure 5-16.

■ To change the metronome range from 60-1500 bpm (beats per minute) to 120-3000 bpm, change C1 and C2 to 1μF. To change to 30-750 bpm, change C1 and C2 to 5μF.

In Case of Difficulty

■ Metronome doesn't work: Check wiring and battery voltage.

■ Metronome won't start: Check polarities of C1 and C2, battery voltage.

■ IC1 gets hot to the touch during operation: Shorted C4.

Specifications

Current consumption: 12mA average, top speed.
Range: Approximately 1 - 25Hz (60 - 1500 bpm).

Figure 5-16

Add the parts indicated with (*) for an amplifier feed; plug into a standard guitar amp or PA. The speaker on-off switch is optional.

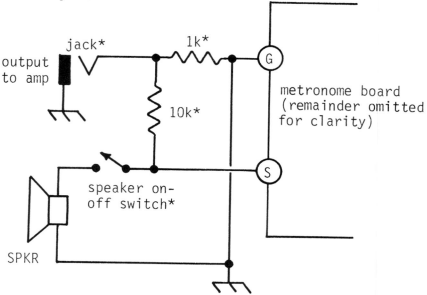

Figure 5-17
*Artwork for the foil side of circuit board, shown 1
to 1.*

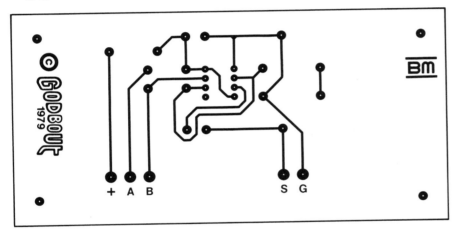

Figure 5-18
Component layout for the metronome.

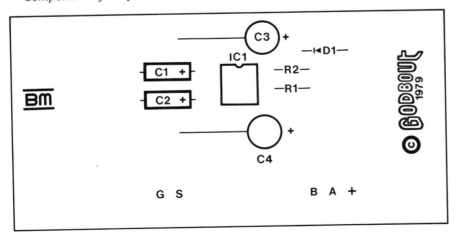

Figure 5-19
Metronome schematic.

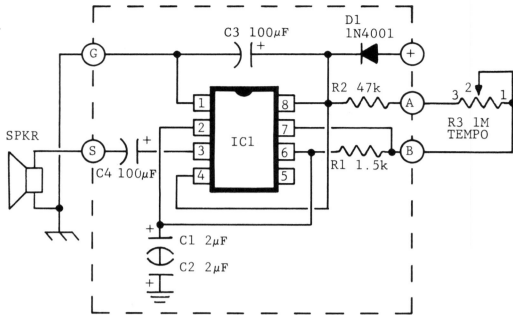

How it Works

The 555 is an integrated circuit developed specifically for industrial control applications. It can give very precise timed functions, and can also deliver a fair amount of power—enough to drive a speaker to more than audible volume. In this particular circuit, tying pins 2 and 6 together forces the 555 to oscillate and therefore generate a continuous stream of pulses, which feed into the speaker through C4. C3 adds bypassing across the supply lines, while diode D1 provides polarity-reversal protection in case you hook up the battery incorrectly.

Project No. 2 PARTS LIST

Resistors (all are 1/4W, 10% tolerance except as noted)

R1	1.5K
R2	47k
R3	1M linear taper pot—controls *tempo*

Capacitors (rated at 10V or more)

C1, C2	2μF, electrolytic or tantalum
C3, C4	100μF, electrolytic or tantalum

Semiconductors

IC1	NE555, LM555, RC555, or equivalent timer
D1	IN4001 or equivalent silicon diode

Mechanical Parts

SPKR	8Ω speaker
Misc.	Case, knob, 8-pin socket, circuit board, solder, on-off switch, etc.

(a)

PASSIVE TONE CONTROL

FREQ   FULL COIL ↑
        HALF COIL ↓   DEPTH

Figure 5-20
(a) Passive tone control mounted in a small box.
(b) The insides of this project.

Project No. 3

PASSIVE TONE CONTROL

Definition: The passive tone control changes the tonal quality of an instrument by putting a <u>notch</u>, or dip in response, at various places in the midrange area of the audio spectrum. It is called "passive" because it requires no source of power for operation.

(b)

Background:

This project uses an electronic component called an inductor. In most modern circuits, inductors have been eliminated in favor of op amp circuits that simulate the properties of an inductor. Nonetheless, for many years inductor/capacitor combinations were the backbone of audio filtering circuits; and the same combination forms the basis of this project, too.

Features

- No power required
- No semiconductor noise
- Choice of 10 different notch frequencies
- Adjustable notch depth
- Very low cost
- Easy to mount inside guitar or keyboard instrument

Level of Difficulty: Beginner.

Construction Tips

I used a small, transistor radio transformer to implement T1 (available from Mouser Electronics; see parts list for specs). Any other transformer with the same specs will do. With this type of transformer, one side will be called the *primary* (usually indicated with a printed designation like the letter "P"), and the other side the *secondary*. We use the primary wires only and leave the secondary wires unconnected.

If you can't find a suitable transformer, obtain two standard 2.5- to 3-henry (a *henry*, abbreviated *H*, is the unit of inductance). Connect one of these inductors between pads F and H on the circuit board (inductors have only two connections, so you can't go wrong), and connect the other one between pads H and J.

Keep T1 out of the way of strong AC fields, like those generated by power transformers, as inductors can pick up hum.

Shield the wires going from pad I and O to the two jacks.

Using the Passive Tone Control

Plug your instrument into J1, and patch J2 to an amp. Turn the *depth* control full clockwise, S2 to *full coil*, play your instrument, and rotate the *frequency* switch throughout its range. Each position should give a different sound. Experiment with the depth control as you listen. Now, repeat the same series of experiments with S1 in the *half coil* position.

This circuit gives a lot more flexibility than the standard treble-cut tone filter found on most guitars, yet it does not add noise or require batteries that could fail at embarrassing moments.

Modifications

■ Bass players may "tune" this circuit one octave lower by doubling the values of C1 - C5.

■ One of S1's positions is unconnected, which cuts the inductor/capacitor combination out of the audio path and eliminates the need for a bypass switch. If desired, this unconnected switch position could also connect to another tuning capacitor (say, $0.005\mu F$) instead.

■ You may elminate the depth control by shorting pad J to ground.

In Case of Difficulty

■ Volume loss through the circuit: There is nothing you can do about this, since a little bit of loss is the tradeoff for not including any active circuits or power supply. Feeding the passive tone control output to a device with a high-impedance input minimizes this loss.

■ Changing S1 has little effect: Make sure T1 is hooked up correctly. Check all ground connections.

■ Hum: Change the orientation of the transformer or inductor away from AC fields. Check all ground connections.

How it Works

Inductor T1 and the capacitor selected by S1 make up what is known as a *resonant* circuit, which will pass some frequencies but not others. For example. if the inductor/capacitor combination has a resonant frequency of 1000Hz, then it will pass 1000Hz signals; however, signals that are lower or higher in frequency will not pass through the inductor/capacitor combination.

Looking at the schematic, we can simplify it and see that basically what we have is the inductor/capacitor combination draped across the signal line to ground. If, for example, this combination has a 1000Hz resonant frequency, then a 1000Hz signal passed through the tone control will go directly to ground (since the inductor/capacitor combination can easily pass this signal), so it will *not* make its way to the output and we won't hear it. Other signals above and below 1000Hz will be rejected by the tuned circuit and not go to ground, so they are free to continue on to the output.

Changing the resonant frequency (by changing either S1 or S2) alters the tonal effect by shunting other frequency bands to ground. In practice, a filter like this is not ideally selective; so, with a resonant frequency of 1000Hz, although it will let through 1000Hz signals the most easily, it will also let through signals close to that frequency by lesser amounts. This is considered a *broad* notch in frequency response, as opposed to a *steep* notch in the response. Steep notches are difficult to create, but luckily for us, broad notches are more musically useful when modifying instruments than steep notches in virtually all applications.

Specifications

Current consumption: 0mA
Resonant frequency chart (all frequencies in Hz):

Switch position (S1)	S2 half coil	S2 full coil
1	1015	540
2	755	380
3	560	240
4	430	170
5	260	107

Headroom ±15V

Figure 5-21
Artwork for the foil side of the board, shown 1 to 1.

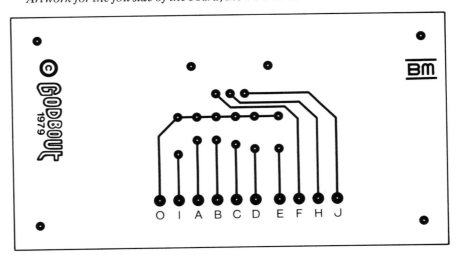

Figure 5-22
Component layout for the passive tone control.

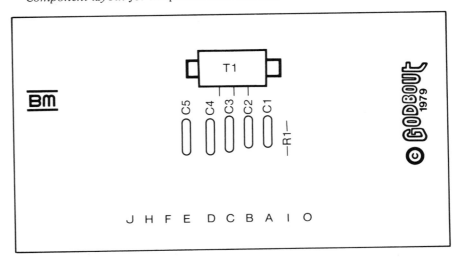

Figure 5-23
Passive tone control schematic.

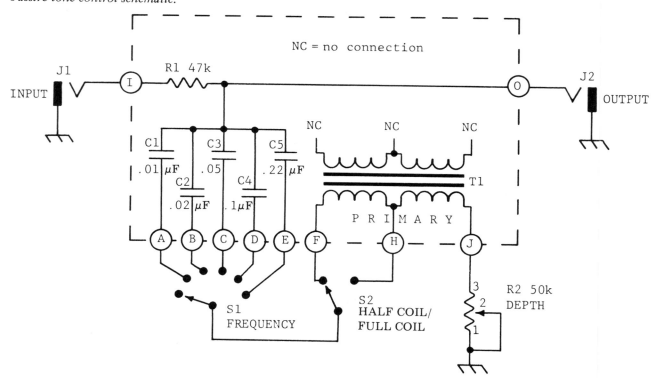

Project No. 3 PARTS LIST

Resistors

R1	47k, 1/4W, 10% tolerance
R2	50k linear taper pot—controls *depth*

Capacitors (rated 10V or more; mylar preferred, disc acceptable)

C1	0.01 μF
C2	0.02 μF
C3	0.05 μF
C4	0.1 μF
C5	0.22 μF

Inductor

T1	5- to 6-H center-tapped inductor (see text)*

Mechanical Parts

J1, J2	Open circuit 1/4" phone jack
S1	SP6T rotary switch
S2	SPDT toggle switch
Misc.	Knobs, case, circuit board, wire, solder, etc.

*T1 is available from Mouser Electronics (see Chapter 2), stock number 42TM-019. Its specs are: primary impedance, 10k at 1Hz; seccondary impedance, 600Ω at 1kHz. Primary DC resistance, 600Ω; secondary DC resistance, 100Ω. Calectro also makes an equivalent audio driver transformer; the part number is D1-711.

Project No. 4

HEADPHONE AMP

Definition: A small hi-fi audio amp that amplifies the output of an instrument to a level capable of driving a set of headphones.

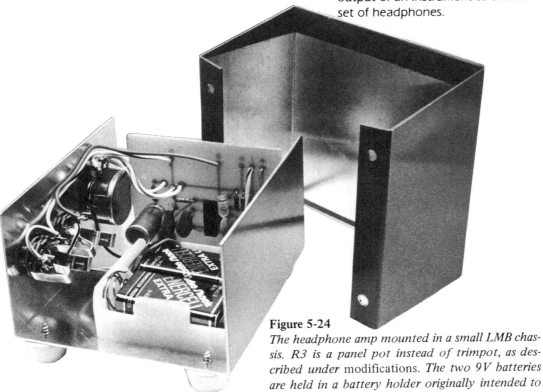

Figure 5-24
The headphone amp mounted in a small LMB chassis. R3 is a panel pot instead of trimpot, as described under modifications. *The two 9V batteries are held in a battery holder originally intended to house two size "D" cells.*

Background:

This project trades off power in order to provide high-fidelity sound at loud, but not ear-shattering, volume levels. If you need more power or want to drive a loudspeaker, skip ahead to Project No. 5

Features

- Portable; requires only two 9V batteries for operation—practice in your van on the way to a gig
- Low power for long battery life
- Dual inputs and dual headphone outputs for jamming with a friend
- Trimpot-adjustable output level
- Allows practice in apartments and hotels without disturbing others
- Tune up on stage through headphones without anyone noticing
- Low-cost, noncritical construction

Level of Difficulty: Beginner

Construction Tips

This is a moderate gain circuit, and requires a few simple precautions.

If you design your own circuit board, make sure that pins 3, 4, 5, 10, 11, and 12 contact as much ground area as possible; this helps IC1 to dissipate any heat it generates while operating. You cannot blow up IC1 if it overheats, as it will simply shut itself off until it cools back down.

Mount R1, C1, and C3 as close to the IC pins as possible.

Keep the input and output leads separated by at least 1 cm (3/8") to avoid unwanted feedback.

Figure 5-25 shows how to hook up power to the headphone amp.

77

Figure 5-25
How to hook up two 9V batteries to create a ±18V supply. The on-off switch is optional; you could also use the input jack switching trick discussed earlier in Chapter 5.

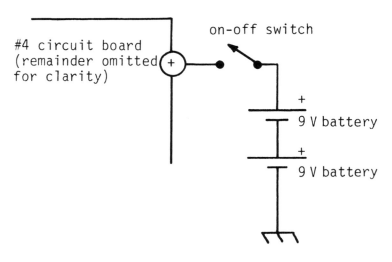

#4 circuit board
(remainder omitted
for clarity)

on-off switch

+
9 V battery

+
9 V battery

Using the Headphone Amp

Start off by plugging your instrument into J1, and a set of phones into J3. Turn on power, play, and adjust R3 for the desired level.

If you're using two sets of headphones, they should be of the same make and model to prevent level mismatches between phones.

Modifications

■ Although R3 is shown as a trimpot, you might want to use a standard pot mounted on the front panel to control volume as shown in Figure 5-24. To do this, remove R3 and run three wires from the trimpot pads out to the panel pot.

■ The headphone amp will also work from +12V DC (car battery voltage) and +15V (found in most synthesizer systems). If small space is a must and you must use a single 9V battery, National Semiconductor makes special LM380s, designated part no. SL61097, that are guaranteed to work down to +8V DC.

■ This circuit is designed to accept low-level signals. If you encounter distortion on the peaks of your playing, and the batteries are *known* to be good, then you are overdriving the amp. To remedy, either lower R4 to 47k (or even less if necessary) or add a volume control similar to the arrangement shown in Project No. 5. For this project, the wiper of the pot would go to an input pad (pad H or I) on the amp.

■ For slightly more power, short out R2. The tradeoff is more noise in your headphones.

In Case of Difficulty

■ Distortion: Check battery voltage; otherwise, change R4 as mentioned under *modifications.*

■ 380 overheats: Add more ground area to pads 3, 4, 5, 10, 11, and 12.

■ 380 still overheats: Eliminate socket and solder 380 directly to board.

Specifications

Quiescent current consumption: 10mA typical

Typical maximum current consumption: 100mA

Frequency response @ 250mW output: ±1dB, 40Hz-20kHz

Maximum input before clipping: 1.7V pk-pk

Power into 8Ω load @ 1kHz, R2 = 10Ω: 250mW

Power into 8Ω load @ 1kHz, R2 = 0Ω: greater than 500mW

All measurements taken with (+) = 15V, R3 at maximum output

Figure 5-26
Artwork for the foil side of the circuit board, shown 1 to 1.

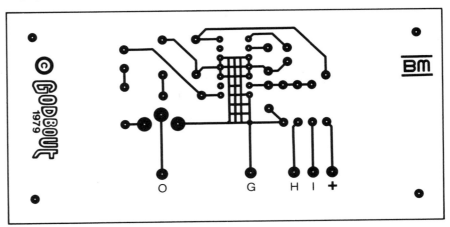

Figure 5-27
Component layout for the headphone amp.

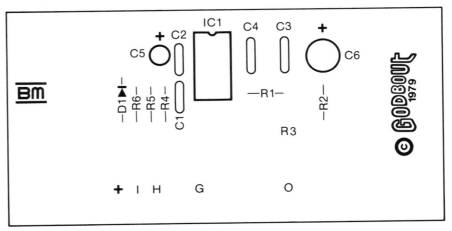

Figure 5-28
Headphone amp schematic.

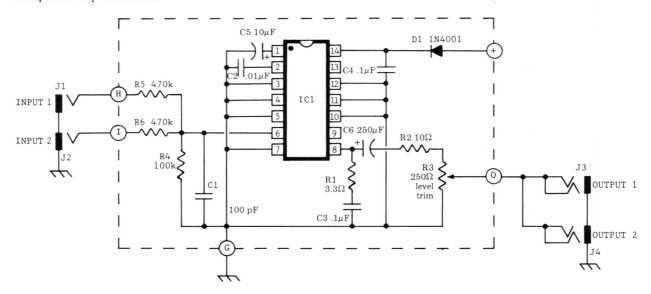

How it Works

IC1 is a power op amp that requires very few external components, and has been designed to deliver a fair amount of output current. Input signals enter the amp through R5 and R6; since the typical guitar puts out too much juice for the 380, resistor R4 adds some attenuation. C1 restricts the supersonic frequency response to prevent oscillations. C2, C4, and C5 are all bypassing capacitors for different sections of the 380. The output of the IC appears on pin 8, which couples through C6, R2, and R3 while working its way to the headphone jacks. R1 and C3 prevent high-frequency oscillations that can occur when the 380 is delivering its maximum power.

Project No. 4 PARTS LIST

Resistors (all are 1/4W, 10% tolerance, except as noted)

R1	3.3Ω
R2	10Ω
R3	250Ω trimpot—controls *output level trim*
R4	100k
R5, R6	470k

Capacitors (rated at more than 20V)

C1	100pF (polystyrene preferred, disc acceptable)
C2	0.01µF, ceramic disc
C3, C4	0.1µF, ceramic disc
C5	10µF, electrolytic or tantalum
C6	250µF, electrolytic

Semiconductors

IC1	LM380 audio power op amp
D1	IN4001 or equivalent silicon diode

Mechanical Parts

J1, J2	Open circuit 1/4" mono phone jack
J3, J4	Open circuit 1/4" stereo phone jack
Misc.	Case, knobs, 14-pin IC socket, circuit board, power supply (see text), solder, wire, etc.

(a)

Project No. 5

MINIAMP

Definition: A portable, low-power audio amp capable of driving a loudspeaker to moderate volume levels.

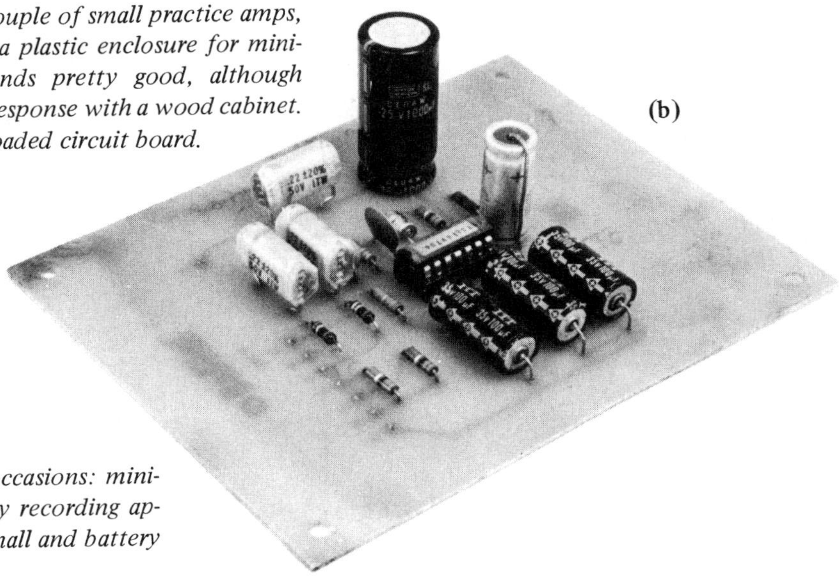

Figure 5-29
(a) I already have a couple of small practice amps, so I built this one in a plastic enclosure for minimum weight. It sounds pretty good, although you'll get better bass response with a wood cabinet. (b) A closeup of the loaded circuit board.

(b)

Background:

Large amplifiers are not needed for all occasions: mini-amps will suffice for practicing and many recording applications. They are usually physically small and battery powered for portability.

Features

- Single IC design, no output transformer required
- Switch-selectable speaker or headphone outputs
- Operates from +12V DC battery pack or car battery
- Reasonable frequency response and distortion characteristics
- Suitable for recording work:
  —Small size allows for unusual miking schemes (see *Using the Miniamp in the Studio*)

  —Simplicity of repair and maintenance

  —Low output power minimizes leakage between instruments, simplifies baffling requirements

  —May be overdriven to simulate large amp sound without large amp power levels

  —Dual, individually mixable inputs for jamming with another player

Level of Difficulty: Beginner to intermediate

Construction Tips

Because this circuit handles more power than other book projects, certain precautions should be followed.

Shield the wires going from the input jacks to both controls, and from the controls to pads A and B. Keep output leads physically separated from the input wires and the area of the board where the input wires terminate.

For best results, build the miniamp into its own case and give it its own power supply. I recommend using a battery holder capable of holding eight "C" cells; for smallest size, use eight "AA" cells. Either of these combinations produces 12 V.

The μA706 uses a nonstandard package. The little dot on the top of most ICs that normally indicates pin 1 is

Figure 5-30

Top view of the μA706. A dot on the bottom of the IC indicates pin 14.

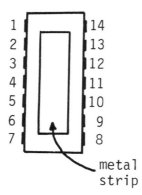

metal
strip

A small speaker baffle makes an excellent enclosure for the miniamp and batteries. Stuff with acoustical padding for best bass response, but *keep the area around the IC heat sink clear of padding.*

If you expect to play at the loudest possible volume level of which this amp is capable for extended periods of time, glue a heat sink to the top of IC1 with a thermally conductive silicone glue (available at hardware stores). Figure 5-34 shows the heat sink attached to the IC.

Figure 5-34

Heat sink mounted on top of the μA706.

on the *bottom* of the μA706 and indicates pin 14. The *top* of the IC has a metal strip that aids in dissipating heat from the IC. (See figure 5-30).

The volume of the miniamp is highly dependent on the speaker it drives. Paradoxically, high-cost/high-quality car radio speakers will usually produce far less volume than the inexpensive speakers you find in table radios and the like. Efficient musical instrument speakers (8" to 15") typically provide the loudest sound pressure levels.

Figure 5-31

Artwork for the foil side of the circuit board, shown 1 to 1.

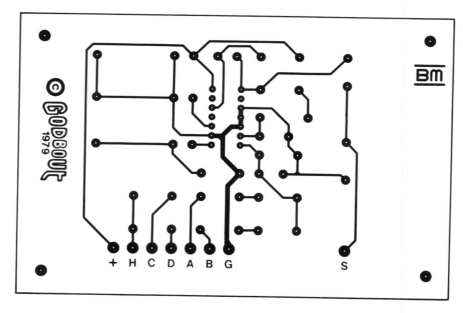

Using the Miniamp, General Instructions

■ Check all connections thoroughly before applying power. Plug one or two instruments into the inputs, select speaker or headphone output, then adjust volume controls to suit.

■ If you hear excessive noise or squealing, or if IC1 gets extremely hot immediately after turn-on, shut down power and determine the source of the difficulty. Otherwise, play away.

■ You may power two sets of headphones without problems; however, these should be of the same make and model.

Using the Miniamp in the Studio

■ There should be no hum (except for stray hum picked up through the instrument being amplified), since the amp is battery powered.

■ The small size allows many unusual mic placements to alter the tonal quality of the miniamp's sound. Here are some . . .

—*Boost bass* by miking close to speaker. *Cut bass* by moving mic further away.

—*Create phase changes* by placing amp on floor; hang mic about 20 cm (8") above the floor, pointing at the floor, about 8-40 cm (4-16") from the amp. Moving the height of the mic in relation to the floor changes the sound by creating phase shifts.

—Point amp at wall; also point mic at wall to pick up the reflected amp sound.

—*Reduce treble* by placing a piece of thin cardboard between the speaker and mic.

—*Boost midrange*, and create resonances, by placing amp and mic inside a large cardboard box with the mic pointing away from a direct line with the speaker. Change size of box, cut holes in box, or change mic/amp positioning to vary the effect.

Figure 5-32
Component layout for the miniamp.

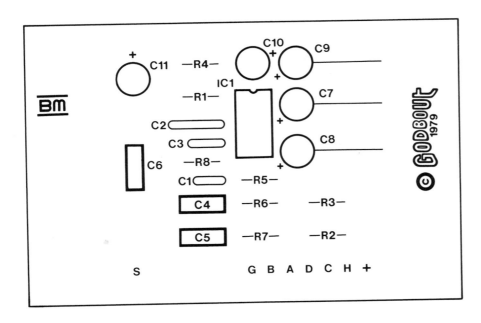

Modifications

■ Reducing C11 to 250μF trades off bass response for longer battery life. This has a negligible effect on the sound, since most small speakers will not respond efficiently to low bass frequencies anyway.

■ For more power, you may use 10 "C" cells connected in series to create a +15V supply. In this case, a heat sink for IC1 will be mandatory.

■ Lowering the values of R2 and R3 (typically to 10Ω) trades off more headphone volume for slightly more noise. Raising R2 and R3 (typically to 56 or 82Ω) trades off less volume for less noise.

In Case of Difficulty

■ Distortion: Back off on input controls. Check power supply voltage *while playing through amp;* if it drops much below 9V or so, the batteries need to be replaced.

■ Low volume: Use more efficient speaker.

■ Oscillations, excessive noise: Check lead layout and shielding, referring to *Construction Tips* section.

■ IC1 overheats or burns out: Increase heat sinking.

■ Resonances, buzzes: Check enclosure for tightness. Make sure all joints are glued together well and are preferably caulked.

Specifications (taken with 12V battery pack)

Quiescent current consumption: typically 15mA
Typical maximum current consumption while playing:
175mA @ 800mW out
Frequency response: ±2dB, 100Hz-10kHz
Maximum input before clipping @ 1kHz: 250 mV pk-pk
Maximum power into 8Ω @ 1kHz: approximately 1W

Figure 5-33
Miniamp schematic.

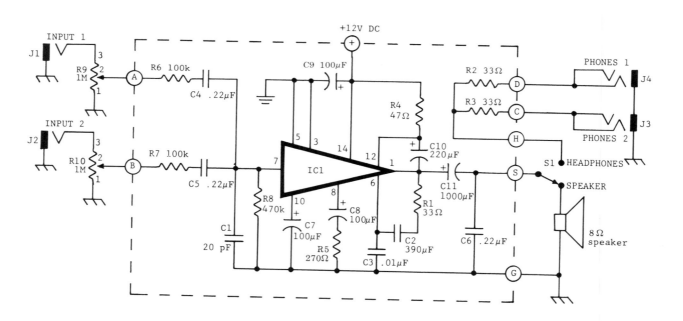

How it Works

The biggest tradeoff in a miniamp is battery life vs. output power; more power means decreased battery life. The chosen output power, approximately 1W, seems like the best compromise between output level and power consumption.

IC1 is an audio power op amp, and is similar to a regular op amp except that it has been optimized to provide large amounts of output current. Signals couple in from the two inputs via R6/R7 and C4/C5. C1 adds stability and discourages radio frequency interference. R5, located between pin 8 of IC1 and ground, sets the overall operating level of the amp. The various other capacitors associated with the op amp provide frequency shaping and/or bypassing to improve stability and power supply rejection.

The output couples into the speaker through C11; C6 is, again, designed to promote stability (power amps do not like feeding inductive loads such as speakers). Switch S1 allows you to choose headphones or speaker, but not both. R2 and R3 cut down on the signal going to the phones in order to attenuate the noise coming out of the amp a little bit, and to bring the output level down to something reasonable for our ears. Use 8- to 16-Ω headphones for best results, although most any type will work satisfactorily.

Project No. 5 PARTS LIST

Resistors (all are 1/4W, 10% tolerance, except as noted)

R1-R3	33Ω
R4	47Ω
R5	270Ω
R6, R7	100k
R8	470k
R9	1M audio or linear taper pot—controls *channel 1 level*
R10	1M audio or linear taper pot—controls *channel 2 level*

Capacitors (rated at 12V or more for +12V supply except as noted)

C1	20pF, ceramic disc
C2	390pF (polystyrene preferred, disc acceptable)
C3	0.01μF (mylar preferred, disc acceptable)
C4-C6	0.22μF, mylar or ceramic
C7, C9	100μF, electrolytic or tantalum
C8	100μF, electrolytic or tantalum, 6V or more
C10	220μF, electrolytic
C11	1000μF, electrolytic

Semiconductors

IC1	Fairchild μA706 or TBA641B audio amplifier

Mechanical Parts

J1, J2	Open circuit 1/4" mono phone jack
J3, J4	Open circuit 1/4" stereo phone jack
S1	SPDT toggle switch—selects *speaker/headphones*
Misc.	Case, knobs, 14-pin IC socket, circuit board, 12V battery pack, solder, wire, loudspeaker, etc.

Project No. 6

ULTRA-FUZZ

Definition: Converts input waveform into a square-wave output, thereby producing a smooth and harmonically intense fuzz effect. Built-in triggering circuitry shuts off the unit between notes for lowest noise.

Figure 5-35
Ultra-fuzz mounted in small Radio Shack box.

Background

Most fuzzes are based on the principle of controlled distortion, usually by overloading some type of amplifier circuitry. The ultra-fuzz is a waveform conversion device that actually transforms the waveform rather than simply adding distortion to an existing waveform. While designed for single-note lines, there are occasional instances where playing two or more notes works well with this fuzz.

A tradeoff in the design of this fuzz eliminates noise at the expense of a somewhat abrupt decay (not unlike the sound of a signal processed through a noise gate). However, with practice and proper adjustment of the sensitivity control, this is generally not a hinderance.

Features

- Single IC construction
- Variable sensitivity (independent of supply voltage)
- Operates from +5 to ±18V
- Choice of line-level or low-level operation set by two components
- High output
- Inherent noise gate action
- Distinctive, "synthesized sounding" fuzz effect
- Excellent sustain characteristics for single-note lead lines

Level of Difficulty: Beginner to intermediate

Construction Tips

This is a high-gain circuit, so keep all leads as short and direct as possible.

Separate input and output leads by at least 1 cm (1/2").

Shield the wires from pad I to J1, and from pad B to R4.

Using the Ultra-Fuzz

Plug your instrument into the input, and patch the output to your amp. Keep the *level* control very low while experimenting, as this unit produces a lot of output and can overload most amps.

Important: Guitarists should use the *bass* or *rhythm* pickup with this fuzz, preferably with the tone control turned all the way down (minimum high frequencies).

- The center of the *sensitivity* control is the most sensitive setting. At this center position, you will probably hear nasty sounds like static, popping, or noise. While *not* playing (preferably mute your instrument by turning down its volume control), turn the control in either direction until the noise/static *just* goes away. Play for a while to familiarize yourself with the triggering action, then experiment some more with the sensitivity control until you find the setting that is most appropriate to your playing.

86

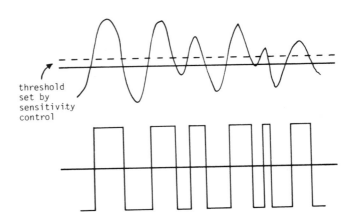

Figure 5-36

The upper drawing shows an audio waveform superimposed on the threshold level set by the sensitivity control. The lower drawing shows the output level of comparator IC1B. When the audio signal exceeds the threshold level, the output of the comparator goes to its maximum level; when the audio signal sinks below the threshold level, the output of the comparator goes to its minimum level. If the audio signal is always below the threshold (which happens after the signal decays past a certain point), then IC1B gives no output and the output of the fuzz is muted.

threshold
set by
sensitivity
control

■ Some players may get best results by turning the sensitivity control clockwise from center; others will find that counterclockwise from center works best. Try both possibilities.

■ If at first the ultra-fuzz seems difficult to "tame," don't get discouraged. As with anything different from the norm, you should allow yourself a sufficient period of familiarzation.

Modifications

■ For *line-level* operation, C1=470pF and R8=100k.

■ For *low-level* operation, C1=47pF and R8=1M.

These two components hold the key to obtaining the best possible sound. For a better understanding of their functions, see *How it Works*.

■ To pad down the output level (you might find it too "hot"), add a 47k resistor between pad O and R5, terminal 3.

In Case of Difficulty

■ "Rough" fuzz sound: Guitarists, use bass pickup; other instruments, turn down tone controls to remove as much treble as possible.

■ Lack of sustain, all notes, even with sensitivity control properly adjusted: Increase R8.

■ Lack of sustain, higher notes only, even with sensitivity control properly adjusted: Decrease C1.

■ Static: Readjust sensitivity control.

Specifications

Current consumption: ±5mA
Frequency response (input = 0.1V pk-pk): ±1dB, 40Hz-20kHz with C1=47pf and R8=100k.
Minimum signal required for full triggering @ 500Hz: less than 10mV pk-pk with R4 near center.
Maximum output signal: 10V pk-pk
Output waveform: square

Figure 5-37
Artwork for the foil side of the board, shown 1 to 1.

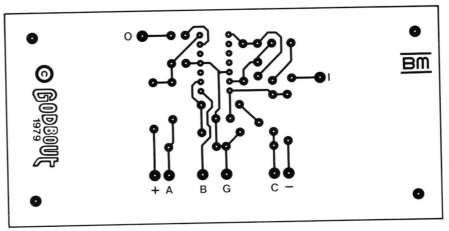

Figure 5-38
Component layout for the ultra-fuzz.

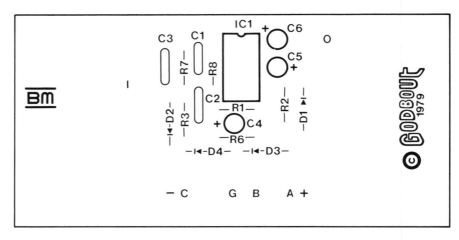

Figure 5-39
Ultra-fuzz schematic.

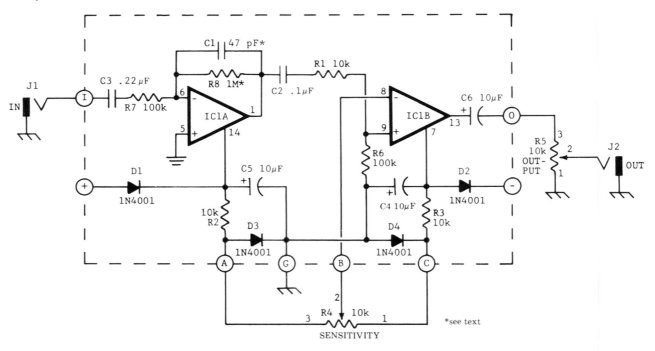

The input signal couples into the circuit through capacitor C3 and sees a 100k input impedance (R7). The gain of IC1A is the ratio of R8/R7. Increasing the value of R8 increases the sensitivity of this stage. C1 is a high-frequency filter that rolls off high frequencies to prevent instability. Increasing the value of C1 gives a "smooth" sound with guitar by filtering out energy above the fundamental frequency of the note.

The output of IC1A couples through C2 and R1 into IC1B. IC1B is an electronic circuit called a *comparator*. It compares the audio signal to the setting of the sensitivity control. Referring to Figure 5-36, if the audio exceeds this setting, IC1B gives an output; if the audio falls below this setting, then IC1B turns off. The output of the comparator couples through C6 and the *output* control into your amp or the next effect.

Resistors R2 and R3, along with diodes D3 and D4, set up a simple voltage reference for the sensitivity pot. These limit the threshold voltages to about +0.7V at the extreme clockwise rotation, and about -0.7V at the extreme counterclockwise rotation. Diodes D1 and D2 are polarity reversal protection diodes, while C4 and C5 add power supply decoupling.

Project No. 6 PARTS LIST

Resistors (all are 1/4W, 10% tolerance, except as noted)

R1-R3	10k
R4	10k linear taper pot—controls *sensitivity*
R5	10k audio taper pot—controls *output level*
R6, R7	100k
R8	100k (line level), 1M (low level)

Capacitors (rated at more than 10V for +9V power supply)

C1	470pF (line level), 47pF (low level)
C2	0.1μF (mylar preferred, disc acceptable)
C3	0.22μF (mylar preferred, disc acceptable)
C4-C6	10μF, electrolytic or tantalum

Semiconductors

IC1	RC4739 or XR4739 dual low-noise op amp
D1-D4	IN4001 or equivalent silicon diode

Mechanical parts

J1, J2	Open circuit 1/4" mono phone jack
Misc.	Knobs, case, 14-pin IC socket, circuit board, wire, solder, etc.

Project No. 7

BASS FUZZ

Definition: A fuzz (distortion circuit) designed specifically for bass.

Figure 5-40
The bass fuzz mounted in a Radio Shack chassis. Note the footswitch added to the unit to control the in/out switching function; this device is most effective when used sparingly.

Background:

Fuzzes designed for guitar add many high-frequency harmonics to the bass sound. So, although the original bass note is still present at the fuzz output, it is reduced to a fraction of the total signal, with the harmonics adding an artificial brightness. This robs some "bottom" from the bass sound. This circuit includes a conventional fuzzing stage, followed by a simple filter that reduces the high-frequency content to achieve a more natural bass sound.

Features

- Switch-selected choice of two filter responses
- Line-level or low-level operation
- Variable intensity control
- Operates from ±5 to ±18V
- Low noise, low cost
- Usable with guitar, piano, etc., to give a muted or "rhythm" fuzz sound

Level of Difficulty: Beginner

Construction Tips

This is a noncritical project, as long as you keep the input and output leads separated by about 1 cm (1/2") and shield the wire going to pad I on the board.

Using the Bass Fuzz

- Plug your instrument into J1 and patch J2 to your amp. Turn the *output* control fully counterclockwise and the *intensity* control halfway up.

- Play and adjust *output* to suit.

- Adjust intensity for desired fuzz effect; readjust the output control to compensate for level changes while setting the intensity control.

- Experiment with the two different switch positions to find the tone most appropriate to your playing.

Modifications

- Too fuzzy: Change R1 to 47k.

- Not fuzzy enough: Increase R5 to 470k or even 1M.

- Less high-frequency response with S1 closed: Increase C2 to 0.005 or 0.01 μF.

- Less high-frequency response for both switch positions: Increase C1 to 0.001 or 0.005 μF, and C2 to 0.002 or 0.01 μF.

- More high-frequency response: Decrease C1 to 10pF.

In Case of Difficulty

■ Gritty or uneven fuzz sound: Check that LEDs are polarized properly. Make sure they have not been burned out while soldering.

■ Intensity control has no effect: Check value of R1.

■ Noisy output but no instrument sound: Check IC1A. Check input wiring.

■ Feedback/squeals: Check lead layout. Install shielded wire between J1 and pad I. Make sure C1 is properly soldered in place.

Specifications

Current consumption: ±4mA
Maximum input before clipping @ 400Hz (R2 up full): 5mV pk-pk
Maximum available output voltage: 2.5V pk-pk
Frequency-response curves: see Figure 5-41

Figure 5-41
Frequency response of the bass fuzz for both settings of S1.

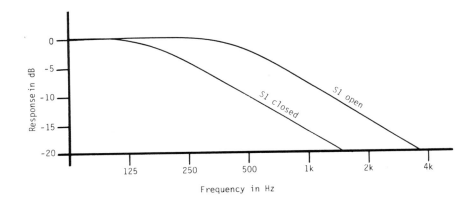

How it Works

The input signal couples into an inverting buffer stage via C3, and sees a 100k or so input impedance represented by R4. This buffer stage couples into the fuzzing stage through C4, R1, and R2. D3 and D4 limit the gain of the op amp; as the signal level increases, D3 and D4 start conducting, which soft-clips the signal and causes a fuzz effect. Note that the LEDs do *not* light up. They are used instead of conventional diodes because they clip at a higher level, thus giving us more overall output.

C1 limits the high-frequency response of the op amp, which is what eliminates the harmonics to give the bass fuzz its distinctively bassy sound. Shunting C2 in parallel with C1 reduces the high-frequency response even more. Diodes D1 and D2 are polarity reversal protection diodes, while C6 and C7 add power supply decoupling/bypassing. The output of the fuzz couples through C5 to R3, the *output* control, and then appears at the output jack.

Figure 5-42
*Artwork for the foil side of the circuit board,
shown 1 to 1.*

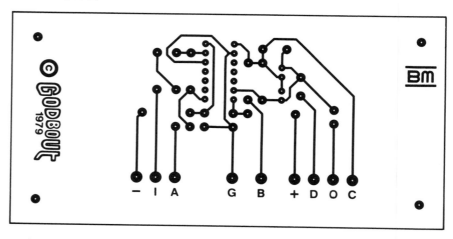

Figure 5-44
Bass fuzz schematic.

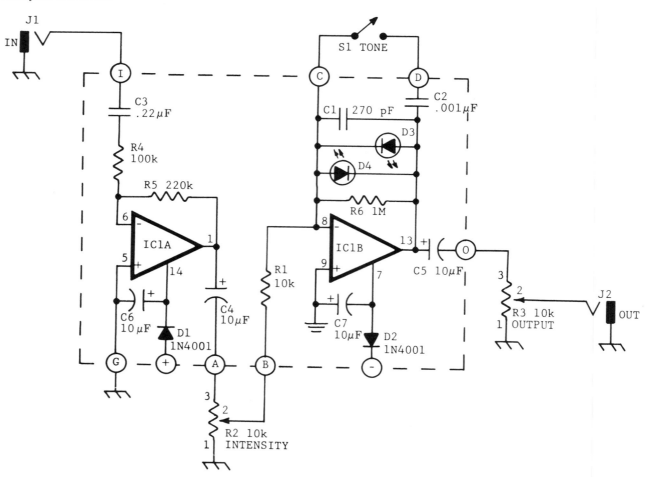

Figure 5-43
Component layout for the bass fuzz.

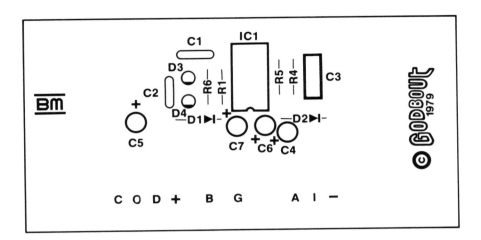

Project No. 7 PARTS LIST

Resistors (all are 1/4W, 10% tolerance, except as noted)

R1	10k
R2	10k audio taper pot—controls *intensity*
R3	10k audio taper pot—controls *output*
R4	100k
R5	220k
R6	1M

Capacitors (rated at more than 10V for ∓9V, more than 15V for ∓15V)

C1	270pF (polystyrene preferred, disc acceptable)
C2	0.001µF (polystyrene preferred, disc acceptable)
C3	0.22µF (mylar preferred, disc acceptable)
C4-C7	10µF, electrolytic or tantalum

Semiconductors

IC1	RC4739 or XR4739 dual low-noise op amp
D1, D2	IN4001 or equivalent silicon diode
D3, D4	General-purpose red LED

Mechanical Parts

J1, J2	Open circuit 1/4" mono phone jack
S1	SPST switch—controls *tone*
Misc.	Knobs, case, circuit board, 14-pin socket, wire, solder, etc.

Project No. 8

COMPRESSOR/LIMITER

Definition: A compressor reduces the dynamic range of a signal by attenuating peaks and amplifying valleys. A limiter only restricts the peaks of a signal. This unit combines elements of both.

Figure 5-45
Compressor mounted in a Vector-Pak card module prior to installation in the pedalboard project (No. 23).

Background:

Compression and limiting have been used for many years in studios, radio stations, commercials, communications, and many other applications. Dynamic range reduction prevents overloading of tapes, thus minimizing distortion; increases the apparent sustain of stringed (percussive) instruments; and improves intelligibility with speech and PA systems. When playing guitar through a compressor, for example, single-note lines or full six-string chords sound equally loud.

Features

- Fast attack, slow decay response
- 10:1 compression ratio over 50-dB range (see *Specifications*)
- Also functions as compressing preamp for converting low-level signals to compressed, high-level signals
- Choice of line-level or low-level operation set by single resistor
- Operates from +9 to +15V
- Separate compression and output controls
- Suitable for recording or stage use
- Excellent frequency response characteristics

Level of Difficulty: Intermediate

Construction Tips;

While not an extremely critical circuit, please note the following precautions.

This project uses a CLM6000 opto-isolator. Refer to the *General Instructions* section at the beginning of this chapter before attempting to solder this part in place.

Keep all wiring as short and direct as possible, especially those wires going to J1, R6, and R7. Keep input and output leads at least 1 cm (1/2") away from each other.

Shield the wires going from pad D to R7, terminal 2, and from pad A to R6, terminals 3 and 2.

Using the Compressor

In many ways, compressors are at their best when used subtly. Use the minimum amount of compression necessary to get the effect you want. Guitar players should note that a compressor only increases the *apparent* sustain of a guitar; i.e., it cannot make a string vibrate any longer, but instead amplifies the string *more* as it decays.

- Plug instrument into J1 and patch J2 to your amp. Start with both controls fully counterclockwise.

- Turn up *output* for a preamping effect. At extreme clockwise positions you may encounter distortion. Return control to about halfway before proceeding to next step.

- Turn up *compression* until you notice a drop in level. The level drop corresponds to the amount of gain reduction introduced by the compressor. Increase output to compensate for this drop. Subtler instrument sounds should now be more prominent.

- With extreme clockwise settings of the compression control, the sound will get noisy and possibly rough-sounding. Avoid overcompression.

- For absolute minimum noise, do not use any electronic devices (fuzzes, etc.) before the compressor. With moderate amounts of compression, including a *low noise* preamp in the signal chain before the compressor will introduce an acceptably low amount of noise. However, in most cases the compressor should come first in the signal chain.

Modifications

- For *line-level* operation, recommended R8=220k

- For *low-level* operation, R8=1M

- For maximum sustain, use 1M for R8, even with line-level signals. The tradeoff is more noise, especially when preceded with other electronic devices or when used in conjunction with an instrument that has a built-in instrument preamp.

- Running the compressor at ±15V increases the amount of sustain slightly.

In Case of Difficulty

- Noise: Reduce *compression* control. Feed instrument directly into compressor.

- Distortion: Reduce *output* control. If distortion persists, reduce *compression* control, and return output to original setting (or until distortion occurs). Make sure you aren't overloading your amp.

- No compression action: First, remember that compressors are not supposed to add much coloration to the sound; compare compressed sound with bypassed sound to determine whether the unit isn't compressing. If compression still isn't evident, check OI1 for proper orientation and installation. Check IC2. Check compression control setting.

Figure 5-46
Compression curve, R8=1M. When R8=220k the curve isn't as dramatic, but I still recommend this value for line-level applications to keep the noise level acceptable.

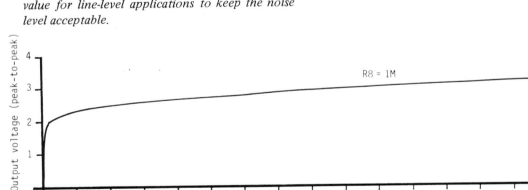

Specifications

Current consumption: ±5mA
Frequency response (any setting of *compression* or *output* control): ±1dB, 50Hz - 20kHz
Output headroom: 14V pk-pk
Compression ratio: 50dB change in input level yields 5dB change in output level; 60dB change in input level yields 10dB change in output level (R8=1M)
Compression curve: see Figure 5-46

Figure 5-47
Artwork for the foil side of the circuit board, shown 1 to 1.

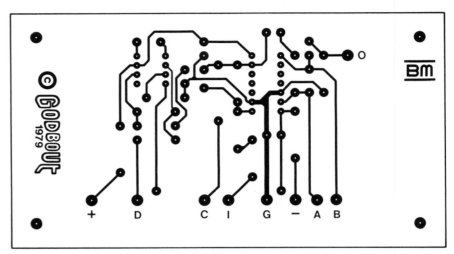

How it Works

To fully understand how this project works, reread the section in the beginning of this chapter on how the CLM6000 opto-isolator works.

The input couples into IC1A through C3 and R9. R8 sets the maximum gain of this op amp stage, but the overall gain is variable because of the photoresistor connected in parallel with R8. *More* light on the photoresistor *reduces* the gain of this stage: *less* light gives *more* gain.

The output of IC1A takes two different paths, one towards IC1B and the other towards IC2. We'll look at IC2 first. This op amp is a high-speed, uncompensated op amp whose frequency response is limited by C2. The signal from IC1A couples into IC2 through C4, compression control R7, and R5. The output of IC2 then drives the LED half of the CLM6000, so the LED brightness corresponds to the loudness of the signal from your instrument. As more signal goes into IC2, the LED gets brighter, which reduces the gain of IC1A and sends less signal to IC2. Thus, as the input signal increases, the compressor is constantly trying to turn itself down, which is what keeps the signal output more or less constant in the face of widely varying input voltages. This action takes place so fast you don't hear the effect as something choppy, but rather as a smooth, compressing effect. R7 determines the amount of signal level going into IC2. Letting more signal through turns on the LED that much sooner, resulting in gain reduction at lower signal levels for more compression.

Because we've cut the gain of IC1A down via the above-mentioned compression action, we need to add some amplification to bring the signal level back up again at the output. This is IC1B's function. R6 sets the gain; C1 limits the high-frequency response of this stage to prevent instability. The output from this amp couples through C6 to J2, the output jack. R3 tries to keep C6 tied to ground; this prevents you from hearing a loud pop when you plug something into the output.

D1 and D2 are polarity reversal protection diodes, while C7 and C8 add power supply bypassing and decoupling.

Figure 5-48
Component layout for the compressor.

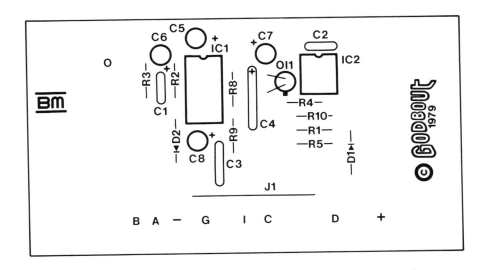

Figure 5-49
Compressor schematic

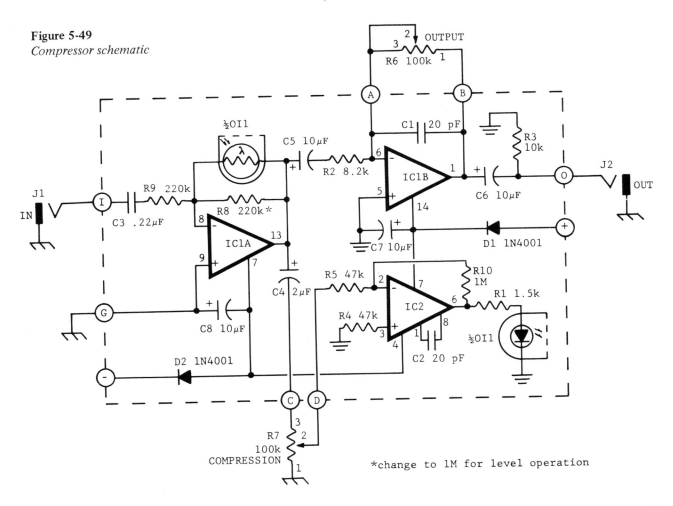

*change to 1M for level operation

Project No. 8 PARTS LIST

Resistors (all are 1/4W, 10% tolerance, except as noted)

R1	1.5k
R2	8.2k
R3	10k
R4, R5	47k
R6	100k audio taper pot—controls *output*
R7	100k audio taper pot—controls *compression*
R8	220k (line level), 1M (low level)
R9	220k
R10	1M

Capacitors (rated at more than 10V for ±9V power supply)

C1, C2	20pF (polystyrene preferred, disc acceptable)
C3	0.22μF (mylar preferred, disc acceptable)
C4	2μF, electrolytic or tantalum
C5-C8	10μF, electrolytic or tantalum

Semiconductors

IC1	RC4739 or XR4739 dual low-noise op amp
IC2	LM201 uncompensated op amp (substitutes: LM301, LM748)
D1, D2	IN4001 or equivalent silicon diode
OI1	CLM6000 opto-isolator (manufactured by Clairex)

Mechanical Parts

J1, J2	Open circuit 1/4" mono phone jack
Misc.	Knobs, case, circuit board, 14-pin IC socket, 8-pin IC socket, wire, solder, etc.

(a)

![Ring Modulator front panel with FREQ, RING, STRAIGHT knobs and treble/bass, in/out switches]

Figure 5-50

(a) The ring modulator mounted in a Vector-Pak card module. The various effects loop jacks are located on the back along with the other connectors. (b) A closeup of the ring modulator circuit board.

Project No. 9
RING MODULATOR

Definition: Accepts <u>two</u> different input signals; output gives <u>sum and difference</u> of the two signals (without either original signal). Example: An input frequency of 220Hz in conjunction with another input frequency of 600Hz produces <u>two</u> notes at the output—820Hz (the sum) and 380Hz (the difference).

(b)

Background:

Ring modulators have many applications, including ones involving radio communications. Musically, they have been used for many years by musicians from Stockhausen, to Jan Hammer, to Devo. The fact that ring modulators produce mathematically *related sounds rather than* harmonically *related sounds has prevented their widespread acceptance in popular music, but for producing atonal effects and percussive and gonglike sounds, or for adding a complex harmonic structure to an instrument, the ring modulator is very useful. Technically speaking, this project isn't a ring modulator but a* balanced modulator, *which is easier to construct. The sound is essentially the same.*

Level of Difficulty: Intermediate

Features

- Low cost
- On-board square-wave oscillator, tunable from 100 Hz to 2kHz, feeds one input of the ring modulator (your instrument provides the other input)
- On-board two-input mixer provides blend of straight (unprocessed) and ring-modulated sounds
- Input overvoltage protection for IC2 allows for increased sustain
- Set-and-forget carrier oscillator rejection trimpot
- Pre-mixer effects loop included in straight signal path
- Choice of line-level or low-level operation, and sustain characteristics, set with single resistor
- Operates from ±9V

Construction Tips

This is a relatively noncritical circuit, and no special precautions are required.

Shield the wire going from pad I to J1.

R7 is a trimpot and not a panel pot.

For best results, follow the circuit board layout as closely as possible, even if you are wiring on a piece of perfboard.

Calibration

- Initially set *straight level* fully counterclockwise, carrier *frequency* halfway, and *ring level* fully clockwise.

- Patch the output to an amp. Leave the input *unconnected* for now.

- Apply power

- You will hear a tone; carefully adjust R7 for the minimum amount of tone. This should occur near the trimpot's midrotation point.

Using the Ring Modulator

Plug your instrument into J1 and patch J2 (output) to your amp. Start with all controls counterclockwise.

- Check ring modulator channel: Turn the *ring level* control clockwise to hear the ring-modulated effect exclusively. Varying the *frequency* control in his mode changes the internal oscillator frequency and therefore changes the "harmony" that tracks along with your instrument. The *tone* switch selects a bright, fuzzy sound when open, and a mellower, bassier sound when closed.

- Blending ring modulator and straight channels: Turning the *straight level* control clockwise adds in some of the unprocessed instrument sound along with the ring-modulated sound. This helps to "tame" the atonality of the ring modulator effect and removes some of the metallic sounding quality associated with ring modulators.

- Using the effects loop: This loop allows for patching of external effects boxes in the straight signal path. Example: To mix ring modulated and fuzzed sounds, patch from J3 (send) to the fuzz, or any other effect, *input*. Then patch the fuzz, or any other effect, *output* to J4 (receive).

- For best results, do not think of the ring modulator as a harmonizing device, but rather as something that lends a harmonically complex, atonal quality to a signal. Example: Plucking short, muted tones on a guitar will sound bell- or chime-like when processed through the ring modulator; drums acquire a more complex timbre; and electric pianos produce very otherworldly sounds when ring modulated.

Modifications

- Resistor R12 programs the ring modulator for line-level or low-level operation, and also sets the "sustain" of the unit. Increased sustain with a percussive instrument, such as guitar or piano, simulates the effect of compressing the input signal. Therefore, for a sustaining, fuzz-like sound, select this resistor for maximum sustain. For a more percussive, bell-like sound, select for minimum sustain.

Line-level operation, minimum sustain: R12=330k
Line-level operation, maximum sustain: R12=100k
Low-level operation, minimum sustain: R12=100k
Low-level operation, maximum sustain: R12=33k

The above are suggested values; however, R12 can be anywhere in the range of 33k to 1M if you wish to experiment further.

- For pedal control of the carrier frequency, mount R15 in a footpedal. It may be necessary to run shielded wires from pads A and B to R15 for long cable runs.

- To lower the frequency range of the internal oscillator by 1 octave, increase C2 to 0.1 μF. To raise the internal oscillator range by an octave, decrease C2 to 0.02 μF.

- If closing S1 results in too muted a sound, change C3 to 0.1 μF or even 0.05 μF.

- Increase the overall ring modulator gain by raising the value of R14; decrease the gain by lowering the value of R14. Doubling its value doubles the gain, and halving its value halves the gain.

- Due to the internal structure of the 565, it is *not* possible to substitute a triangle- or sine-wave oscillator in place of the on-board square-wave oscillator.

- Operation is optimized for +9V. Do not run on higher supply voltages, unless R1 and R2 are increased in value so that the voltage on pin 1 of IC2 is in the range of -5 to -6V and the voltage on pin 10 of IC2 is +5 to +6V.

In Case of Difficulty

- No straight channel sound: Make sure J3, and particularly J4, are wired correctly (see Chapter 1, section on jacks).

- Effects loop doesn't work: See above. Also, while all book projects are compatible with the effects loop, some commercially available effects may not be.

- If a 2.5k trimpot is not available for R7, use a 5k trimpot and change R4 to 3.3k.

- Excessive carrier feedthrough: Check supply voltage. Make sure R1, R2, C7, and C9 are the exact values given in the parts list. Check instrument feeding the ring modulator for hum (this can cause strange-sounding problems, especially when R12 is set for high sustain values). Check all ground connections. Readjust R7.

- Effect is "unusable" in musical contexts: The proper use of this device is not something that is intuitively obvious, so allow yourself a period of time to become familiar with its operating characteristics and distinctive sound. Experiment with different settings of the frequency control and straight level control.

Figure 5-51
Artwork for the foil side of the circuit board, shown 1 to 1.

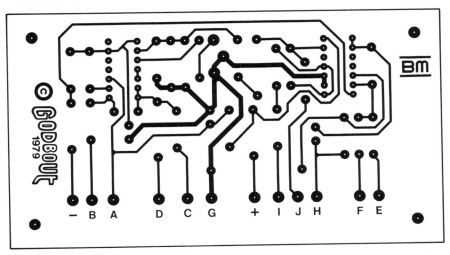

Figure 5-52
Component layout for the ring modulator.

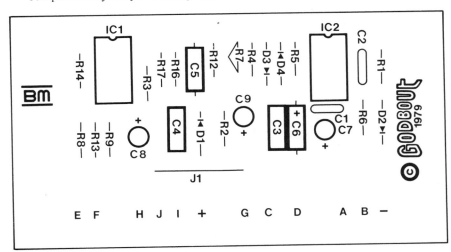

Specifications

Current consumption: ±11mA
Maximum recommended input level: less than 3V pk-pk*
Frequency response (S1 open)† : ±1dB, 40Hz-20kHz
Maximum available output, ring modulator channel: 3V pk-pk minimum
Maximum headroom, straight channel: 10V pk-pk
Carrier frequency (typical) 100Hz-2kHz
Carrier rejection (R15=0Ω, R7 adjusted for minimum feedthrough): -40dB typical

*Signals above this level will not damage the circuit, but increase the apparent amount of sustain.

†This represents an averaged frequency response. At certain frequencies, cancellations can occur that change the response drastically (but only at a single frequency). With S2 closed, high-frequency response starts rolling off around 1kHz.

Figure 5-53
Ring modulator schematic.

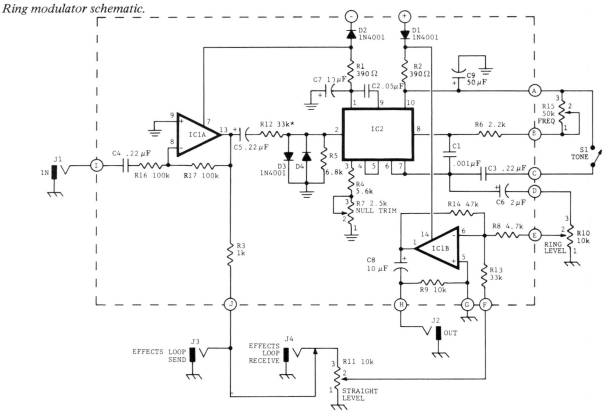

How it Works

Signals couple into the input through C4 and R16. IC1A is a unity-gain buffer amplifier that inverts the signal phase and drives both the effects loop send and IC2's input. The signal couples into IC2 through C5 and R12. Diodes D3 and D4 prevent excessive signal levels from reaching IC2, preventing possible damage to the IC.

R1 and R2 drop the power supply voltage to about $\pm$6V for feeding IC2, while C7 and C9 add decoupling and D1 and D2 provide polarity reversal protection. R15 sets the frequency of IC2's internal oscillator. C3 bypasses high frequencies away from the output with S1 closed. IC2's ouput couples through C6 into R10, which then couples through R8 into IC1B. IC1B forms a two-input mixer, and R10 mixes in the appropriate amount of ring-modulated signal.

The unmodified signal leaving IC1A also couples through R3, R11, and R13 into IC1B. R11 mixes in unmodified sound. The mixer inverts the phase of the unmodified signal once again, so between the inversion provided by IC1A and the inversion provided by IC1B, the unmodified signal comes out of the unit noninverted. The output of the mixer couples through C8 to output jack J2. R9 ties one end of C8 to ground to minimize "popping" when you initially plug into the output.

Here's how the effects loop works: J3 taps off the output of IC1A, and feeds the external effect. J4 is a closed-circuit-type phone jack. With nothing plugged into J4, the unmodified signal connects directly to R11. With an effect output plugged into J4, the unmodified signal is disconnected from R11 and must pass through the effect before appearing at R11.

Project No. 9 PARTS LIST

Resistors (all are 1/4W, 10% tolerance, except as noted)

R1, R2	390Ω
R3	1k
R4	5.6k
R5	6.8k
R6	2.2k
R7	2.5k trimpot—controls carrier *null trim*
R8	4.7k
R9	10k
R10	10k audio taper pot—controls *ring level*
R11	10k audio taper pot—controls *straight level*
R12	33k, 100k, or 330k (see *modifications*)
R13	33k
R14	47k
R15	50k linear taper pot—controls oscillator *frequency*
R16, R17	100k

Capacitors (rated at more than 10V for ±9V operation)

C1	0.001μF ceramic disc
C2	0.05μF (mylar preferred, disc acceptable)
C3-C5	0.22μF (mylar preferred, disc acceptable)
C6	2μF, electrolytic or tantalum
C7, C8	10μF, electrolytic or tantalum
C9	50μF, electrolytic or tantalum

Semiconductors

IC1	RC4739 or XR4739 dual low-noise op amp
IC2	NE565 or LM565 phase-locked loop
D1-D4	IN4001 or equivalent silicon diode

Mechanical Parts

J1-J3	Open circuit 1/4" mono phone jack
J4	Closed circuit 1/4" mono phone jack
S1	SPST toggle switch—controls *tone*
Misc.	Knobs, case, circuit board, two 14-pin IC sockets, wire, solder, etc.

Project No. 10

DUAL FILTER VOICING UNIT

Definition: Combines a preamp, two variable bandpass filters, and a three-input mixer in one unit for flexible tone-shaping capabilities.

(a)

Figure 5-54

(a) Dual filter voicing unit mounted in a typical Radio Shack chassis. (b) Note that the board is mounted close to the pots for minimum possible lead lengths.

(b)

Background

Some combinations of effects work very well together; for example, two filters in parallel allow you greater control over frequency response than a single filter. This project is like a "minipedalboard" where several projects work together to create a wide variety of sounds.

Level of Difficulty: Intermediate

Features

- Multiple module configuration, yet only requires 1 IC

- Accepts line-level or low-level inputs

- On-board mixer allows blend of filtered and straight voices

- Provides sufficient output level to allow overdrive of instrument amplifiers; also includes internal overdrive (fuzz) capability

- Operates from ±5 to ±18V

- Dual bandpass filters are tunable over a 10:1 range, and staggered to cover two different frequency ranges.
- Configurable as wa-wa, or wa/reverse wa, foot pedal
- Can simulate the sound of old amps when recording direct
- Adds response anomalies to purely electronic instruments

Constructions Tips

Despite the number of connections and controls, this is a relatively noncritical circuit.

Keep the input and output leads separated by a least 1 cm (1/2").

Shield the wire going from J1 to pad I on the board.

Use short, direct wiring when connecting the board pads to R11-R15 and especially R21.

Following the control layout shown in Figure 5-54 results in the shortest average lead lengths when connecting board pads to outboard components.

Using the Dual Filter Voicing Unit

It takes some time to get fully acquainted with the functions of the various controls, and how to use them to get a specific sound. *Spend time practicing* to get the most out of this unit.

- Set all controls fully counterclockwise, then plug your instrument into J1 and patch J2 to your amp. Apply power, then play; there should be no output. If there is, recheck all control settings.

- Check straight channel: Turn the *straight level* control clockwise to hear the instrument's unmodified sound. Next, turn the *overdrive* control clockwise; the overall volume should increase to the point where you will have to turn down the straight level to compensate for the extra volume boost. Extreme clockwise settings of the overdrive control produce fuzz (especially with line-level signals).

- Check filter 1 channel: Set all controls fully counterclockwise. Turn *freq 1 level* clockwise for a muted, filtered sound; adjust *freq 1* for the desired tonality. Rapidly turning the control should give a wa-wa effect. Experiment with different settings of the overdrive control to overdrive filter 1.

- Check filter 2 channel: Return all controls to full counterclockwise. Turn *freq 2 level* clockwise to listen to the second filter channel; this channel is tuned to a higher frequency range than channel 1. Adjust freq 2 for the desired tonality. Experiment with different settings of the overdrive control to overdrive filter 2.

- Check blend of straight and filtered sounds: Try various combinations of settings for the freq 1 level, freq 2 level, and straight level controls. Suggested order for setting a sound:
    1. Adjust straight level for a comfortable listening level.
    2. Adjust overdrive to add distortion or a volume boost. You may have to readjust the straight level to compensate for the extra boost.
    3. Add in filter channel 1 by turning up freq 1 level. and adjusting freq 1 for the right sound.
    4. Add in filter channel 2 by turning up freq 2 level, and adjusting freq 2 for the right sound.

Figure 5-55
Block diagram of the dual filter voicing unit.

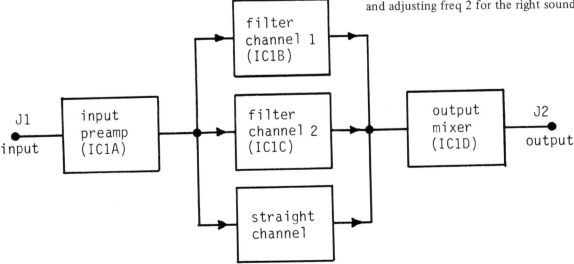

Modifications

■ C4 and C5 tune filter 1, while C2 and C3 tune filter 2 (refer to *Specifications* for the frequency ranges of these filters). Bass players may *double* the values of both sets of capacitors to tune the unit down one octave, or *quadruple* the values of both sets of capacitors to tune the unit down two octaves. Decreasing the value of these capacitors tunes these filters higher. When experimenting with different filter tunings, make sure C4=C5 and C2= C3.

■ R17 and R18 determine the sharpness, or resonance, of the filters. For a sharper sound, increase these to around 100k or more. This will affect the tuning range of the filter somewhat.

■ The overdrive control is designed more for overdriving conventional amps then actually acting as a fuzz tone, although fuzz effects are possible. For a fuzzier effect, drop the power supply voltage down to +5V or so.

■ For the cleanest possible sound, use +15 or +18V.

■ For a wa-wa pedal, mount a dual-ganged 10k pot in a foot pedal. Replace R11 with one pot and replace R12 with the other (use shielded cable between the foot pedal and pads A and D). For a wa/reverse wa pedal, change C2 and C3 to 0.05μF so that both filters are tuned to the same range. Replace R11 and R12 with a dual-ganged pot in a pedal as described above, but this time *reverse* the connections going to terminals 1 and 3 of R11. With this wiring, pushing the pedal down will cause filter 1 and filter 2 to sweep in opposite directions.

■ The dual filter voicing unit is an excellent processor for low-level instruments such as guitar. For stand-alone use with stock guitars, short out C6 and remove R19 from the circuit board for minimum noise and maximum input impedance. Next best option, should that cause problems: Change C6 to 0.05μF and R19 to 470k or 1M.

In Case of Difficulty

■ Distorted sound: Back off on overdrive control; back off on R13-R15. Increase power supply voltage.

■ Not enough filter level: Lower R6 and R10 to 4.7k.

■ Hum: Shield wires going from pad C to R21, and from pads A and D to R11 and R12. Check orientation of instrument with respect to transformers, amps, AC lines, etc.

■ Excessive noise: Place the dual filter voicing unit *first* in the signal chain, after the instrument.

Specifications

Current consumption: +7mA
Straight channel maximum input before clipping,
R21=1M: 250mV pk-pk
R21=0Ω: 6V pk-pk
(Filter channels clip at somewhat lower input levels)
Filter 1 frequency range: +3dB, 250-2500Hz
+1.5dB, 250-1500Hz
Filter 1Q: Approximately 1.1
Filter 2 frequency range: +1dB, 1200Hz-12kHz
Filter 2Q: Approximately 1.1

Figure 5-56
Artwork for the foil side of the circuit board, shown 1 to 1.

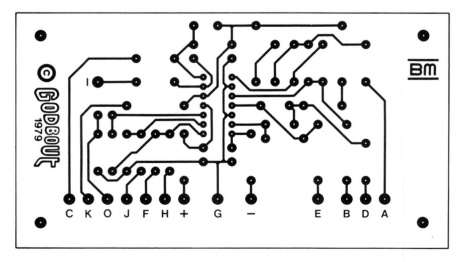

IC1A is a preamp stage whose gain (controlled by R21) is variable from X2 to X45. IC1B and IC1C make up the two filters, and IC1D is the output mixer. The input signal couples into IC1A through C6, and sees an approximate 120k input impedance across R19. The gain of this stage is determined by the ratio of R20 to R21 + R16; thus, as the resistance of R21 becomes *smaller*, the gain *increases*. This produces the overdrive effect. Capacitor C1 helps to preserve stability with high-gain settings of R21.

The output of IC1A couples through C9/R13 into the output mixer (IC1D), through C7/R9 into filter 1, and through C8/R8 into filter 2. With filter 1, capacitors C4 and C5 set the general frequency range, with R11 setting the specific resonant frequency. C2 and C3 set the general frequency range for filter 2, with R12 setting the specific resonant frequency.

The output of IC1B couples through C10, R14, and R10 to the output mixer; the output of IC1C couples C11, R15, and R6 to the output mixer. One trick used in this mixer to keep all the signals in phase is to mix the straight signal into the noninverting input via R13 and R7 while the inverted filtered signals terminate in the inverting input.

The output of IC1D couples through C12 into the output jack. Resistor R5 ties to C12 to ground to minimize "popping" when plugging into J2. D1 and D2 provide polarity reversal protection; C13 and C14 add power supply decoupling.

Figure 5-57
Component layout for the dual filter voicing unit.

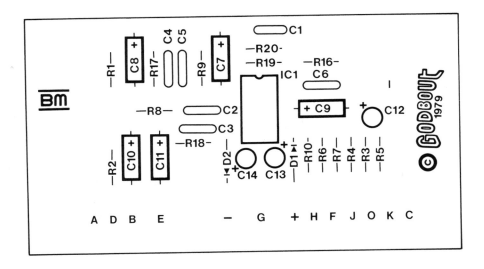

Figure 5-58
Dual filter voicing unit schematic.

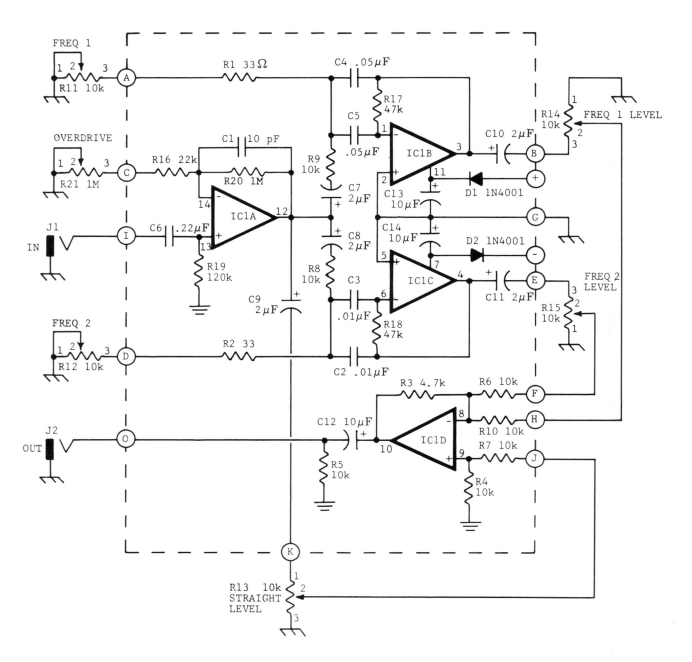

Project No. 10 PARTS LIST

Resistors (all are 1/4W, 10% tolerance, except as noted)

R1, R2	33Ω
R3	4.7k
R4-R10	10k
R11	10k linear taper pot—controls *filter frequency 1*
R12	10k linear taper pot—controls *filter frequency 2*
R13	10k audio taper pot—controls *straight level*
R14	10k audio taper pot—controls *filter 1 level*
R15	10k audio taper pot—controls *filter 2 level*
R16	22k
R17, R18	47k
R19	120k
R20	1M
R21	1M linear taper pot—controls *overdrive*

Capacitors (rated at more than 10V for ±9V)

C1	10pF, ceramic disc
C2, C3	0.01μF (mylar preferred, disc acceptable)
C4, C5	0.05μF (mylar preferred, disc acceptable)
C6	0.22μF (mylar preferred, disc acceptable)
C7-C11	2μF, electrolytic or tantalum
C12-C14	10μF, electrolytic or tantalum

Semiconductors

IC1	RC4136 or XR4136 quad low-noise op amp
D1, D2	IN4001 or equivalent silicon diode

Mechanical Parts

J1, J2	Open circuit 1/4" mono phone jack
Misc.	Knobs, case, circuit board, 14-pin socket, wire, solder, etc.

Project No. 11

ADDING BYPASS SWITCHES TO EFFECTS

Definition: Many players do not wish to use an effect all the time, but only in specific sections of a piece. A bypass or in/out switch allows you to choose between the straight and modified sounds. Fuzz tones, wa-wa pedals, and many other effects usually include bypass switches.

Background

The various modification devices in this book have no provision given for switching the effect in and out of circuit, since there are many possible ways to accomplish the bypassing function. Rather than including bypassing circuitry for each project, this section treats the subject as completely as possible to allow you to choose whichever approach best suits your purposes. There is additional information on adding improved bypassing to commercially available effects.

Features

- Requires no power, adds no noise
- Does not degrade signal quality
- Minimal clicking or popping during switching
- Simple installation
- Suitable for footswitch control

Level of Difficulty: Beginner

Adding Bypassing to Book Projects

All effects projects have an input jack that goes to the circuit board, and an output jack that either goes to the circuit board or to an output level control (see Figure 5-59). To add true bypassing, we need to break the connections indicated with an "X" on Figure 5-59, and then add a DPDT switch as shown in Figure 5-60.

With S1 in position A, the signal from the input jack goes directly to the input of the effect; meanwhile, the output of the effect (either from the circuit board or the level control) goes to the output jack. With S1 in position B, the input jack signal flows directly to the output jack, bypassing the effect completely.

Figure 5-59
The upper drawing shows a project whose output pad connects directly to the output jack; the lower drawing shows a project whose output pad passes through an output level control before reaching the output jack. (In both cases, power supply and other connections are not shown for clarity.) Breaking the connections between the jacks and the effects, where marked with an "X," allows you to add a bypass switch.

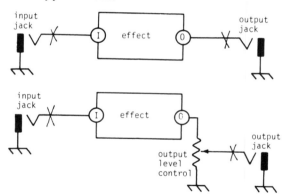

Figure 5-60
With S1 in position A, the effect is in the audio signal path. With S1 in position B, the effect is bypassed and out of the signal path.

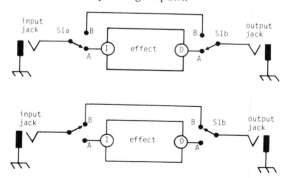

Adding Bypassing to Commercially Available Effects

Some effects boxes detract from the quality of a signal even when they are (supposedly) switched out of the signal path. Before we get into the cure, let's investigate why this happens.

Many commercial effects, in order to keep costs down, switch the effect in and out through the use of an SPDT switch as shown in Figure 5-61. In position A, the switch connects to the output of the effect and you hear the modified instrument sound. In position B, you hear the sound of the instrument itself—but note that the instrument is still connected to the *input* of the effect, which affects your signal by shunting some of the signal's power to ground.

Additional effects only serve to compound the problem, as shown in Figure 5-62. When the effects are switched out, the instrument is not just shunted by the input of one effect, but by several effect inputs—each of which lowers the input impedance even further and contributes to the degradation of the overall sound.

Figure 5-61

Even though the effect is theoretically "bypassed," note that the instrument still connects to the input of the effect.

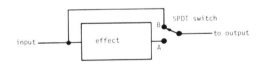

Figure 5-62

While both effect 1 and effect 2 are supposed to be bypassed, note that the instrument still connects to the inputs of both effects. This often has a detrimental effect on the sound of the instrument.

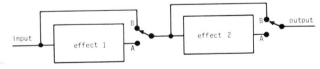

One partial solution is to add a buffer board (see Project No. 26) between the instrument and chain of effects. The buffer converts the relatively high-impedance output of a guitar pickup to a relatively low-impedance output that is far less affected by the shunting action of the effect's input stage. The input of the effect is still draped across the signal line, though, so a better solution is to use a DPDT switch to accomplish the switching function as we did for the book projects. Basically, we replace the SPDT switch with a DPDT switch. The con-

nections are again broken in the same places as for the previous modification (right at the input and output jacks), and are wired up to the switch as shown in Figure 5-63.

Figure 5-63

Here's how to convert an effect to true bypassing. Begin by unscrewing the SPDT footswitch from its case, and screw in the DPDT replacement. I'd also advise making a sketch of the original wiring, just in case you run into some kind of problem and need to convert back to the original wiring. Next, follow the steps below while carefully observing the pin numbers we've arbitrarily assigned to the terminals of the DPDT switch.

1. Disconnect the wire going from the output jack to S1 at the S1 end, and connect it to S2, terminal 2.

2. Trace the wire coming from S1 that works its way back to the input of the effect. Cut this wire at the effect input end.

3. Unsolder the remaining wire going to S1. Connect it to S2, terminal 3.

4. Disconnect the wire going to the effect's input jack at the jack and connect this end to S2, terminal 6.

5. Run a wire from the input jack (the same terminal we disconnected a wire from last step) to terminal 5 of S2.

6. Connect terminals 1 and 4 together on S2.

7. Check the bypassing switch to make sure it is wired correctly.

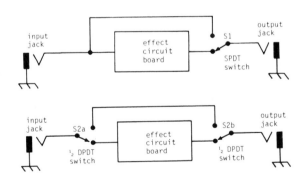

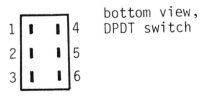

bottom view,
DPDT switch

Eliminating Clicks and Pops

Switching an effect between the straight and modified modes should produce no clicks or pops in the output as long as you are *not* playing your instrument when you do the switching. If you are playing, you may get minor pops that are unavoidable. Should popping occur even when you aren't playing, you may need to add two "tie down" resistors to the DPDT bypass switch as shown in Figure 5-64.

For all book projects, the 100k resistor will *not* be necessary, and the 1M resistor will only be required under some conditions. On commercially available projects, you may need to add one or both resistors to minimize popping.

If you're interested in the theory behind why this eliminates pops, remember that most effects have coupling capacitors at their inputs and outputs. When the end of the capacitor is disconnected, that end can build up a voltage charge. Switching the effect "in" deposits the capacitor's charge on the signal line, creating a pop. The tie down resistor holds the free end of this coupling capacitor at ground (zero voltage) level; so, no charge can build up to cause pops.

What Type of Switch is Best to Use?

A miniature toggle switch is the simplest way to do in/out switching. Toggle switches are easy to find and easy to mount on an effects box front panel.

Footswitches are for those who seldom have a hand free for flicking switches. You must use a *push-on/push-*

off type. This means that you push it once to switch the effect in, and push it again to bypass the effect.

Unfortunately, heavy-duty DPDT push-on/push-off footswitches are not too easy to find. As of this writing, Musician's Supply (PO Box 1440, El Cajon, CA 92022) and Burstein-Applebee (3199 Mercier Street, Kansas City, MO 64111) carry suitable types.

Another problem with footswitches is that since they carry an audio signal, you must use shielded cable on all connections going to the footswitch. If the effects box mounts in a floor unit along with the switch there should be no real problem, but if you want to run the footswitch remotely from the effect you'll need to use quite a bit of shielded cable.

An alternative to mechanical switching is the electronic footswitch project (No. 15) in this book. It not only uses an easy-to-find SPST push-on/push-off switch (available at auto supply, hardware, and electronics stores), but all the audio switching happens at the effect itself, which means that no audio passes through the SPST footswitch since the footswitch is there merely to instruct the circuitry what to do. Finally, an LED indicates whether the effect is on or off, which can be very helpful. However, now we run into the problem of having to spend additional money and effort on building an electronic circuit . . . so the electronic footswitch is not without its complications, although from a convenience point of view it's hard to beat.

As a compromise, I'd suggest using toggle switches for those projects that you don't switch in and out too often, and electronic footswitches for those projects that you switch in and out a lot.

Figure 5-64
Tie-down resistors added to the circuit of Figure 5-63. Project No. 15, the electronic footswitch, includes tie-down resistors as part of the switching circuit.

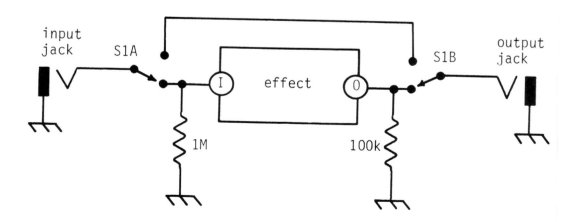

Project No. **12**

GUITAR REWIRING

Introduction

The art of rewiring guitars could easily take up a book in itself, for a number of reasons:

■ There are many possible ways to modify the wiring of a guitar; some are more musically useful than others, or more applicable to one style of music than another.

■ Different guitars lend themselves to different modifications. For example, a good Stratocaster modification would not necessarily apply to a Les Paul, because the Strat has three pickups compared to the Les Paul's two pickups. Humbucking pickups offer several modification options not available with single-coil pickups, and tapped pickups allow for another, entirely different, set of modifications.

■ Since you're working with a musical instrument, you have to work very carefully. If you blow up something like a treble booster, you can chalk it up to experience without too many regrets . . . but put a file gash in your prized guitar, and you'll feel a whole lot worse.

Rather than try to cover all possible bases, then, we'll examine the basic principles of guitar rewiring and a specific example of how to modify the ubiquitous Fender Telecaster. This information will hopefully give you a feel for how to go about adapting what we'll be covering to your own specific instrument and needs.

Pickup Basics

A pickup basically comprises a coil (or number of coils) of fine wire housed in a metal or plastic case. With ordinary, high-impedance pickups (found on the majority of guitars), two wires trail out from the case.

Plucking a string induces a signal into the coil(s); a varying voltage—the electrical equivalent of the note being plucked—appears at one end of the coil, and a counterpart signal 180 degrees out of phase with respect to the first signal appears at the other end (see Figure 5-65). One side of the coil generally goes to ground, and the other lead (the "hot" lead) goes to the pickup selector or other electronics (see Figure 5-66). However, we also have the option of using a switch to listen to *either*

Figure 5-65
Phase relationship of the signals coming out of a guitar pickup.

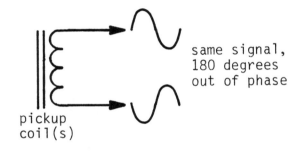

same signal,
180 degrees
out of phase

pickup
coil(s)

Figure 5-66
How to listen to two different signals from the guitar pickup.

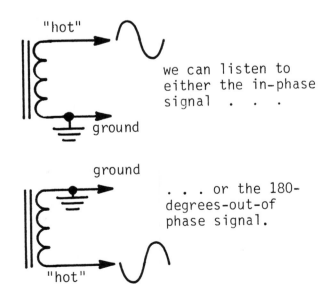

"hot"

we can listen to
either the in-phase
signal . . .

ground

ground

. . . or the 180-
degrees-out-of
phase signal.

"hot"

113

end of the coil, and therefore have a choice of pickup outputs; Figure 5-67 shows a switching circuit using a DPDT switch that allows you to listen to either the in-phase or 180-degree-out-of-phase signal generated by the coil.

Figure 5-67

Using a DPDT switch gives you in-phase and out-of-phase options.

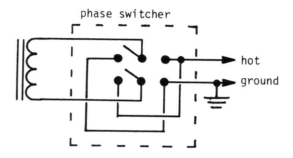

Interestingly, though, the ear is *not* sensitive to phase changes. In other words, whether we listen to the signals present at one end or the other end of the pickup, they sound the same—even though they are 180-degrees-out-of-phase with each other. So, why bother to change the phase? Because if you have a two-or-more-pickup guitar, by listening to more than one pickup while changing the phase of *one* of them, cancellations and reinforcements occur between the two pickups that produce interesting changes in the overall sound.

Combining Pickups

Let's say we have a guitar with bass and treble pickups, and that the treble pickup has an out-of-phase option. If we listen to only the treble pickup and flick the phase switch, there is no audible difference. But if we select the bass and treble pickups at the same time, as shown in Figure 5-68 (this is the middle position on most selector switches). we get two distinct sounds, depending on the treble pickup's phase setting. The in-phase position gives the regular sound of both pickups together; the out-of-phase position gives cancellation effects between the two pickups to create a thin, bright sound.

The aforementioned situation had the pickups connected in *parallel.* Although this configuration is very common, it is not the only way to combine two pickups. Figure 5-69 shows how to connect them in *series,* and by changing the treble pickup phase, you can acquire two additional sounds. With the treble in phase, your output becomes much hotter compared with a parallel connection, and the response is very full bodied—sort of like an acoustic guitar sound. With the treble out of

phase, you have a peaked midrange response that gives a kind of honky-tonk guitar sound.

So, with a two pickup guitar we now have six basic sounds to choose from: treble pickup only, bass pickup only, both pickups in parallel with the treble pickup out of phase, both pickups in parallel with the treble pickup in phase, both pickups in series with treble in phase, and both pickups in series with treble out of phase. All these different combinations have their specific uses and characteristic sounds.

Figure 5-68

Two pickups in parallel, with a phase switcher connected to the treble pickup.

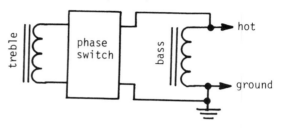

Figure 5-69

Two pickups in series, with a phase switcher connected to the treble pickup.

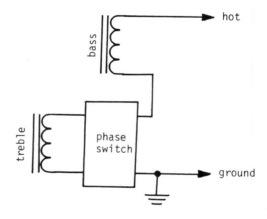

Constructions Tips

Now, this probably doesn't sound like too difficult a wiring job, especially the out-of-phase wiring switch, but there's big catch. Most pickups have two leads coming out of them, but unfortunately for us, they often take the form of a piece of shielded cable with the ground part connected to a metal shield of casing (see Figure 5-70a). Attempting to reverse the wires to throw the pickup out of phase means that the whole pickup plate or shield becomes "hot," which can cause hum and generally act like an antenna for noise. What we need to do is electrically disconnect the pickup leads from the case and wire the pickup shield or plate to ground *after* going through the magic

114

phase change switch (see Figure 5-70b). With some pickups, it's easy to remove the coil lead from the shield ground; with others, it's almost impossible. I hope your pickups fall into the former category if you want to try this modification. If things look too difficult, don't mess around or get in over your head. Pickups are quite fragile, and it's easy to damage the tiny wires used for the coil.

After isolating the pickup terminals from the shield, remove the shielded cable coming from the pickup coil, since you don't want the shield to become hot when you flip the phase switch. Either use two wires twisted lightly around each other, or better yet, use a piece of shielded cable for each lead going to the phase switch, and another piece of shielded cable to connect the output of the phase switch to the rest of the guitar's electronics.

Low-impedance pickups will often have a balanced configuration, which simplifies matters considerably. The ground line is already brought out separately from the coil leads, so simply adding a DPDT switch in the two "hot" coil lines in a manner similar to that shown in Figure 5-67 does the phase reversal job.

Modifying the Fender Telecaster

That pretty much sums up the background information we need to know about rewiring pickups. Now, let's look at a specific example of how to rewire a guitar.

Figure 5-71 shows a Telecaster rewiring that uses the stock Fender pickups; however, you will need two additional parts, one of which is a five-position pickup switch. While originally designed for Stratocaster guitars, the five-position switch is equally applicable to the Telecaster. This switch is made by several companies that specialize in replacement parts for guitars. You will also need a DPDT switch to accomplish the phase reversal function.

Our first step is to separate the treble pickup ground wire from the treble pickup ground plate/bridge assembly. With the Tele, this is a particularly easy job: Simply remove the strings, and then unscrew the treble pickup plate assembly. Now take a good look at the underside of the pickup. The coil connections to the pickup should be obvious; one of the them is "hot," while the other

Figure 5-70

How to reconnect the pickup plate or metal cover to avoid picking up hum.

(a)

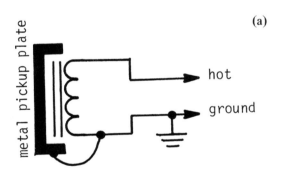

(b)

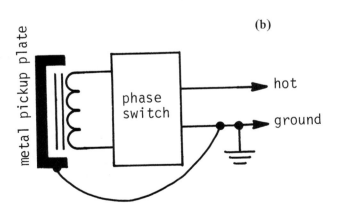

Figure 5-71

Modified Telecaster schematic. See text for explanation of the different switch positions.

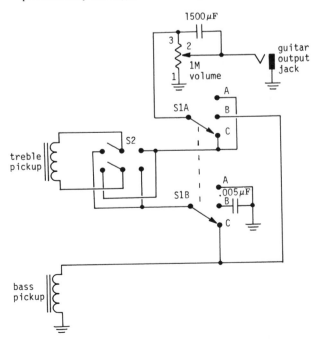

jumpers to the pickup plate assembly via a short length of wire. Cut this ground jumper, wire two new pickup coil leads to the phase reversal switch, and run a *separate* ground wire from the pickup plate to the ground tab of the output jack. To add some shielding, I wrapped this ground wire around the two coil leads. So, both pickup coil leads for the treble pickup should now be disconnected from ground and connected to the phase reversal switch, but the pickup plate and tailpiece should still connect to ground via a separate wire.

Next, you need to replace the old Tele pickup selector switch with the new five-position switch, and rewire the whole mess according to the schematic. Note that with the five-position switch, in position 1 (treble pickup only) the wiper of the switch connects to contact A only; in position 2 (both pickups in parallel) the wiper connects to both contacts A and B; in position 3 (bass pickup only) the wiper connects to contact B only; in position 4 (bass pickup with treble cut) the wiper connects to both B and C; and in position 5 (both pickups in series), the wiper connects to contact C only. S2 provides the in-phase/out-of-phase choice for the treble pickup.

Since position 4 gives bass pickup with treble cut, I decided that a tone control wasn't all that necessary (I usually only use the tone control with the bass pickup, anyway). So, S2 can mount in the hole normally reserved for the tone control, which means you can add this modification without changing your guitar from

stock should you ever decide to return to the standard wiring.

If you wish to replace your stock pickups with "hot rod" pickups in the above modification, try to locate pickups that are tapped at the halfway point of the coil. This will allow you to get the original "Fender sound" along with the louder, hot-rod sound. To add a switch that chooses between the full coil and tapped coil (or half coil) modes, refer to Figure 5-72. You may add one of these switches for each pickup if desired.

Final Comments

I've purposely kept this section rather general (some might say vague!) in order to discourage those who don't have a lot of experience from destroying their guitars. On the other hand, I believe that enough information has been presented to allow those with some electronic experience to do some rudimentary, but very effective, guitar rewirings. Humbuckers are another matter altogether; while there are many modifications you can make to humbucking pickups, humbuckers are more fragile and difficult to work with . . . so, I've limited this section to single-coil pickup modifications. You can also treat the humbucker as a single-coil pickup composed of two smaller coils if you want to try the series/parallel and in-phase/out-of-phase switching tricks. Good luck with your experiments.

Figure 5-72
Using an SPDT switch to choose between the full coil and half-coil sounds available from tapped pickups.

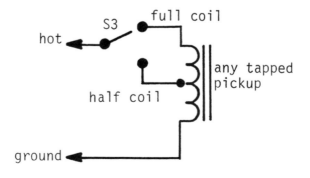

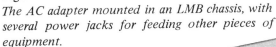

Project No. 13

BIPOLAR AC ADAPTER

Definition: A bipolar supply provides two power sources that are equal and of opposing polarities. This supply gives approximately ± 9V DC, and is suitable for powering projects presented in this book as well as for powering many commercially available effects.

Figure 5-73
The AC adapter mounted in an LMB chassis, with several power jacks for feeding other pieces of equipment.

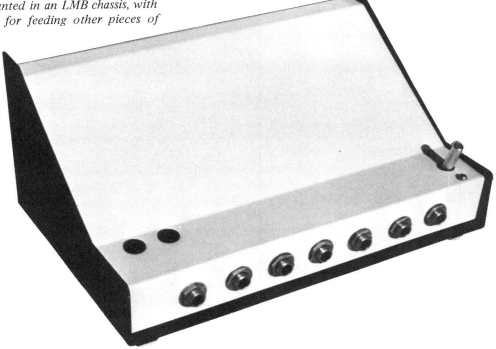

Background

While most projects in this book may be battery-powered, batteries are the least cost-effective way to power your projects. A supply like this costs less than $20 to build; think of how many alkaline batteries that will buy, and you'll see that an AC adapter is the only way to go. Batteries are also much more likely to fail at unexpected moments.

Level of Difficulty: Beginner to intermediate

Features

- Provides enough current to power all book projects (except those that use speakers) simultaneously, with reserve capacity left over

- Simplified construction due to IC regulation

- Short-proof and protected against thermal overload

- Immune to brownout conditions; maintains full regulation with a ±200mA load down to 90V AC

- Less than 10mV output variation between no-load and ±200mA load

- Power on indicator LEDs

- On-board heat sinking

- Extremely low ripple, hum, and output noise

Construction Tips

CAUTION! This project uses AC house current. Make sure the wires going from the line cord to the fuse holder and transformer are well insulated, and kept well away from the chassis. Mount all terminal strips, circuit board, jacks, etc., *very securely* to prevent vibration and mechanical "hum."

The regulators require *heat sinking.* A heat sink is a piece of metal that attaches to the IC package to help dissipate heat and thereby prevent overheating. Figure 5-74 shows how to mount the heat sink between the regulator and board, using a nut, screw, and lockwasher. Optional: Smear a *thin* coating of heat sink compound on the side of the regulator that faces the heat sink.

Figure 5-74

How to mount the heat sink between the regulator and circuit board.

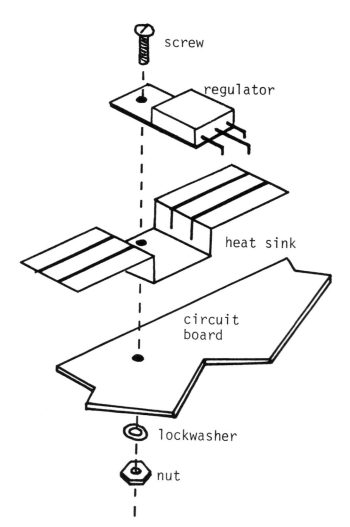

Avoid mounting the heat sinks too closely to the electrolytic capacitors for best results.

Use heavy-gauge wire (no. 20 or no. 22) for common (ground) connections and power supply line connections. Connecting the ground points for each regulator, the filter caps, and the center tap of the transformer to a common ground point (as shown in the schematic) is the best way to ground things with this supply.

It is vital to hook the transformer up correctly. In all probability, your transformer will have five wires coming out of it. Two of them will be black (or perhaps, one black and one white); these are called the *primary* leads and connect to the AC line. The other ones will be two of one color, and the third will be a different color (for example, two reds and a yellow). The two *like-colored* leads connect to pads A and B on the circuit board, while the odd color connects to pad CT (which, not surprisingly, stands for *center tap*).

Before plugging in, check everything over carefully—especially the diodes and electrolytic capacitors. With most other projects a wiring error won't cause something to burn to a crisp, but with this project that is a possibility. Don't plug in until you're satisfied that all is well.

Using the Bipolar AC Adapter

■ When building the AC adapter into a case with other projects, simply run wires from the power supply (+) to the (+) pads on the circuit boards, the power supply (-) to the (-) pads on the circuit boards, and connect the power supply ground and point G from each board to a common ground point. When using the AC adapter as part of a modular system, refer to figure 5-75. The supply output is paralleled among several stereo 1/4" phone jacks. Connect the power supply connections for each project to a matching stereo jack, and supply power to the project through a three-conductor (stereo) cord. To minimize the overall number of stereo cords required, you may attach the power supply connections from several projects to a single stereo jack, which then connects through a single cord to the supply's jack. Other three-conductor connectors (see Project No. 23) are suitable if you don't wish to use standard stereo jacks.

■ When plugging the adapter in both LEDs should immediately light up. If not, shut down power *immediately* and refer to the "In Case of Difficulty" section.

■ Voltmeter checkout: Connect the voltmeter (-) or black probe to pad G and the (+) or red probe to pad (+) on the supply; the meter should read +8.7V, +5%. Now, connect the (+) probe to pad G and the (-) probe to the supply (-); the meter should read -8.7V, +5%. If during testing anything smokes, belches fire, or shows other signs of distress, shut down the supply until you find out what is wrong.

Figure 5-75

You may connect as many output jacks as you wish to the power supply, but make sure that you wire them up in a consistent fashion. Each project has an associated power jack, that can be patched into the AC adapter via a stereo (three-conductor) patch cord.

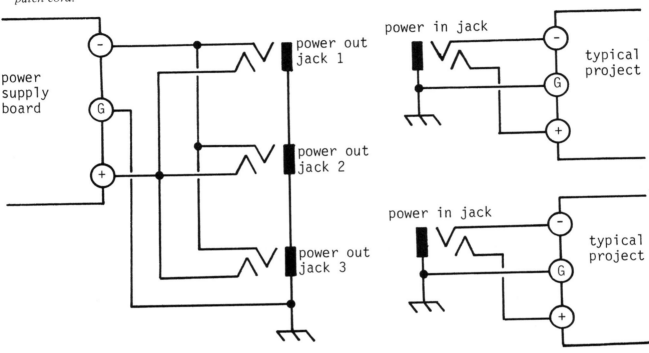

In Case of Difficulty

■ No voltage, either side: Check fuse. Check transformer wiring. Check that LEDs and diodes are properly polarized, and have not been overheated during soldering.

■ No positive voltage: Check polarity of D5, D7, D9, and D11.

■ No negative voltage: Check polarity of D6, D8, D10, and D12.

■ Filter capacitors get warm: Check polarity of C1 and C2.

■ Excessively high positive voltage output: Check for shorted D7.

■ Excessively high negative voltage output: Check for shorted D8.

■ Supply shuts off under constant use: Increase heat sinking on IC1 and IC2.

■ Supply works OK, but doesn't seem to provide power to effect: Check wiring between supply and effect. If using stereo cord to transfer power, check cord and check wiring of stereo jacks.

Modifications

■ If you wish to add an on-off switch, wire it between the fuse and transformer primary as shown in Figure 5-76.

■ A three-wire AC plug is recommended, although a two-wire AC plug is acceptable. To connect a three-wire plug, connect the third wire (ground) to a common ground point on the chassis.

Figure 5-76

Adding an optional on-off switch to the AC adapter.

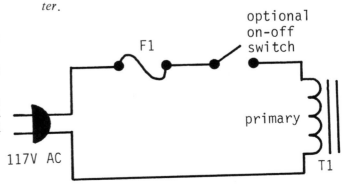

Specifications:

Recommended continous output current (maximum): ±250mA

Recommended intermittent output current (maximum): ±600mA

Line regulation (output variation with AC input varied between 85 and 135V AC, with ±200mA supply load): less than 10mV

Load regulation (output variation from no load to ±200mA load): less than 5mV

Residual noise/hum at output: 0.5mV pk-pk no load, 2mV pk-pk with ±200mA load

---

How it Works

This supply is based on a pair of IC regulators. When you feed unregulated but filtered DC into the regulator, it magically delivers tightly regulated and virtually hum-free DC at its output. Regulators are available in various fixed voltages for either positive or negative regulation; typical choices are 5, 6, 8, 12, 15, 18, and 24V. However, I've never seen a 9V regulator, so we need to add a few parts to a stock 8V regulator to persuade it to give out a nominal 9V.

We start off with a 20-24V AC center-tapped transformer. By feeding the transformer secondary through a full-wave rectifier (D1-D4), we obtain a DC voltage. The two large filter capacitors smooth out the DC to minimize ripple and hum; they also improve the stability of the supply. The voltage at each capacitor must be at least 3V or so higher than the desired output voltage to properly feed the regulators. Since this voltage will depend on the current load, we use capacitors rated at 25 or more volts to accommodate light or no-load conditions.

The section that gives us +9V is built around regulator IC1, a 7808 regulator. Adding a diode between the ground pin of the IC and the circuit ground raises the output voltage up an additional 0.7V, giving us +8.7V DC at the output-almost exactly what you'd get from a battery. The D11/R1 combination assures that enough current will flow through the diode to insure that it will act as a stable reference. D11 simultaneously indicates that the +9V section of the supply is working. The diode strapped across the input and output of the 7808 protects the chip if the output voltage should exceed the input (which can happen if C1 is accidentally shorted to ground during operation—say, by a slipped test probe). The diode at the output of this supply insures that only positive voltages appear at the output of the supply; any negative voltages shunt to ground through the diode.

The -9V regulator section is very similar to the +9V section, but uses an equivalent negative regulator, the 7908. Again we must change the operating voltage, and again we use a diode/LED/resistor combination to do the job. The remaining diodes perform protective functions, but are oriented differently because we are dealing with a negative regulator.

Figure 5-77
*Artwork for the foil side of the circuit
board shown 1 to 1.*

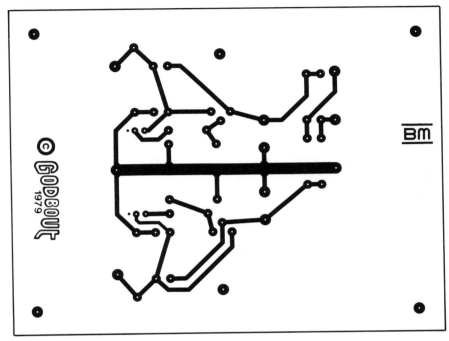

Figure 5-78
*Component layout for the AC adapter. Note that
the diodes are designated "CR" instead of "D" for
this project.*

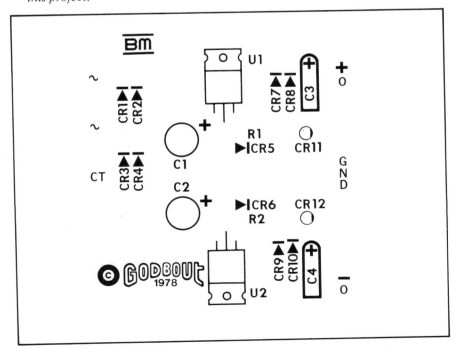

Figure 5-79
AC adapter schematic.

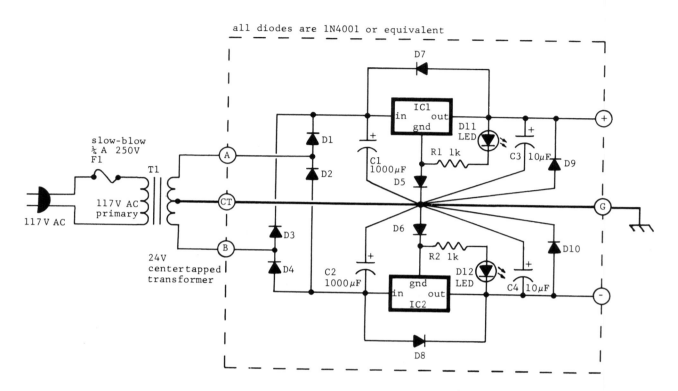

Project No. 13 PARTS LIST

Resistors (all are 1/4W, 10% tolerance)

R1, R2	1k

Capacitors

C1, C2	1000μF, electrolytic, 25V or more
C3, C4	10-50μF, electrolytic or tantalum, 10V or more

Semiconductors

IC1	μA7808 or LM7808 positive 8V regulator
IC2	μA7908 or LM7908 negative 8V regulator
D1-D10	IN4001 or equivalent power diodes
D11, D12	LEDs (your choice of color)

Mechanical Parts

T1	24V AC center-tapped transformer, 1A or more
F1	1/4A slow-blow fuse and fuse holder
(2)	heat sinks (TO-220 style)
Misc.	Circuit board, chassis, wire, solder, terminal strips for connecting wires, etc.

Project No. 14

TREBLE BOOSTER

Definition: Boosts the high frequency control of a signal to give a brighter, crisper sound.

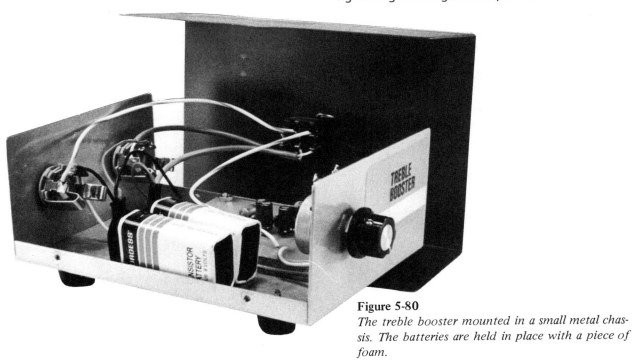

Figure 5-80
The treble booster mounted in a small metal chassis. The batteries are held in place with a piece of foam.

Background

The treble booster was one of the earliest effects offered to musicians; but due to its normally high noise level, it wasn't too widely accepted. This modern version uses low-noise circuitry to boost treble while contributing a minimal amount of noise.

Features

- Line-level or low-level operation
- Allows instruments to cut through at lower volume levels
- Compensates for lack of high frequencies in other parts of an amplification system
- Applicable to guitar, keyboards, bass, vocals
- Single IC construction
- Easily modified for custom response

Level of Difficulty: Beginner

Construction Tips

Shield the wire going to pad I; separate the input and output leads by at least 1 cm (1/2").

Mount C1, C2, C6, and C7 as closely as possible to the IC socket.

Keep the wires going from pads A and B to R4 as short as possible.

Using the Treble Booster

- Plug your instrument into J1 and patch J2 to your amp.

- Adjust the *gain* control for the desired volume level.

- CAUTION: Many people find prolonged exposure to high-frequency sounds very irritating. High frequencies also tend to dull the ear's response over a period of time; at the very worst, they can cause physical pain. Be judicious in the use of this box—too much of a good thing can turn into a bad thing.

- If the treble booster cuts out too much straight sound, use a splitter with a two-channel amp in the following manner:

—Split the output of your instrument with a Y cord or "Spluffer" (Project No. 26).

—Run one split into one amp channel; run the other split to the treble booster input. Patch the treble booster output to the second amp channel.

—Channel 2 level adjusts the amount of treble-boosted sound; channel 1 level adjusts the amount of straight sound. Adjust for proper balance. This technique works particularly well for bass, as channel 2 accents harmonics and pick sounds, while channel 1 gives the bass "bottom."

Modifications

■ Decrease C3 to roll off even more bass. Increase C3 to increase the bass response.

■ To get more gain or fuzz the high frequencies, use a 50k pot for R4.

■ For lowest noise, refer to "How it Works."

Figure 5-81

Frequency response curve for the treble booster with a 0dB input.

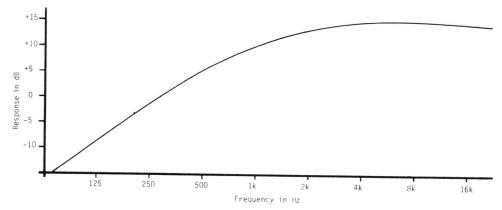

In Case of Difficulty

■ No treble-boosting action: Check wiring. Check C3 for short.

■ Distortion: Back off on *gain* control.

Specifications

Current consumption: ±3mA

Maximum input before clipping, R4=0Ω, @ 20kHz: 6V pk-pk

Maximum input before clipping, R4=10k, @ 500Hz: 4V pk-pk

1kHz: 2.5V pk-pk

5kHz: 1.8V pk-pk

20 kHz: 1.5V pk-pk

Maximum available output: 10V pk-pk

Frequency response (0dB signal input): see Figure 5-81.

Figure 5-82

Artwork for the foil side of the circuit board shown 1 to 1.

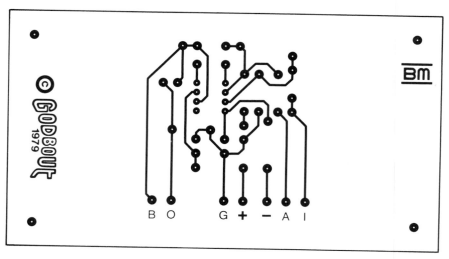

How it Works

IC1 is configured as a standard noninverting type of amplifier, with one important exception: capacitor C3 attenuates the low frequencies (refer to Figure 5-81, the frequency response graph). Capacitors C1 and C2 add stability, and discourage oscillations at high frequencies. The *gain* control sets the overall gain of the amplifier, while C5 couples the signal to the output.

By using a socket, you may substitute various op amps to try for the lowest possible noise. Here's the procedure.

The first op amps introduced to the market used a specific pinout which has, in many cases, been retained through the years. As a result, quite a few op amps have similar pinouts (for example, the 748, 201, 301, 1556, and several others can all plug into the same socket). This has also led to companies bringing out improved op amps with the same pinout as the op amps they're designed to replace; thus, a company marketing an improved 741 would put it in a 741-type package, so that you can just unplug the 741 and put in the replacement.

Since a treble booster increases the highs, and since that's where noise is most objectionable, we would ideally like to have a *very* low noise op amp for IC1. When I was prototyping the treble booster, just for the fun of it I took a bunch of 741s and plugged them into IC1's socket. Interestingly enough, some had low noise, some had lots of noise, and others fell in between these two extremes. I then tried a 201, which was noisier than about half of the 741s I tested and quieter than the others, and then checked out a Signetics 5534 (which has very low noise specs), and it was indeed audibly quieter, although not by an earth-shaking amount. So, not only does the treble booster make good musical sense, but when you're selecting op amps for the lowest possible noise the booster can also come in handy as a sort of "noise tester." The parts list mentions several ICs that may be used with the treble booster, in the approximate descending order of noise. Use the best one that is available and affordable.

Figure 5-83
Component layout for the treble booster.

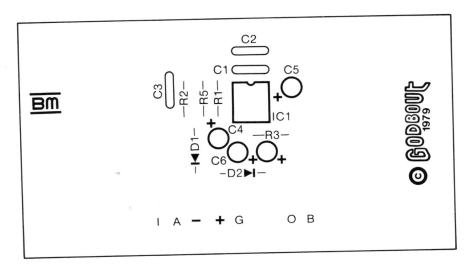

Figure 5-84
Treble booster schematic.

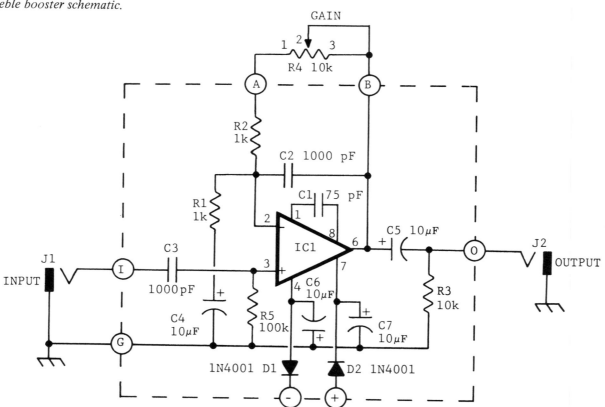

Project No. 14 PARTS LIST

Resistors (all are 1/4W, 10% tolerance, except as noted)

R1, R2	1k
R3	10k
R4	10k linear taper pot—controls *gain*
R5	100k (5% preferred)

Capacitors (rated at more than 10V for ±9V, more than 15V for ±15V)

C1	75pF, ceramic disc
C2, C3	1000pF (polystyrene preferred, disc acceptable)
C4-C7	10μF, electrolytic or tantalum

Semiconductors

IC1	NE5534, LM1556, LM201, LM748, LM741 or equivalent op amp
D1, D2	IN4001 or equivalent silicon diode

Mechanical Parts

J1, J2	Open circuit 1/4" mono phone jack
Misc.	Case, knob, 8-pin socket, circuit board, wire, solder, etc.

Project No. 15

ELECTRONIC FOOTSWITCH

Definition: Replaces a DPDT bypass switch (see Project No. 11) with an electronic switching network, controlled by an easy-to-find and inexpensive SPST footswitch.

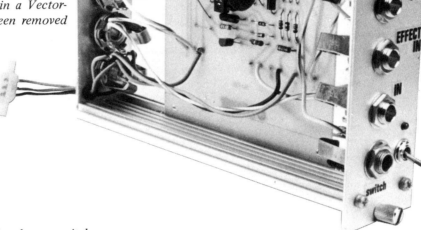

Figure 5-85
The electronic footswitch mounted in a Vector-Pak module. The side panels have been removed to show the inside construction.

Background

While DPDT footswitches make excellent bypass switches for controlling one or two projects, for multiple device setups ("pedalboards") they have several drawbacks (difficult to control remotely, no status indicator to show whether the project is in the signal path or not, wires going to the switch must be shielded, and so on). This project solves those problems, while offering several unique advantages.

Features

- LED status indicator shows whether effect is in or out
- Compatible with ±9V supplies
- Switches low- or high-level signals
- Very low noise, hum, distortion, and crosstalk
- Ideal for pedalboard and remote control applications
- Slow make/fast break switching action minimizes pops and clicks
- Wires leading to footswitch need not be shielded
- Simplifies control of multiple projects (Example: A mechanical DPDT footswitch requires at least 4 wires for each switch; therefore, to switch six different effects you would need 24 shielded wires. With the Electronic Footswitch you only need 7 unshielded wires to control the same number of effects (1 for each pad A on the various switch boards, and a separate common lead for pad B).

Level of Difficulty: Intermediate to advanced

Construction Tips

This circuit uses a CMOS integrated circuit designed for computer applications. CMOS is an acronym that refers to the internal electrical structure of these ICs, which offer the benefits of low power consumption, uncritical operation, and tolerance of a wide range of supply voltages.

CMOS ICs are tolerant of abuse, with one very important exception: They hate static electricity charges. Simply putting a CMOS IC in a plastic bag on a dry day can generate thousands of volts (!) of static charges, which can get into the IC via its pins and damage the internal structure. BE SURE TO OBSERVE THE FOLLOWING PRECAUTIONS WHEN HANDLING CMOS ICs:

■ Store CMOS ICs in aluminum foil or similar conductive substance with all pins touching the foil.

■ Avoid excessive handling. Leave the IC tucked away until absolutely needed.

■ USE SOCKETS. Soldering irons, and soldering guns in particular, build up electric fields that can harm the IC. If you *MUST* solder, unplug your iron immediately before soldering the IC pins. The iron will retain enough heat to solder, although it technically isn't on. Rechargeable DC-operated soldering irons are also acceptable.

■ Make sure power to the circuit board is off before installing or removing a CMOS IC.

Additionally, you *cannot* substitute for the 4016-type IC specified in this project. While some switching ICs are considered as identical plug-in replacements for the 4016 (4066 and 4116, among others), they will *not* work in our circuit.

Finally, make sure that the transistor leads are installed correctly on the board. The E, B, and C designations embossed or printed on the transistor should match up with the E, B, and C designations on the circuit board.

Principles of Electronic Switching

The 4016 quad switch IC contains four miniature electronically controlled switches; each one is an SPST type. With a mechanical switch, the operator usually selects whether it's open or closed by pushing a button or operating a toggle. With an electronic switch, since we can't get inside the IC and switch the electrons around with our hands, we introduce a new concept—a control terminal for the switch (see Figure 5-86). Applying a voltage equal to the positive supply *closes* the switch, while applying a voltage equal to the negative supply *opens* the switch. Pretty tricky.

Figure 5-86
The CMOS switch is functionally equivalent to a mechanical switch, with the exception of the control terminal. When a negative voltage connects to the control terminal, the switch is open; a positive voltage closes the switch.

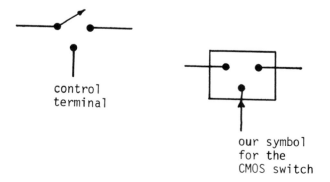

control terminal

our symbol for the CMOS switch

So, how do we use this to control an effect? Figure 5-87 shows the basic scheme. If S1 and S3 are closed while S2 is open, then the signal flows into and out of the effect. However, if S1 and S3 are open while S2 is closed, then the signal going to the effect is interrupted and the effect is bypassed. We need to also include some circuitry to make sure that the switches open and close in the right sequence; this is discussed more fully under the *How it Works* section.

Figure 5-87
Simplified block diagram of the switching system. As shown, the switches are bypassing the effect.

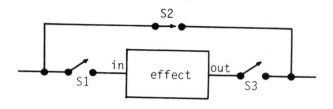

Using the Electronic Footswitch

■ Look over Project No. 11 (bypass switching) to refresh your memory of how effect switching is supposed to work. Once that's clear, then test out the electronic footswitch.

■ Plug your instrument into J1 and patch J2 into your amplifier. Now, take the effect you wish to control; plug its *input* into J3 ("to effect input") and plug its *output* into J4 ("from effect output").

■ Next, provide power to the electronic footswitch board. If you're controlling a project that uses ±9V, simply tap power from the effect's power supply. Note that this module is not designed to work with voltages higher than ±9V; if you're using something like ±15V synthesizer supply, I'd advise building a separate ±9V unit for the footswitches.

■ With pads A and B left unconnected, the effect should be out of the signal path and you should hear your regular instrument sound. Connecting A and B together puts the effect in the signal path, without any loud clicks or other problems. Note that LED D1 is an integral part of the circuit and *must* be included for the footswitch to work properly.

■ You may build the electronic footswitch in the same case as one of the other projects in this book, which eliminates the need for J3 and J4. As an illustration of how to do this, Figure 5-88 shows how to control a typical effect (in this case, the ring modulator) with the electronic footswitch. You may connect the footswitch to other projects in a similar manner. If you're controlling a project mounted in a Vector-Pak enclosure, there is usually enough room to slide the footswitch circuit board in next to the effect circuit board.

Controlling Multiple Effects

Many times, you'll want to have your effects controls at arm level, with the footswitches on the floor. Suppose you want to control four effects with individual electronic footswitches; Figure 5-89 shows how you would run the wires down to a separate, remote footswitch box. Since pad B on each board connects directly to the negative power supply line, connecting the footswitch common line to *any* pad B or to the -9V line coming from the power supply connects to the pad B on every board.

Modifications

■ A 4016 with a "B" suffix (such as CD4016B) indicates that the part can withstand ±9V. If you use this type of IC, you may replace D6-D11 with wire jumpers.

■ For use with power supplies of ±7.5V or lower, replace D6-D11 with wire jumpers.

Figure 5-88

How to connect the electronic footswitch directly to a project instead of using patch cords. Notice that most of the connections to both projects have been eliminated for clarity; we're only talking about the audio signal paths here. If the project you're controlling has no output control, then connect pad O directly to footswitch pad P.

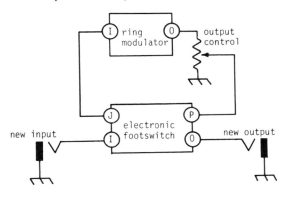

In Case of Difficulty

■ Incorrect switching action: Check polarities of all diodes, including the LED.

■ Bypass mode doesn't work, but effect in mode works correctly: Check D1.

■ Squeals occur while switching: Check D2-D5.

Specifications

Current consumption, effect out: ±8mA
Current consumption, effect in: ±18mA
Feedthrough at 1kHz between pads I and O, effect in mode: -75dB
Maximum input signal before clipping: ±7V pk-pk
Switch frequency response: ±1dB, 40Hz-20kHz

Figure 5-89

Controlling multiple footswitches. We're assuming here that the LEDs are mounted at the effect itself rather than at the footswitch, however, if you wish to have LEDs at the footswitch itself you may run line L down to the footswitch box. Also, although the control lines generally are immune to hum, it doesn't hurt to connect the case of the remote footswitch box to chassis ground.

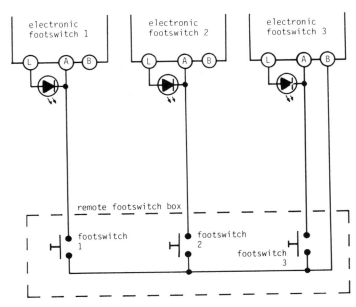

Figure 5-90
*Artwork for the foil side of the circuit board,
shown 1 to 1.*

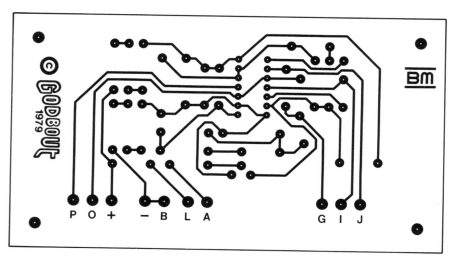

How it Works

I know we went over the basic idea earlier, but there are other aspects of the switch that might interest you.

One unfortunate aspect of CMOS switches is that they can produce a click or pop when you switch them. Another possible switching problem arises if the bypassing switch is closed at the same time as the other switches; this connects the output of the effect right back into the effect input, which is undesirable and may produce feedback.

The way we get around both problems is by controlling the rate at which the switches open and close. Analyzing how this happens may be a little difficult, but try to trace things through—it will probably be quite educational

When the effect is switched out, pads A and B are unconnected. Therefore, current flows through the LED into pad A (although not enough current to cause the LED to glow). This makes transistor Q1 conduct, which forces the voltage at the collector (C) of Q1 to be low.

R2-D2, C2, and D3 form a little timing circuit that makes IC1B and IC1C close slowly, but open rapidly. R3, D4, C3, and D5 do the equivalent timing function for IC1D. The slow closing effect eliminates pops and similar problems, while the fast opening means that it's impossible for IC1B, C, and D to all be "on" at the same time, thus surmounting our possible feedback problem. IC1A is not a part of the audio switching network; it's hooked up as an inverter (which means that IC1D always acts in opposition to IC1B and IC1C—when B and C are closed, D is open; and when D is closed, B and C are open).

This design comes pretty close to the ideal of a noiseless, clickless, and simple electronic switching device; it has enabled me to easily control multiple effects, and I hope it does the same for you.

Figure 5-91
Component layout for the electronic footswitch.

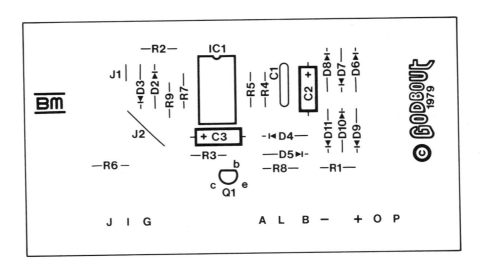

Figure 5-92
Electronic footswitch schematic.

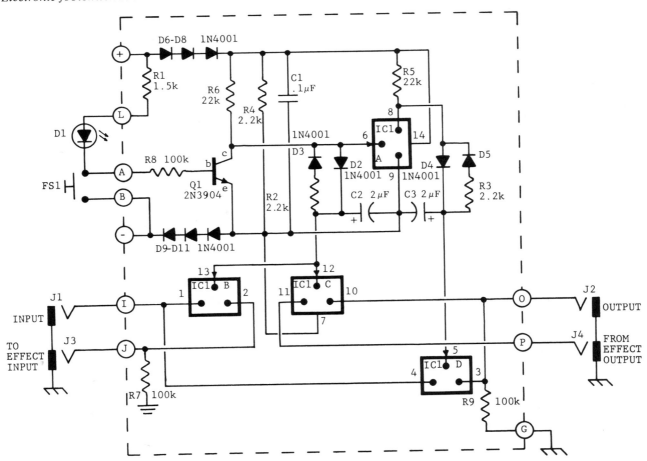

Project No. 15 PARTS LIST

Resistors (all are 1/4W, 10% tolerance, except as noted)

R1	1.5k
R2-R4	2.2k
R5, R6	22k
R7-R9	100k

Capacitors (rated at more than 10V)

C1	0.1 μF, ceramic
C2, C3	2 μF, electrolytic or tantalum

Semiconductors

IC1	CD4016 quad analog CMOS switch
D1	red LED
D2-D5	1N914, IN4001, or equivalent silicon diode
D6-D11	1N4001 or equivalent silicon diode
Q1	2N3904 or equivalent general-purpose NPN transistor

Mechanical Parts

J1-J4	Open circuit 1/4" mono phone jack
FS1	SPST push-on/push-off footswitch (available at many hardware stores and auto supply houses)
Misc.	14-pin IC socket, circuit board, wire, solder, etc.

Project No. 16

TUNING STANDARD

Definition: Generates all 12 notes of the even-tempered chromatic scale, over a five-octave range, with extreme accuracy.

Figure 5-93
The tuning standard mounted in an LMB enclosure. This enclosure has the speaker grille holes already drilled in place. In order to eliminate the need for a separate on-off switch, I used a level control pot that had a DPST switch mounted on the back and switched the batteries with that.

132

Background

Tuning forks are accurate tuning references, but lack volume and cannot generate a continous tone. Strobe tuners and frequency counters are often expensive, and subject to "jitter." This tuning standard is accurate and relatively inexpensive, and generates all the notes needed to tune up a variety of instruments at reasonable volume levels from the internal speaker.

Features

- 0.01% or better accuracy for each note
- Multi-octave range allows for intonation adjustments on guitars, tuning checks on synthesizers and other keyboards, and tuning of bass guitars
- Built-in speaker output (with level control)
- Optional output jack (with associated volume control) can feed amplifier inputs when more volume is required
- Simplifies and speeds up tuning of all fretted instruments
- Battery-powered for portable operation

Level of Difficulty: Intermediate to advanced

Constructions Tips

- This project uses CMOS ICs; *be sure to reread* the instructions on handling CMOS ICs included in the "Construction Tips" section of Project No. 15.

- We will be using a part in this project called a *crystal* that is not mentioned in Chapter 1. This part looks like a miniature sardine tin, has two leads sticking out of it, and acts as a stable tuning reference. The two leads are nonpolarized (i.e., either lead can go in either designated board hole), but crystals are heat-sensitive—so make your solder connections as quickly as possible.

- Plug the ICs into their sockets *after* the wiring is completed but *before* you apply power to the unit.

- Use a printed circuit board; a sloppy layout could cause problems due to the high frequencies involved.

- As mentioned in Project No. 5, devices with built-in speakers tend to draw a lot of current. For battery power, use 12 penlight ("AA" type) cells—6 in series for +9V, and 6 in series for -9V (see Figure 5-94). Commercial battery holders are available that hold 6 penlight batteries per holder. Nine-volt transistor radio batteries are not acceptable as they cannot supply enough current. An AC power supply such as Project No. 13 is also fine, although of course you sacrifice portability. Note that this project is *not* designed to work with a ±15V supply.

Using the Tuning Standard

- Turn on power, then turn up control R9; you should hear a tone coming through the speaker (if not, shut down power and determine the source of the problem).

- The lowest note selectable by S2 is C; the scale progresses upwards in half-tone steps, until you come to B.

- When S2 selects A, with the octave switch in the middle position that A is an A 440Hz.

- Tune by selecting the desired note on the standard and playing the same note on your instrument. Adjust the instrument's tuning until the two notes are exactly the same pitch.

- For louder volume levels, patch J1 to an amp and adjust the level with R10.

- To put a tuning tone on tape, patch J1 to the tape recorder's input and record about 20 or 30 seconds of tone. This will give you a reference to tune to during future overdub sessions.

- Since the tuning standard generates all notes of a scale, guitarists may check the intonation of a guitar neck and synthesizer players may check the intonation of a keyboard to check its accuracy. Don't be surprised if there are slight discrepancies (it's impossible for an even-tempered scale, such as a guitar fretboard scale, to

Figure 5-94

How to connect up 12 penlight batteries to create a suitable supply for the tuning standard.

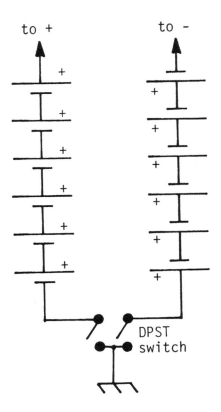

Figure 5-95

Artwork for the foil side of the circuit board, shown 1 to 1.

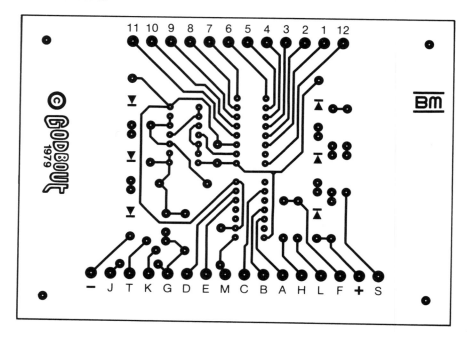

be perfectly in tune at all times), but the correlation between the standard's notes and the instrument's notes should be pretty close.

■ This standard is not necessarily satisfactory for tuning a standard acoustic piano, unless you know how to "stretch" the notes properly.

■ Under normal usage the batteries should last quite a while; however, the negative supply battery pack does not supply as much current during operation as the positive supply pack. Therefore, the negative suppy batteries will last longer than the positive supply batteries.

Modifications

■ The tuning standard can run from ±6V DC if you wish to minimize the number of batteries (although the speaker output level will drop). Use the same wiring as if you were installing a ±9V supply *except* replace D1-D6 with wire jumpers.

■ If you don't plan on using the speaker output, you may eliminate R6, R7, R9, Q1, and leave pads S and T unconnected.

■ An additional note, C an octave above S2's lowest note, is available from pin 15 of IC3.

■ Bass players who wish to add an additional range one octave below the lowest range already available can use a six-position switch for S1, and wire the sixth position to pin 4 of IC3. The lowest C available then becomes C1, or 32.7Hz.

In Case of Difficulty

■ Auxiliary output works, but speaker doesn't: Check Q1; replace if bad. Check R9 level and associated wiring.

■ Notes missing as you go through S2: Check wiring going to S2.

Specifications

Current consumption: ±30mA (minimum speaker output); +100, -30mA (maximum speaker output)

Range: 65.4Hz (C2) to 1975Hz (B below C7)

Auxiliary output level: 5V pk-pk minimum

134

Figure 5-96
Component layout for the tuning standard.

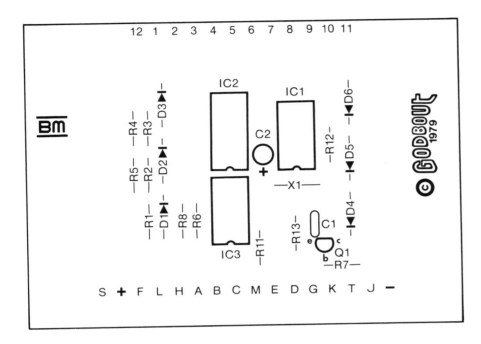

How it Works

IC1A and IC1B form an oscillator that resonates at X1's frequency, which in this case is 1MHz. (A fine point: note that although IC1 is composed of NOR gates, I've drawn these gates as inverters on the schematic because that is their function.) This precision 1MHz signal then feeds IC2, which is an organ chip called a "top octave divider." It generates all the notes of a scale by taking the ultrahigh reference frequency and dividing it down electronically to create a scale of notes in the audio range. The various outputs from IC2 feed S2, which chooses the desired note; this then goes to IC3, which divides this notes down in octaves. S1 selects the desired octave range for the note. The signal proceeds down two different paths after leaving S1; one is a direct out that passes through R10 to J1. The other feeds a transistor driver that is capable of driving a speaker to moderate volume. Resistors R1-R5 limit the current passing through Q1 to a safe value to prevent destroying the transistor. The reason for using a number of resistors like this is so that the power dissipation is shared by the resistors, eliminating the need for a single, high-power resistor.

Figure 5-97

Tuning standard schematic.

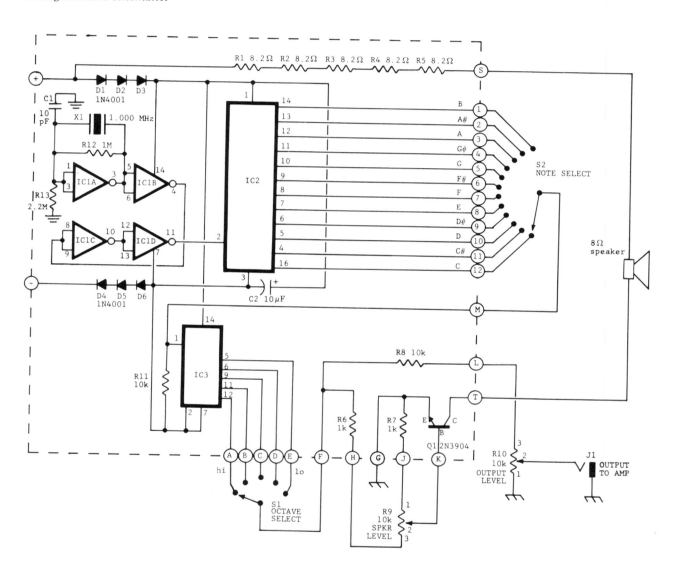

Project No. 16 PARTS LIST

Resistors (all are 1/4W, 10% tolerance, except as noted)

R1-R5	8,2Ω
R6, R7	1k
R8	10k
R9	10k audio or linear taper pot—controls *speaker level*
R10	10k audio or linear taper pot—controls *amp output level*
R11	10k
R12	1M
R13	2.2M

Capacitors (rated at more than 15V)

C1	10pF, disc ceramic
C2	10μF, electrolytic or tantalum

Semiconductors

IC1	CD4001 CMOS quad NOR gate
IC2	MK50240 (Mostek) top octave divider
IC3	CD4024 binary counter
D1-D6	1N4001 or equivalent silicon diode
Q1	2N3904 or equivalent general purpose NPN transistor
X1	1.000-MHz series mode crystal

Mechanical Parts

S1	SP5T rotary switch
S2	SP12T rotary switch
SPKR	8Ω loudspeaker
J1	Open circuit 1/4" mono phone jack
Misc.	Circuit board, one 16-pin socket and two 14-pin sockets, wire, solder, knobs, etc.

Project No. 17

SUPER TONE CONTROL

Definition: Offers flexible control over tone by creating several different response options. Low pass response boosts low frequencies, and attenuates high frequencies; high pass response boosts high frequencies, and attenuates low frequencies; bandpass response boosts a specific frequency range; and notch response attenuates a specific frequency.

Figure 5-98
I mounted this particular project in a panel for inclusion in the pedalboard project (No. 23). The text for this project tells how the super tone control was modified to fit into the available space.

Background

The "state variable" filter is a type of filter used in several synthesizers to control timbre; this circuit is a variation of the state-variable filter that has been optimized for tone control purposes. It offers considerably more sonic flexibility than the tone controls found on most instruments and amplifiers.

Features

- Single IC construction
- Operates from ±5 to ±18V DC
- Variable *resonance* control changes "sharpness" of the sound
- Easily resettable to flat response
- Low-pass, high-pass, the bandpass outputs are individually mixable via an onboard mixer to create highly complex responses
- Useful as recording studio or PA equalizer
- Operates at low level or line level
- Highly cost-effective

Level of Difficulty: Beginner to intermediate

Construction Tips

- Follow standard cautions about keeping lead lengths short, and shielding the lead going from the input to pad I.

- Please note that there are many connections between the board and external parts, and they all must be correct for the unit to work properly. Double check all wiring carefully before applying power.

Getting Acquainted with the Super Tone Control

- Plug your instrument into J1 and patch J2 to your amp. Start with the *resonance select* switch on low, the *resonance* control fully counterclockwise, all *level* controls fully counterclockwise, and the *frequency* control about halfway up.

- Play and turn up the *low pass* control; this brings up the bass channel of the filter. Turn the low pass control down, and turn up the *high pass* control; this brings up the treble channel of the filter. Return the high pass control to full counterclockwise, and this time bring up the *bandpass* control to hear the midrange channel of the filter.

■ After getting a feel for these various responses, repeat the above steps but this time experiment with varying the frequency control.

■ Next, repeat the above experiments but vary the mix of the low pass, high pass, and bandpass controls while varying the frequency control.

■ Finally, experiment with different settings of the resonance select switch and resonance controls.

■ NOTE: The first time I checked out my prototype Super Tone Control, it took me quite some time before I started getting musically useful results out of this device. There are so many controls and options that it's very easy to get ugly sounds as well as pleasing ones . . . if any project in this book requires practice to obtain optimum results, it's this one. So, take your time while experimenting, and think about what you're doing as you play with the various controls; this will make it much easier for you to reconstruct your favorite settings in the future.

Using the Super Tone Control

Start off with all controls set to the midposition or thereabouts (*resonance select* switch on low), and carefully analyze the sound you wish to modify. If it lacks bottom, for example, turn up the *low pass* control and adjust the *frequency* control until the sound is "right." If, on the other hand, the bottom is too heavy, turn down the low pass control a bit and again adjust the frequency control to taste. Turning up the *high pass* control adds brightness, while turning it down takes some of the brightness away. Increasing the *bandpass* channel adds definition to a sound; again, adjust the frequency control for the most desirable effect. Don't overlook the importance of the *notch* position (low pass and high pass up, bandpass all the way down) to attenuate resonances that occur in instruments.

Another application of the Super Tone Control involves PA work and the control of feedback. If a mic starts feeding back, put the filter in the notch position (with a fair amount of resonance) and vary the frequency control until the feedback goes away, which it often will. Although this filtering does affect whatever signal you're putting through the PA, the difference is not all that noticeable—and it's a difference you'll probably be willing to tolerate when the alternative is a nasty feedback squeal!

Modifications

■ To make the *frequency* control respond to the dynamics of the input signal, see Project No. 25.

■ While this circuit is optimized to cover the audio range, it can be used for control voltage processing in modular synthesizer systems by replacing capacitors C4 and C5 with wire jumpers, and using large capacitors (1-20μF) for C2 and C3. C2 and C3 should be equal in value.

■ For more overall gain, increase R11.

In Case of Difficulty

■ "Tinny" sound: Reduce *resonance* control, or change S1 to *low* position.

■ Distortion: Reduce resonance control or reduce input signal level; check power supply.

■ Oscillations or squeals: Check lead layout; shield wires going to the resonance control.

■ No output: Check R7-R9 levels; check that the frequency control is operating at a high (or low) enough frequency to pass the input signal.

Figure 5-99
Artwork for the foil side of the circuit board, shown 1 to 1.

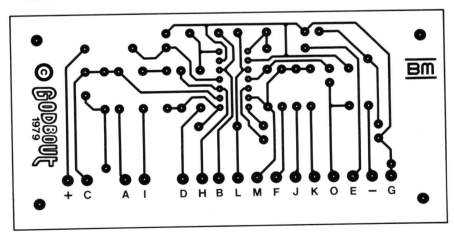

Figure 5-100

Component layout for the Super Tone Control

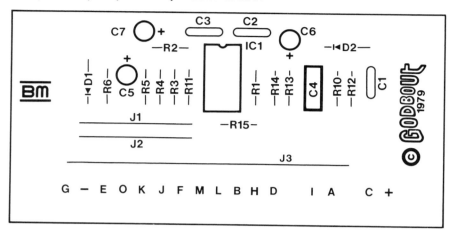

Figure 5-101

Super Tone Control schematic.

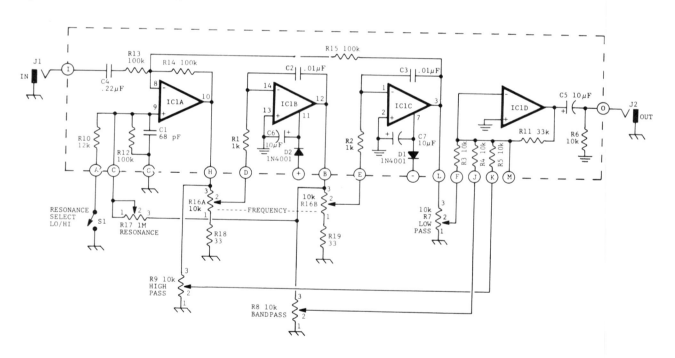

Specifications:

Current consumption: $\pm$7mA

Filter range: 50Hz-15kHz minimum

Maximum input before clipping @ 1kHz; minimum resonance: 8V pk-pk

Maximum input before clipping @ 1kHz; maximum resonance: 100mV pk-pk

Maximum available output: 10V pk-pk

IC1A is basically a mixer that mixes the input signal and feedback from the output of the filter (via R15). It also accepts feedback from IC1B; this feedback increases the overall resonance of the filter.

IC1B and IC1C are called integrators (in mathematical terms), or filters (in audio terms). R16A/C2 and R16B/C3 form a pair of tuned circuits that determine the tuning of the filter. IC1D is another mixer; this one sums together the various responses (low pass, high pass, and bandpass). R11 is selected to give some gain through the filter. C6/D2 and C7/D1 add power supply decoupling.

Project No. 17 PARTS LIST

Resistors (all are 1/4W, 10% tolerance, except as noted)

R1, R2	1k
R3-R6	10k
R7	10k audio taper pot—controls *low pass* level
R8	10k audio taper pot—controls *bandpass* level
R9	10k audio taper pot—controls *high pass* level
R10	12k
R11	33k
R12-R15	100k
R16	Dual-ganged 10k linear taper pot—controls *frequency* (any dual-ganged pot from 10k to 100k will work, although with higher value pots R18 and R19 will need to be increased)
R17	1M linear taper pot—controls *resonance.*
R18, R19	33Ω

Capacitors (rated at more than 10V for ±9V, more than 15V for ±15V)

C1	68pF (polystyrene preferred, disc acceptable)
C2, C3	0.01 μF, mylar
C4	0.22μF (mylar preferred, disc acceptable)
C5-C7	10μF, electrolytic or tantalum

Semiconductors

IC1	RC4136 or XR4136 quad low-noise op amp
D1, D2	1N4001 or equivalent silicon diode

Mechanical Parts

J1, J2	Open circuit 1/4" mono phone jack
S1	SPST switch—controls *resonance hi/lo select*
Misc.	Knobs, case, 14-pin IC socket, circuit board, solder, wire, etc.

Project No. 18

EIGHT IN, ONE OUT MIXER

Definition: Electrically combines several different input signals into a composite output signal.

Figure 5-102
Mixer module mounted in the Vector-Pak enclosure . Note that only four mixer inputs are used, and that the master ouput control has been eliminated to conserve panel space.

Background

"Eight-in, one-out" refers to the fact that this mixer can accept up to 8 inputs (expandable to 16), and combine them into one output. This master output can then go into a PA, guitar amp, headphone amp, or whatever.

Features

- Suitable for pedalboard, home recording, and PA applications
- Operates from ±5 to ±18V DC
- Handles line level signals
- Choice of three outputs: low-impedance unbalanced, inverting or noninverting, for use with guitar amps, some tape recorders, hi-fi power amps, etc.; and low-impedance balanced, for use with professional studio equipment.
- Expandable to 16 inputs
- Low noise, distortion, and crosstalk
- Single IC construction
- Includes master output control

Level of Difficulty: Beginner to intermediate

Construction Tips

This is one project that is so versatile that it's impossible to give any recommended type of packaging. You might want to include the mixer, along with several preamps and the like, in a large console suitable for studio use. Or, you might just need a simple two-input mixer to combine a couple of effects box outputs, in which case this project could be built into the same enclosure as the effects. On the other hand, just having one of these mounted in a small box is useful to have around (mixers are pretty universal devices). So, read the text for this project thoroughly to get an idea of the many modifications you can make to this device to customize it to your needs; then decide on the most suitable form of packaging. Other tips:

- Shield the wires going from the mixer input pots to input pads 1-8 if these leads exceed about 5 cm (2"). Note that there is an extra hole near each board input pad for attaching the shield.

- Shield the wire between pad A and the *master output* control.

Using the Mixer

Please note that for lowest noise this mixer is designed to accept line level signals only. Its relatively low input impedance (10k for each of the eight inputs) means that attempting to plug a device with a high output impedance (such as a stock guitar, microphone, or even some effects boxes) into the mixer will audibly degrade the sound. As a result, make sure that anything feeding the mixer is either buffered or going through one of the other book projects, and is preferably running at line level. This insures optimum signal transfer into the mixer.

Another basic rule when mixing is to keep the individual channel controls up as *high* as possible, and the master output control as *low* as possible, for the best signal-to-noise ratio.

Finally, before attempting to use the mixer determine which output is most suited to your application. Use *J10* for feeding devices with *unbalanced, high-level* inputs. These include power amps such as BGW, Crown, McIntosh, and the like; budget PA mixers; most semipro and consumer tape recording equipment; line level studio effects; most synthesizer modules; and synthesizer *external-input* jacks. Use *J11* for feeding devices with *balanced, high-level* inputs. These include studio mic preamp inputs, most studio patch bay patching points,

professional tape recorder inputs, some studio effects inputs, and professional-level mixers. Use *J9* for applications similar to J10, but where phase is unimportant. Using this output will give slightly better noise performance compared to J10.

Here are some typical mixer applications:

■ *Combining outputs of effects.* As mentioned in Project No. 23, effects may be combined either in series or in parallel. Figure 5-103 shows how a keyboard player might combine some effects into the mixer (note that we're only using three of the mixer's inputs; you can simply ignore the other inputs). By turning up channel 1, you hear the phase-shifted piano sound. Turning up channel 2 gives you the piano sound through the Super Tone Control, while turning up channel 3 gives you the straight piano sound. You may combine these individual elements in any proportion you want. One possible sound combination: turn the straight channel up most of the way, with a little phase shifter added in the background along with a little extra treble (provided by the Super Tone Control). As shown, the preamp output feeds the inputs of three separate effects; however, because all of these projects have been designed to work efficiently together, you do *not* need to use something like Project No. 26 to do the splitting. Any simple Y cord or similar passive signal splitter will do the job.

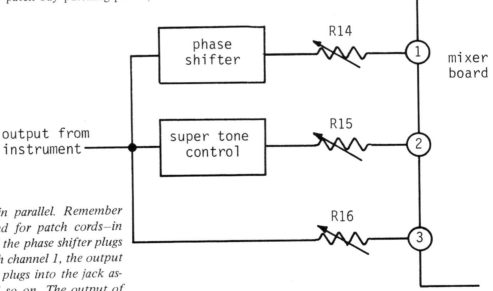

Figure 5-103

How to combine effects in parallel. Remember that the various lines stand for patch cords—in other words, the output of the phase shifter plugs into the jack associated with channel 1, the output of the Super Tone Control plugs into the jack associated with input 2, and so on. The output of the instrument feeding the effects splits to the various inputs through a Y adapter or multiple box (see text). However, if the various effects and mixer board are being built into a single unit, patch cords may be eliminated by wiring the output of an effect directly to the mixer channel fader. Finally, note that for clarity, only the pertinent connections to the mixer are shown; all the other pads are wired up as described elsewhere in the text.

■ *Monaural recording mixer.* Most home recording machine outputs can plug directly into the mixer. Figure 5-104 shows an example using four of the mixer's inputs. After recording on all four tracks, we can combine them into a monaural output suitable for sending to a monitor amp or mixdown recorder. Additional effects may be patched between the tape outputs and the mixer inputs (tone controls, phase shifter, etc.). Many readers have built home recording setups based around this mixer; for more information on studio mixers, see my *Home Recording for Musicians* book, which covers the subject in much greater detail.

Another mixer trick allows you to generate more than four tracks from a four-track recorder. Let's say you have recorded signals on tracks 1, 2, and 3. You can combine these three tracks through the mixer and send the mixer output to track 4. After getting the correct mix, record the signals from tracks 1-3 on to track 4. This allows you to erase the material on tracks 1-3, thus leaving room for three more tracks of new material since your original tracks reside (in mixed form) in track 4.

■ *PA/mic mixer.* Figure 5-105 shows a typical PA or recording application for multiple microphones. We can feed a high-impedance, unbalanced mic output directly into the preamp (Project No. 1) and then feed the preamp output into one of the mixer inputs . . . in this case, input 2. The preamp is necessary in order to keep the noise down, and the signal level up. If you have low-impedance, balanced line microphones instead of the high-impedance types, don't worry; find a suitable low-impedance and balanced to high-impedance and unbalanced adapter and connect it up as shown for input 1. Any low-level signal will need to go through something like the premap, although many high-level instruments can feed the mixer directly. Don't forget that you can plug other effects in the signal path between the signal source and mixer inputs.

Figure 5-104
Run the outputs from your tape recorder into the mixer inputs, and you've got a way to mix down your multitrack tapes. Note that most of the mixer connections are omitted for clarity.

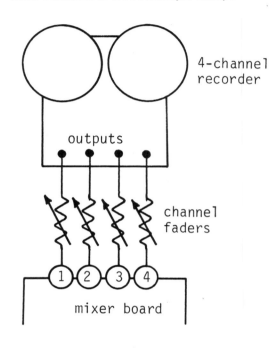

Figure 5-105
Using the mixer as a mic or PA mixer. Again, most of the mixer connections are omitted for clarity; and again, either patch the various modules together with cords, or if the preamps and mixer are built into one unit, make the connections directly.

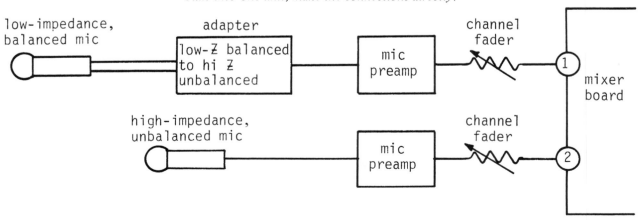

Modifications

■ Fewer inputs: Wire up only as many channels as you need; for example, if you need a four-input mixer, then ignore pads 5-8.

■ More inputs: Figure 5-106 shows how to add 8 extra inputs to create a 16-in, 1-out mixer. All you need is one jack, one pot, one resistor, and one capacitor for each extra channel.

■ Extra output channel: This creates an eight-in, two-out (stereo) mixer. Duplicate the eight-in, one-out setup you already have—that is, another set of pots, another mixer board, and so on. Figure 5-107 shows that by paralleling the mixer pots together at each channel, you can feed one mix into one output buss or channel, and a different mix into the second output buss. By considering one output buss the right channel buss, and the other output buss the left channel buss, you have a stereo setup. You can put a signal into the left channel by turning up one knob, into the right channel by turning up the other knob, or into both channels by turning up both knobs. You can even *pan* (spatially change the sound) by turning up one knob at first, then fading out that knob while turning up the other one. The sound will appear to move from one channel to the other.

(Please note that this is not an entirely satisfactory way of implementing a mixer; the most popular approach is to have one knob [called a *panpot*] that determines the stereo placement, while another knob controls the overall level. There are many ways to implement panpots, some of which require more gain in the mixer, some of which add noise, some of which require hard to find parts, and so on. Many people wrote in after the first edition of the book was published and asked how to add panpots to this mixer; unfortunately, a true stereo mixer with panpots that retains excellent performance is not a trivial design chore, and needs to be designed as part of a complete system. So, if you want to go stereo, I'd suggest going with the scheme shown in Figure 5-107. Other than that, you're on your own; there just isnt't enough space here to discuss how to make a spiffy stereo mixer.)

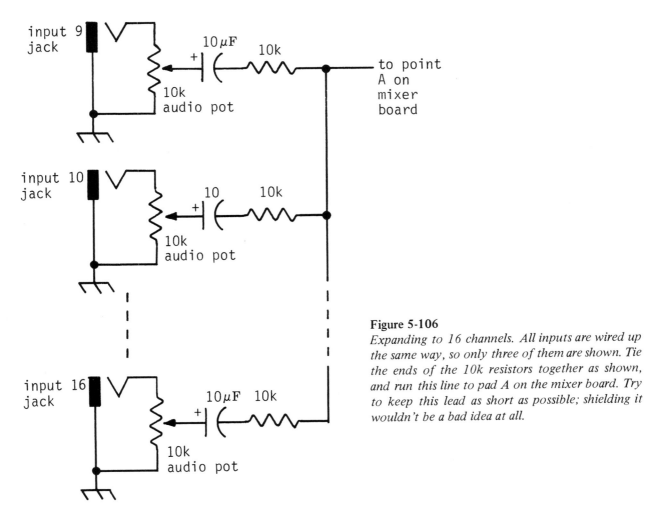

Figure 5-106
Expanding to 16 channels. All inputs are wired up the same way, so only three of them are shown. Tie the ends of the 10k resistors together as shown, and run this line to pad A on the mixer board. Try to keep this lead as short as possible; shielding it wouldn't be a bad idea at all.

145

■ Having a mixer with two independent outputs is also useful when you want a separate mixer for main and monitor amp systems. One mixer output can go to the monitor system, with the other output going to the main amp. Another less obvious use is to consider the second channel as a reverb line, as shown in Figure 5-108. Treat mixer A as a straight mono mixer; then connect a reverb unit input to the output of mixer B, and connect the reverb output to one channel (let's say channel 8) of mixer A. By turning up channel 8 in mixer A, you hear the reverb line, and select which channel you wish to have "reverbed" by turning up the appropriate pot on mixer B. For example, if you want to put reverb on channels 1, 4, and 5, then turn up faders 1, 4, and 5 on mixer B. This feeds these signals into the reverb unit, and turning up channel 8 on mono mixer A allows you to hear the reverb effect. This technique works with effects other than reverb such as tape echo, phasing, flanging, and so on.

■ If you need to conserve space, you may eliminate R22 by jumpering pads **A** and **B** with a 10k resistor.

■ Increasing input impedance: For applications where 10k is too low an input impedance, you may increase the input impedance to 100k by replacing all 10k resistors with 100k resistors, all 10k pots with 100k pots, and changing C1-C8 to 0.22μF capacitors.

In Case of Difficulty

■ Noise: Increase channel level pots and decrease *master output*. Increase strength of input signal via preamp or similar device.

■ "Thin" instrument sound when feeding mixer: Instrument probably has a high-output impedance. Add buffer board (Project No. 26) or preamp (if gain is required) between instrument output and mixer input.

■ Not enough "headroom" for recording applications: Use ±15 to ±18V supply.

■ Distortion: Reduce *master output* or channel input pots.

Specifications:

Current consumption: ±5mA

Gain: Unity

Frequency response: ±0.5dB, 20Hz-20kHz

Maximum available output, noninverting output: 10V pk-pk

Maximum input before clipping: 10V pk-pk

Maximum available output into 600Ω load, noninverting output: 4V pk-pk minimum.

Figure 5-107

Here we're using two mixer boards to create two output busses, useful for stereo mixing and other applications. J1 connects to two input level controls so that turning up one control puts the input signal in the right channel, while turning up the other control puts the input in the left channel. Turning up both pots puts the input signal into both channels.

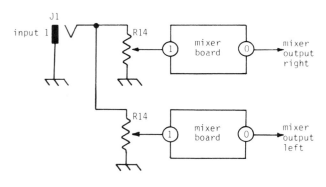

Figure 5-108

This setup is similar to the previous figure, except that the second channel feeds a reverb unit. The reverb mixer board combines the signals to be reverberated; its output feeds directly into the reverb unit. Turning up R21 on the main mixer board allows you to hear the reverb output.

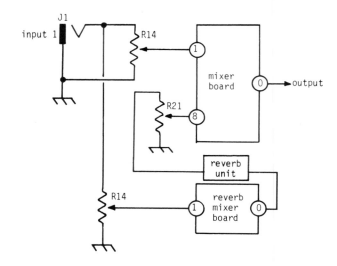

Figure 5-109
Artwork for the foil side of the circuit board, shown 1 to 1.

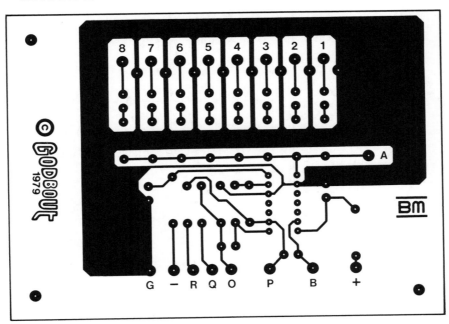

Figure 5-110
Component layout for the mixer.

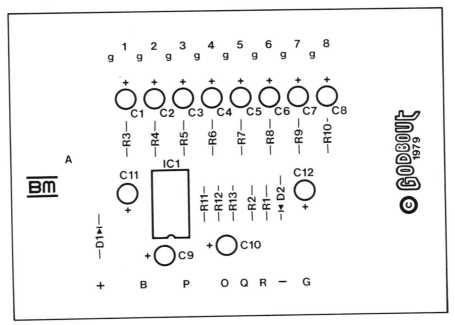

Figure 5-111
Mixer schematic.

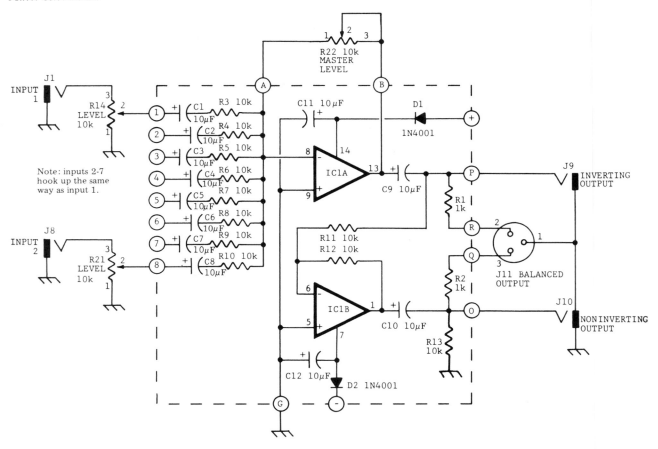

How it Works

Op amps were originally designed to perform mathematical operations, and one of the operations they do best is addition . . . and that is exactly what this mixer is all about: adding signals together. IC1A is a *summing amp*, one of the applications most suited to op amps, and it sums together the various inputs. R22 determines the master output level (required for doing fadeouts and the like). The output of IC1A couples into J9 and also into IC1B, which simply inverts the signal so that the mixer can offer a noninverting output. The outputs of these two op amps also feed J11 to give a balanced output. D1/C11 and D2/C12 add power supply decoupling.

Project No. 18 PARTS LIST

Resistors (all are 1/4W, 10% tolerance, except as noted)

R1, R2	1k
R3-R13	10k
R14-R21	10k audio taper pot—controls *channel levels*
R22	10k audio taper pot—controls *master output level*

Capacitors (rated at more than 10V for ±9V, more than 15V for ±15V)

C1-C12	10µF, electrolytic or tantalum

Semiconductors

IC1	RC4739 or XR4739 dual low-noise op amp
D1, D2	IN4001 or equivalent silicon diode

Mechanical Parts

J1-J10	Open circuit 1/4" mono phone jack
J11	Optional XLR female connector
Misc.	Knobs, 14-pin IC socket, solder, wires, circuit board, etc.

Project No. 19

USING A VOLT OHM-MILLIAMMETER

Figure 5-112
Two different types of analog VOMs. The larger one is designed for bench work, while the smaller is meant for portable service applications.

How to Use a Volt-Ohm-Milliammeter for Musical Applications

The volt-ohm-milliammeter (or VOM for short) is a common, inexpensive test instrument for electronic work. A few years ago, there was only one type of VOM; Figure 5-112 shows a picture of this type, called an *analog* VOM which has a meter and pointer, just like the VU meters on tape recorders. Different voltages deflect the pointer by different amounts, and you can read the numerical values of the voltage on the meter's calibrated scale. Recently, though, the same technology that brought us calculators and microcomputers has created the *digital* volt-ohm-milliammeter, or simply DVM for short (Figure 5-113). Instead of a pointer and meter scale, there are a bunch of digits, just like a calculator; these digits display the voltage under test. Digital meters

Figure 5-113
A typical compact digital VOM.

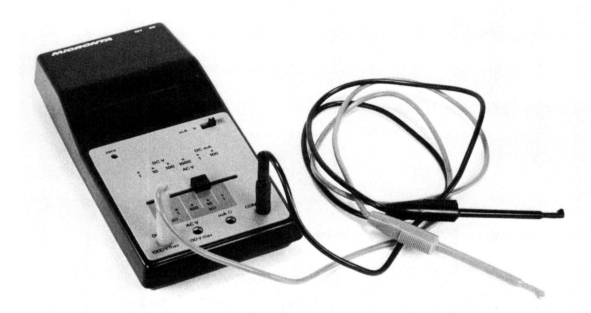

have several advantages: they are more tolerant of mechanical abuse, they are less ambiguous to read, and they are often more compact. However, they are also more expensive . . . but I'm sure that in time the DVM will eventually replace the analog meter.

Anyway, no matter which type you use, they both have certain common characteristics. These are:

■ **Test Probes.** The test probes connect the meter to the circuit you want to measure. One will be color coded black (for negative), and the other will be color coded red (for positive). If you're measuring a positive (+) DC voltage, the black probe connect to ground and the red probe connects to the test point. If you're measuring a negative (-) DC voltage, the red probe connects to ground and the black probe connects to the test point. Don't know whether what you're measuring is positive or negative? Then just arbitrarily hook up the probes; if the meter deflects to the right, you have them hooked up correctly. If you accidentally reverse the probes with an analog VOM, chances are you won't damage the meter (most have overload protection), but the pointer will deflect to the left and not give you a correct reading. With DVMs, an overload or reversed probe condition will trigger some type of indicator to let you know that there's something strange going on.

Before we get off test probes, though, remember that VOMs can also measure resistance, AC voltage, and DC current; when measuring resistance or AC voltages, it generally doesn't matter which probe you use. Measuring current consumption is a whole other subject—we'll get into that later.

■ **Test Probe Jacks.** Any voltmeter will have a number of jacks; plugging the probes into different jacks sets up the meter for different functions. There will usually be one ground jack, and that's easy to deal with; the black probe plugs in there. The other jacks are for the "hot" probe, and their functions vary considerably from model to model. Plugging the hot probe into the jack labeled "ohms" will allow you to take resistance measurement; plugging into the one labeled "DCV" sets the meter up to measure DC volts; and so on. Other jacks might be included for measuring exceptionally high voltages, AC voltages, etc. In any event, the instructions provided with any meter will explain these different jacks—the important thing to remember is that if you're plugged into the wrong jack, you'll end up with inaccurate readings.

■ **Ohms Adjust Control.** Most DVMs don't need one of these, but the analog types do. This is a control that allows the ohms scale to be calibrated when you initially set up the meter. Since the ohms scale (and only the ohms scale) uses an internal battery, as the battery ages you'll have to readjust this control. You may also have to readjust as you change from range to range, which leads us right into the next section.

■ **Multiposition Range Switch.** The highest voltage a meter can measure is around 1000V. But what happens if you want to measure, say 2.5V? On a meter scale that goes from 0 to 1000, that amount of voltage would hardly cause the meter to budge at all, and in any case would be very hard to read. As a result, it's much better to be able to change the *sensitivity* of the meter for measuring different voltages. For measuring low voltages, a 0 to IV range would be useful. For measuring something like a 9V transistor radio battery, a 0 to IV range would be insufficient and a 0 to 10V range would be more practical. For measuring even larger voltages, then a 0 to 100V or even a 0 to 1000V range, would be useful. So, you'll have a

Now we run into a snag, however; since there is a limited amount of space on the face of the meter, there isn't enough room to print a separate scale for each range. So the best short cut is to simply label the scale 0 to 10. In the 0 to 1V range, you mentally divide the reading by 10 to arrive at the correct voltage; for example, if the meter reads 5, then in the 0 to 1V range the true reading is 0.5V. If you're switched to the 0 to 10V range, then whatever the meter reads is the actual voltage. But if you're switched to the 0 to 100V range, a reading of 5 would be *multiplied* by 10 so that the reading would be 50V. Getting the hang of this? Here's one more example. In the 0 to 1000V range, a 5 reading translates as 500V. It's all basically a question of moving the decimal point around, like you learned about in math class.

Resistance measurements also have various ranges. One range might multiply the resistance reading by 1000, or by 10,000, or whatever; again, either the meter or the instructions will explain this. However, the ohms scale will be different from the volts scale . . . and to avoid confusion, it will usually be printed on the meter in a different color.

That pretty much covers what you'll find on a basic voltmeter. There may be additional scales for measuring AC volts or special options that a particular meter offers, but again, this varies a lot and your best bet is to study any accompanying manual thoroughly.

By the way, don't feel bad if it takes you a while to get the hang of converting from the meter reading to the voltage reading. It confused the heck out of me at first, but the whole thing becomes really obvious after a little while.

Taking Care of Your Meter

Some analog meters will have an "off" position that damps the meter movement to prevent the pointer from swinging around wildly while you're transporting the VOM from place to place. As one who has damaged a meter that didn't have an "off" switch by taking it for a ride in a friend's Porsche, I'd advise finding one with the damping option.

Another tip that's always good practice when making any measurements is to start off with the highest range available on the meter (i.e., the least sensitive range), then switch down to more sensitive ranges to actually measure the voltage. Otherwise, if your meter is set to a 1V scale and you try to measure 100V, the pointer will swing violently to the right—so much so that the pointer may bend, making the thing useless for further measurements. Many meters are overload protected, but it's best to play it safe.

When using the resistance scale, don't let the probes touch each other for extended periods of time, as this wears down the battery. For best results, if you don't have an "off" position, switch to a voltage scale when the meter is not in use.

Musical Applications

Ok . . . now that we have all those basics out of the way, let's look as some typical musical applications for the VOM. These examples will assume you have an analog meter, since this requires somewhat more complex procedures. Those of you who have DVMs will no doubt be able to translate these instructions so that they apply to your meter.

■ **Measuring 9V Batteries.** Many effects use 9V, transistor-radio-type batteries, and will not give optimum results when the battery wears down. When you check the battery, *make sure it is connected to the circuit that it powers and that the circuit is turned on* (usually by plugging mono cords into the input and output jacks, or via a switch). A battery may read 9V when not connected, but drop to an unacceptable voltage under the load of the circuit.

Set the selector switch to a relatively low-voltage DC range, like 0-10V; then connect the red probe to the (+) end of the battery and the black probe to the (-) end of the battery. The pointer of the meter should deflect to the right. If the pointer deflects downward to the left, reverse the probes and make sure you have them connected up correctly. If you're switched into a 0 to 10V range, you can then read the battery voltage directly from the DC volts scale. A new 9V battery will read from 8 to 10V, while a bad one will read anywhere from about 7V on down. For reading other DC voltages, change the selector to the appropriate scale and go to it.

■ **Making Continuity Measurements (short circuit/open circuit).** To do this we need to use the resistance (ohms) scale. First, make sure the probes are in the right jacks, then touch the two probes together. The pointer should swing over to the right (unlike measuring volts, where a rightward deflection means *more* volts, a rightward deflection of the pointer means *fewer* ohms). If it doesn't, chances are either you don't have a battery in the VOM or the battery is dead . . . of course, now you have a way to test it. After touching the probes together, adjust the ohms adjust control for a 0Ω reading. If this is not possible, you need a new battery. By the way, many VOMs come with a battery, but the battery will invariably be a real cheapie. Get an alkaline battery to replace the original one; it will last a lot longer, and not leak all over the place if it gets too old.

■ **Checking Speakers for Burned-Out Voice Coil.** Set selector switch to the *lowest* resistance range (like R x 1 or R x 10. If in the R x 1 scale, read the resistance directly from the meter; if in the R x 10 scale, multiply all readings by 10). With the speaker disconnected from its amp, connect the two probes to the speaker's two terminals. This should indicate a very low resistance, on the order of a few ohms. If the meter doesn't budge, make sure you're making a good connection with the speaker. If the pointer still doesn't move, the speaker coil is *open* and needs to be repaired.

■ **Checking Pickups for Open and Short Circuit Conditions.** With the same settings as before and with the pickup out of circuit, touch both probes to the two pickup wires with the pickups out of circuit. If the pointer indicates 0Ω, your pickup has a short in it. If the pointer doesn't move, switch to a higher resistance scale (like R x 1000) and see if you get a reading. If the pointer still doesn't move, your pickup has an open circuit and probably has a break in the winding somewhere.

■ **Checking Patch Cords.** With the same meter settings as for the speaker coil test, touch one probe to the tip of the plug on the end of a cord and the other probe to the tip of the other plug. This should indicate 0Ω, showing conduction from one end of the cord to the other end. Then, touch one probe to the shield or ground of one plug, and the other probe to the shield or ground of the other plug. This should also indicate 0Ω to show that the grounds on each of the ends connect together. Finally, touch one probe to the *tip* and one probe to the *ground* of the same plug. This should indicate a very high resistance; in fact, the pointer shouldn't really move at all. Note that if your probes are making good contact with the cord connections but the pointer swings erratically, then that probably means your cord is intermittent (or "crackly") and should be fixed.

■ **Checking String Grounding.** Many people feel that guitar strings should not be grounded in the interests of safety, although this does increase the chance of your pickups picking up noise under certain conditions. To check whether your strings are grounded, touch one probe to the ground of the guitar's output jack and the other to your strings. If the meter reads 0Ω, the strings are grounded. To unground them, find the wire going from a ground point on the guitar to the bridge, tailpiece, or other conductive part connected to the strings, and remove it. Guitarist/inventor Dan Armstrong recommends replacing the wire with a 0.1µF disc ceramic capacitor rated at 250V or more to swamp out hum but still provide isolation.

■ **Measuring Current Consumption.** Current, you will remember, is measured in a unit called the *ampere*; however, something like an effects box will draw current that's measured in much smaller units, such as the milliampere. Refer to your selector switch, and you'll see some scales calibrated in mA; you usually read these from one of the voltage scales. So, let's say your scale goes from 0 to 10, and your selector switch says 10mA. That means you can read the current consumption, in milliamperes, directly from the face of the meter. If the selector switch says 100mA, multiply all meter readings by 10 . . . you get the idea. Current is measured by putting the VOM in series between a power source and the device being powered, as we'll see in the next two examples.

■ **Measuring Effects Box Current Consumption.** Start off with the selector switch set to the highest current range in order to protect the meter. Then, *with the effect turned on,* disconnect *one* of the battery terminals from its battery connector. Connect one VOM probe to the disconnected battery terminal, and the other probe to the disconnected battery connector terminal. If the meter deflects downward, reverse the two probes; if the deflection is very slight, switch to a more sensitive range. Carefully note the range you're switched to, then read the current in milliamperes. If there are two batteries in

Figure 5-114

How to measure current of the book projects. (a) The voltmeter (set for current measurements) connected in series with the lead going from the positive supply to the project's (+) pad. This measures the current drawn from the positive supply. (b) The meter measuring the current drawn from the negative supply. If the positive current reading is, say, 10mA, and the negative current reading is also 10mA, then the project is said to have a current consumption of ±10mA.

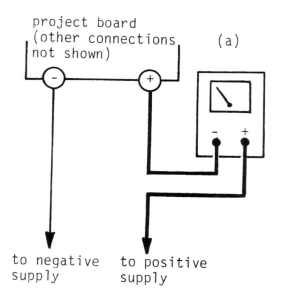

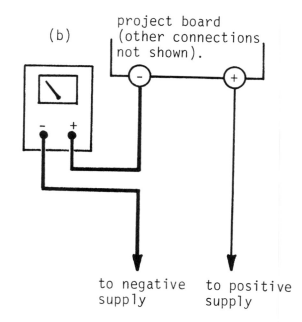

a bipolar arrangement, measure the current drawn from each battery and add these figures together to arrive at the total consumption. Incidentally, you may note that changing control settings or altering your playing style can cause minor changes in the current consumption. *Never* attempt to measure the AC current drawn by something by connecting your VOM in series with the AC line; you'll regret it.

Figure 5-114 shows how to measure the current consumption of the various book projects.

Measuring AC Voltages

Like the ohms scale, the AC voltage scale doesn't differentiate between the black and red probes. One thing, though: When you're measuring high AC voltages, like the kind that come out of wall outlets, BE VERY CARE-FUL!! Those probes are carrying the full 115V AC, and are just as dangerous as an exposed line cord. So make sure you aren't standing in a pool of water, or on a conductive surface, when you're making measurements . . . and spend as little time as possible making the measurement to minimize the chances of mistakes or slipped probes.

■ **Measuring the Voltage at AC Outlets**. With the scale set on the highest AC scale, carefully insert the probes into an AC outlet. Check the reading on the face of the meter, then multiply by the appropriate amount as indicated by the selector switch. For example, if you have a 1 to 10 scale, and the selector switch says "AC V x 100," then a line voltage of 115V AC would read 1.15 on the meter face.

■ **Checking for Leakage**. Sometimes you can have AC leakage in equipment which is responsible for those nasty shocks you can get while touching guitar strings and a microphone at the same time. First of all, hopefully you've ungrounded your guitar strings according to the directions given earlier to minimize your chance of shock, but you could still be in trouble if you touch your mic stand and guitar output jack at the same time. To check for leakage, put your selector switch on a medium-high AC voltage range and connect one probe to your jack and the other probe to your microphone. If the meter budges at all, you've got leakage. Even a couple of volts can be nasty, so if you encounter this leakage, either change polarity switches and plug orientations until the problem goes away (and if your equipment has three-wire AC connectors, *don't cheat*), or connect a large-diameter wire between your amp ground and the PA amp ground. In an extreme case, connect this wire between something like your foot pedal and the mic stand. The problem of AC leakage can be compounded if you have a defective piece of equipment, which could make the situation potentially lethal. Make sure *all* your equipment is fused, in case trying to ground something to something else causes a direct short or other problem due to equipment malfunction. By the way, you can also check whether the fuse is good by using the resistance scale techniques mentioned earlier.

Human bodies are most susceptible to shock when tired and wet, and that's what happens when you're on the road in front of hot lights. So, please be careful.

A Final Note

For many years, the only piece of test equipment I had was a VOM, and it did a good job of telling me what was happening in various circuits. Best of all, you can get VOMs that are small enough and inexpensive enough so that you can afford to keep one in your instrument case. You can bet it will come in handy someday (like the time I wondered why my amp wasn't putting out, and found that the line voltage was about 85V AC).

153

Project No. 20

PRACTICE PLAY ALONG

Definition: When used with a typical stereo hi-fi amplifier or receiver, this project mixes the sound of any electrified instrument in with whatever you're listening to (record, tape, FM, etc.) so that you can "play along" and hear the results on speakers or headphones.

Figure 5-115
The Practice Play Along mounted in a small metal box with the cover removed. The left channel pot has a DPST switch mounted on the back to turn the batteries on and off.

Background

Playing along with records or the radio is an excellent way to build your musical expertise, both in terms of ear training and improvisation; the PPA allows for playing without the need of another, separate amp for your instrument. Incidentally, for repeated practicing, tapes or FM radio work best. Playing records over and over again wears them out much faster than playing them once every 24 hours (the "rest period" recommended by some hi-fi purists).

Level of Difficulty: Beginner to intermediate

Features

- Single IC construction
- Operates from +5 to +18V DC
- Converts standard hi-fi amp into an instrument amp if desired
- Places instrument anywhere in the stereo field (left, right, or in between)
- Set-and-forget gain trimpot accommodates instruments with a wide variety of output levels.
- Use your hi-fi amp to practice through headphones
- Interfaces with virtually any hi-fi amp or receiver
- High-input impedance for accurate reproduction of instruments with high output impedances

154

Construction Tips

Since there are only a handful of parts and the circuit runs at low gain, you don't have to pay too much attention to lead layout. However, if the leads connecting to pads I, B, C, F, and H are more than about 12 cm (5") long, you might want to shield them.

Patching the PPA into Your System

■ With cassette deck only (see Figure 5-116): Connect the tape recorder outputs to J2 and J4, then connect J3 and J5 to the *tape* input on your amplifier. Set the *amp* selector switch for *tape*, then with the volume on your amp at a minimum, apply power to the PPA. Finally, plug your instrument into the input.

Figure 5-116

How to practice with something like a tape recorder. Don't forget to make sure that the amplifier source selector is set to tape.

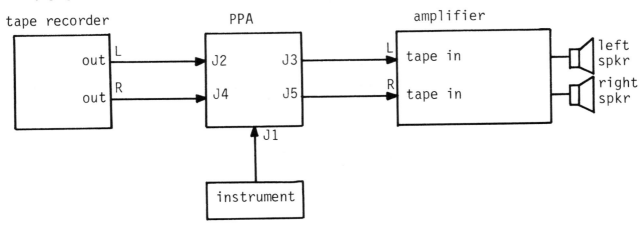

■ Interfacing via the amp's *tape output* jacks (see Figure 5-117): Patch the *tape output* connections from your amp to J2 and J4; this way, any source selected by the amp (tuner, phono, etc.) feeds the PPA input. To listen to the PPA output, connect J3 and J5 to the *tape monitor* jacks of the amplifier. There is usually a front panel switch associated with this function; with the *tape mon* switch in the *out* position, you will hear whatever signal source has been selected. But when the *tape mon* switch is in the *in* position, you'll be listening to the PPA. For more information on the way a *tape mon* switch works, refer to the manual for your amp.

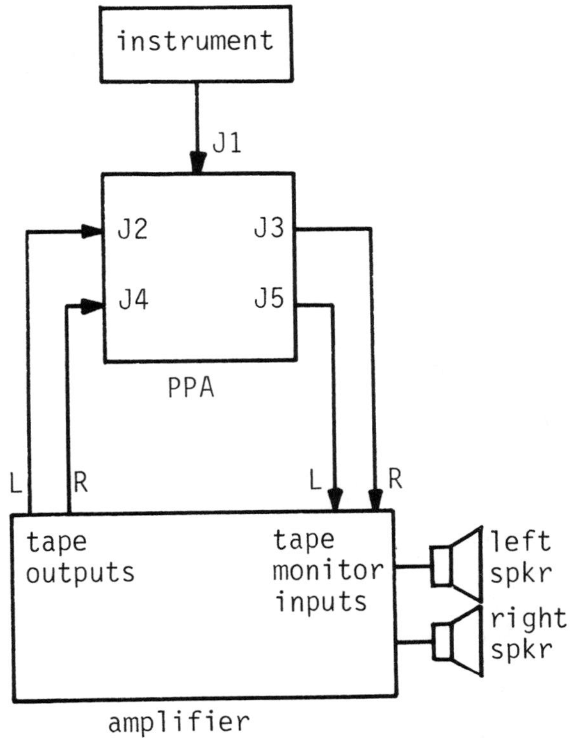

Figure 5-117

Here's how to hook the PPA into a standard hi-fi amp so that you can play along with FM, tape, or phono. Select your signal source with the amp's selector switch, then push the tape mon *button in so that you can hear the PPA output.*

Checking Out the PPA

Now that it's hooked up and your instrument is plugged into the input of the PPA, turn on power to the PPA *first*, then turn on the rest of your system. Listen to something like FM radio (and if necessary , depress the *tape mon* switch). You should hear the sound of the FM. Turn up R10 while playing your instrument; its sound should appear mixed with the FM in the left channel. Turning up R11 mixes your instrument in with the right channel. If your instrument's volume doesn't match the source signal level, adjust R2 for the best possible match.

How to Use Your Hi-Fi as an Instrument Amp

■ Referring to Figure 5-118, ignore J2 and J4; connect J3 and J5 to the *auxiliary* or *aux* input on your amp. Set the amp's source selector switch to *aux*, plug in your instrument with the amp volume turned down, and adjust R10 and R11 to suit. You'll probably be quite surprised to hear what your axe sounds like going through a really clean system . . . and most hi-fi systems are *very* clean compared with the average instrument amplifier.

Figure 5-118
In this application, the PPA interfaces your instrument to a standard hi-fi amp. Leave J2 and J4 unconnected, and set the amplifier selector switch to aux. *In this application, the* tape mon *switch should not be engaged.*

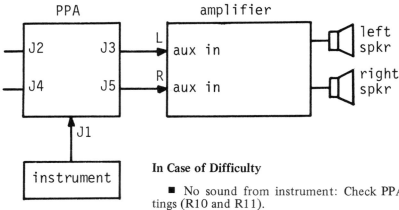

■ CAUTION: Hi-fi speakers, unless they are of the super high power variety, are not designed to handle the types of signals that emanate from "live" musical instruments. For example, adding something like a fuzz to your guitar will increase the harmonic content, and thus the higher overtones, by a significant amount—possibly to the point where your tweeter would cease to tweet. So, be sparing with the volume. You can always use headphones to keep the overall noise level down while still giving yourself the illusion of a big sound.

Modifications

■ Not enough gain, even with R2 up all the way: Change R2 to a 10k trimpot *or* lower R1 to about 220Ω to take care of instruments with very low outputs.

■ Lower noise: If you use a stock, nonpreamplified guitar with the PPA, you may replace C1 with a wire jumper to minimize the noise contributed by IC1D.

In Case of Difficulty

■ No sound from instrument: Check PPA level settings (R10 and R11).

■ Neither the signal selected by the amp, nor the instrument, is audible: Check for improper patching; make sure *tape monitor* switch is correctly set on amp.

■ Distorted input signal: Reduce R2. Reduce input level via R10 and R11.

■ Speakers crackle: Check for intermittent patch cord; turn down volume (you may be blowing a tweeter).

Specifications

Current consumption: ±7mA

Instrument input, maximum input before clipping, R2= 0, channel level controls full up: 8V pk-pk

Instrument input, maximum input before clipping, R2= 5k, channel level controls full up: 600mV pk-pk

Instrument input frequency response: ±1dB, 40Hz-20kHz

Channel inputs, maximum input before clipping: 10V pk-pk

Channel inputs frequency response: ±1dB, 40Hz-20kHz

Figure 5-119
Artwork for the foil side of the circuit board, shown 1 to 1.

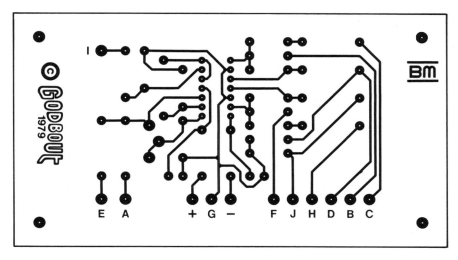

Figure 5-120
Component layout for the PPA.

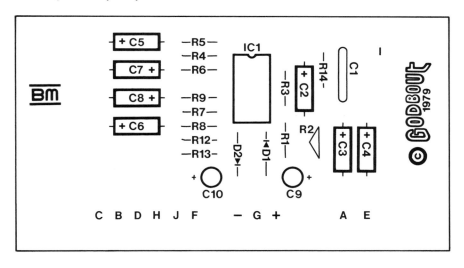

Figure 5-121
PPA schematic.

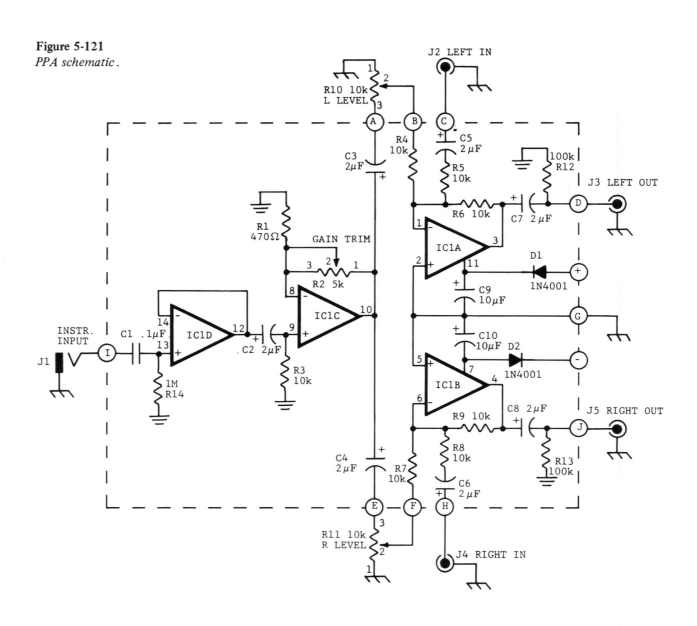

How it Works

IC1D is a buffer stage that protects the instrument signal from subsequent loading. IC1C is a gain stage that amplifies low-level signals up to compatibility with the line-level signals found in hi-fi equipment. In practice, these two stages could have been combined into one stage, but since this circuit requires at least three op amps, I used a quad op amp and had an extra amp left over . . . hence the separate gain stage.

From here the signal couples into two two-input mixers, one for the left channel and one for the right channel. R10 and R11 inject the desired amount of instrument sound into the mixer, while the signals from the hi-fi are mixed in at unity gain. If the hi-fi outputs are relatively high impedance there might be some volume loss when using the PPA; this can be compensated for if necessary by turning up the amp volume a bit.

The outputs of the two mixers couple into the output jacks through C7 and C8. R12 and R13 tie the ends of these capacitors to ground to minimize popping when plugging into the PPA.

Project No. 20 PARTS LIST

Resistors (all are 1/4W, 10% tolerance, except as noted)

R1	470Ω
R2	5k trimpot—trims *input gain*
R3-R9	10k
R10	10k audio taper pot—controls *left channel level*
R11	10k audio taper pot—controls *right channel level*
R12, R13	100k
R14	1M

Capacitors (rated at more than 10V for ±9V, more than 15V for ±15V)

C1	0.1μF, disc ceramic
C2-C8	2μF, electrolytic or tantalum
C9, C10	10μF, electrolytic or tantalum

Semiconductors

IC1	RC4136 or XR4136 quad low-noise op amp
D1, D2	IN4001 or equivalent silicon diode

Mechanicals parts

J1	Open circuit 1/4" mono phone jack
J2-J5	RCA phono jack
Misc.	Circuit board, 14-pin IC socket, solder, wire, case, knobs, etc.

Project No. 21

PHASE SHIFTER

Definition: Imparts an ethereal, animated timbre to electrified instruments or voice (refer to soundsheet).

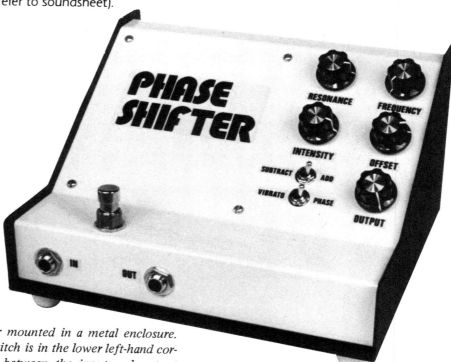

Figure 5-122
The phase shifter mounted in a metal enclosure. An in/out footswitch is in the lower left-hand corner of the box, between the input and output jacks.

Background

Phase shifters were originally introduced in the early '70s to fill the need for an effects box, suitable for on-stage use, that simulated the sound of tape "flanging" (for many years, the flanging sound was only obtainable in recording studios using sophisticated equipment). In the late '70s, the flanger (a new type of device based on time-delay technology) gave an even closer approximation of the flanging sound. However, flangers do have certain drawbacks such as greater expense, higher noise levels, and poor high-frequency response; as a result, they have not replaced phase shifters, but rather, flangers and phase shifters now coexist as equally valid and musically useful effects.

Level of Difficulty: Advanced

Features

- Line-level or low-level operation set with single resistor
- Resonance control adds "sharpness" to the phase-shifted sound
- Add/subtract switch gives two different phase shifter timbres
- Switchable vibrato option
- On-board LFO (low-frequency oscillator) has adjustable frequency and offset controls
- Easily adapted to envelope control (see Project No. 25)
- Low-noise operation (-80dB typical below full output)
- Variable intensity

160

Construction Tips

■ This project uses four CLM6000 opto-isolators. Please refer to the *General Instructions* section at the beginning of this chapter before attempting to solder these parts into place. Suggestion: Mount all four opto-isolators on the board at the same time, and solder 1 lead from each part sequentially until all 16 leads are soldered. This is preferable to soldering all 4 leads of one CLM-6000 and then moving on to the next part, as it reduces the heat build-up for any given part.

■ Lead layout is important. The leads going from R23 to pads K and L should be routed away from the wires going to pads I, A-E, and Q-T, and also away from C6. This minimizes the chances of the audio circuitry picking up any "ticking" sounds from the oscillator.

■ Shield the wires connecting to pads I, B, and D.

■ Due to the relatively heavy current consumption of this device, an AC adapter is recommended. Otherwise, use alkaline batteries.

■ Double-check all connections before applying power.

Using the Phase Shifter

■ Begin checkout with S1 in the *phase* position, S2 in the *add* position, R22-R24 at their midpoints, and R25 and R26 fully counterclockwise. Plug your instrument into J1, patch J2 to your amplifier, and apply power to the phase shifter.

■ You should now hear the unmodified sound of your instrument as you play; turning up the *intensity* control adds phase-shifted sound in with the straight sound. If you advance R26 too far, the phase-shift effect will become less apparent and sound more like vibrato. Suggestion: Adjust R26 for the most intense (not necessarily the loudest) phase-shifted sound, and then use the *output* control to adjust the overall level.

■ Experiment with R22 (*offset*) and R23 (*frequency*). R23 varies the rate of the phaser's sweep, while R22 varies the range of the sweep. At slow sweep speeds, R22 will need to be turned further clockwise compared with its setting at faster sweep speeds.

■ Turn up R25 and experiment with different resonance effects; at extreme clockwise settings, you'll hear a whistling sound.

■ Return R24 to its full counterclockwise position, and change S1 to *vibrato*. This effect is most pronounced at relatively fast sweep speeds. Adjust *offset* for the most natural sound.

■ Finally, change S1 back to *phase* and change S2 to *subtract*. Experiment again with the different controls; the subtract sound resembles a wa-wa, while the *add* sound gives the traditional phasing sound.

Getting the ideal combination of resonance, intensity, LFO frequency, and offset may take a little time . . . but the experimentation is worth it if you expect to get the most out of this device.

Modifications

■ Lower noise: Some of the phase shifter's noise output lies outside the audio band; to get rid of it, add a 270 to 300pF capacitor in parallel with R19. This will make no audible difference.

■ More control over the LFO speed: Change C9. A larger value gives slower speeds, while a smaller value gives faster speeds. A further refinement is to add a switch that selects between a couple of different capacitor values (see Figure 5-123).

■ Less resonance at low frequencies: Reduce C7's value.

■ For low-level operation, R2=470k. For line-level inputs, R2=200k.

■ To make the sweep range narrower, reduce R28 to 24k or 22k.

Figure 5-123
How to switch between two different LFO capacitors. Connect the wires from these components to C9's pads, as indicated on the illustration.

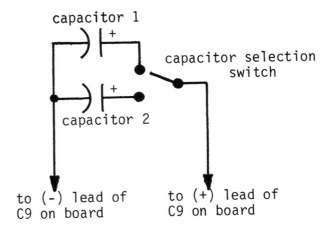

In Case of Difficulty

■ Distortion: Back off on *resonance* control or attenuate input signal.

■ Sweep is irregular (hits low point, stops, then starts sweeping up again): Turn R22 further clockwise until sweep is regular.

■ Weak vibrato sound: Make sure *intensity* control is full up. S2 should be in the *add* position.

■ Clicking sound in output: Carefully review the section on lead layout and shielding under *Construction Tips*. In extreme cases, C6 can pick up clicking from the wires connecting to pads K and L. If routing these wires away from C6 still doesn't solve the problem, wrap some wire tightly around the capacitor and ground one end. This creates a shield that completely eliminates the problem. You should be able to dress the leads so that there is no audible clicking at all in the audio output.

■ Loud whistling sound: Back off on the *resonance* control.

■ Weak phasing sound: Control misadjusted, or burned-out CLM6000. To test the CLM6000s, adjust R23 for a medium-speed sweep, and clip an ohmmeter across the photoresistor leads of each CLM6000. If the meter pointer swings back and forth at the same speed as the LFO (use the R x 100 or R x 1000 range), the CLM6000 is good. If the pointer doesn't move after repeated tests, the CLM6000 should be replaced. Do not listen to the phase shifter output as you perform this test, as clipping the ohmmeter leads to the photoresistor leads causes a pop.

Specifications

Current consumption: ±15mA

Number of notches in passband: 2

Maximum input before clipping:
    R32=470k 1.1V pk-pk
    R32=220k 2.2V pk-pk

Maximum available output: 10V pk-pk

LFO waveform: triangle

LFO frequency range: 0.2-8Hz

Signal-to-noise ratio: greater than -70dB under least favorable control settings (typically -80dB in normal use)

How it Works

The phase shifter has four basic sections: Input buffer/preamp (IC2A), phase shift stages (IC1A-IC1D), output mixer (IC2B), and low-frequency oscillator (IC3A and IC3B). The output of the buffer/preamp feeds both the phase-shift stages and the output mixer. When S1 is closed, the phase-shift stages' output is combined at the mixer with the normal signal to give a phase-shifted sound. Preventing the normal signal from reaching the output mixer by opening S1 gives a vibrato effect.

Each phase-shift stage contributes somewhat less than 180 degrees of phase shift. Looking at the stage built around IC1B, when the photoresistor in the CLM6000 is in the high-resistance state (which also means that very little current is flowing through the CLM6000's LED), the signal mostly feeds into the noninverting input of IC1B via C2. As the photoresistor resistance decreases, more signal goes into the inverting input. This action produces the phase-shift effect.

To vary the current flowing through the CLM6000 LEDs, and therefore vary the resistance of the four photoresistors, we use a low-frequency oscillator that produces a subsonic triangle wave at at its output. You can think of the triangle wave as being a series of rising and falling voltages; this rise and fall serves to modulate the LEDs by sending varying amounts of current through them.

The *add/subtract* switch is a little unusual, and gives you the choice of changing the phase of the output of the phase-shift stages when it joins with the normal signal. In the add position, the two waveforms add together to produce a phaser sound. In the subtract position, the phase-shift stages' output is subtracted from the straight signal, giving a filtered type of sound.

You may wonder why there are two pads for N and P, since they connect together. This configuration allows you to easily attach the envelope follower (Project No. 25) to the phase shifter so that the phasing effect follows the dynamics of your playing instead of the internal LFO. If you're interested in getting a different type of phaser sound from what you normally hear on records and in concert, then look into this combination.

Figure 5-124

Artwork for the foil side of the board, shown 1 to 1.

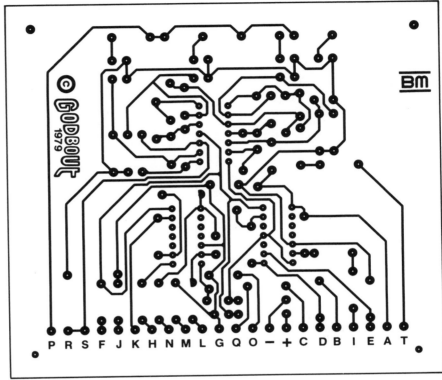

Figure 5-125

Component layout for the phase shifter.

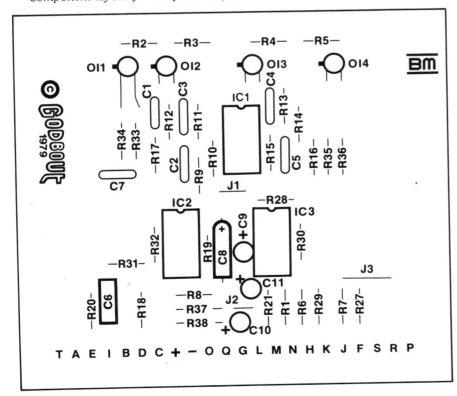

Figure 5-126
Phase Shifter schematic

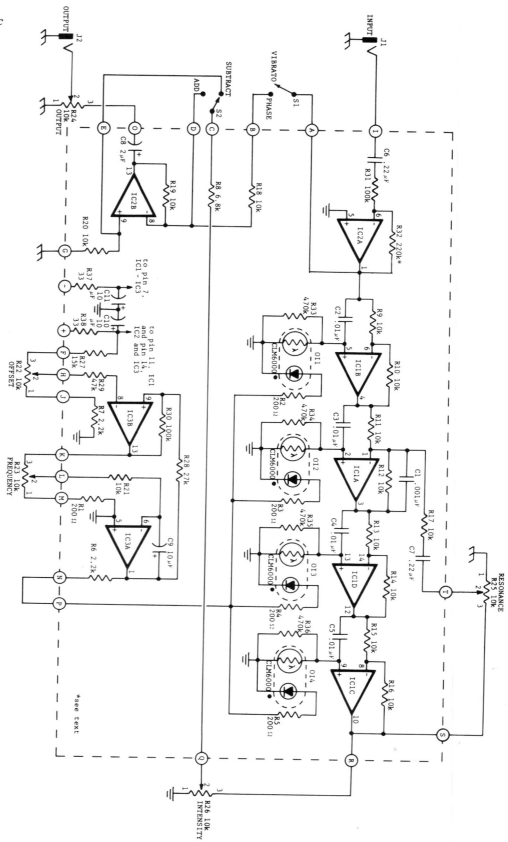

164

Project No. 21 PARTS LIST

Resistors (all are 1/4W, 10% tolerance, except as noted)

R1-R5	200Ω
R6, R7	2.2k
R8	6.8k
R9-R21	10k
R22	10k linear taper pot—controls *LFO offset*
R23	10k linear taper pot—controls *LFO frequency*
R24	10k audio taper pot—controls *output*
R25	10k linear taper pot—controls *resonance*
R26	10k audio taper pot—controls *intensity*
R27	15k
R28	27k
R29	47k
R30, R31	100k
R32	220k (line level), 470k (low level)
R33-R36	470k
R37, R38	33Ω

Capacitors (rated at more than 10V)

C1	0.001μF, disc ceramic
C2-C5	0.01μF (mylar preferred, disc acceptable)
C6, C7	0.22μF (mylar preferred, disc acceptable)
C8	2μF, electrolytic or tantalum
C9-C11	10μF, electrolytic or tantalum

Semiconductors

IC1	RC4136 or XR4136 quad low-noise op amp
IC2, IC3	RC4739 or XR4739 dual low-noise op amp
OI1-OI4	CLM6000 opto-isolator (Clairex)

Mechanical Parts

J1, J2	Open circuit 1/4" mono phone jack
S1	SPST toggle switch—selects *vibrato/phase*
S2	SPDT toggle switch—selects *add/subtract*
Misc.	Case, circuit board, three 14-pin IC sockets, knobs, solder, wire, etc.

Project No. 22

MAKING PATCH CORDS

Definition: Patch cords connect the inputs and outputs of various effects together in order to complete the audio signal path.

Figure 5-127

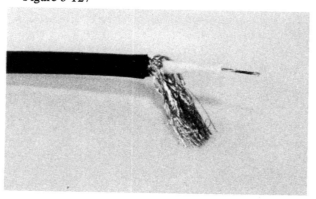

Figure 5-128

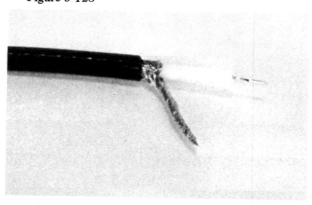

Background

While often neglected, patch cords are an important part of your system. Cords that snap, crackle, or break down can wreck an otherwise good performance; so, it pays to put together the very best cords you can, and to keep the cords you already have in good repair.

How to Make a Patch Cord

1. *Choose the shielded wire for your cord.* There are many low-capacitance cables designed specifically for audio use: TEAC, for example, sells its wire through pro audio dealers. Additionally, music stores often carry cable for "do-it-yourself" cord makers.

2. *Strip both ends of the cord* (Figure 5-127). This photo shows the outer insulation removed, the braid pulled away from the center conductor, and about 50mm (1/4") of insulation removed from the inner wire to expose the center conductor. Be especially careful not to nick the shield as you strip away the outer layer of insulation.

3. *Tin the center conductor and shield* (Figure 5-128). Twist the strands of the center conductor together, and melt a little solder onto these strands to hold them together. Likewise, twist the braid carefully and melt some solder onto the braid to hold its strands together. When tinning the shield, make sure it doesn't get hot enough to melt through the inner conductor insulation.

4. *Attach the end of the cable to one plug* (Figure 5-129). Some plugs have a little hole in the ground lug; you can feed the tinned braid through this hole. Then connect the inner conductor of the cable to the hot lug of the plug. Pull gently on the braid until the cord rests in between the two strain relief clamps on the side of the ground lug.

5. *Solder the inner conductor to the hot lug of the plug, solder the braid to the ground lug of the plug, then crimp the strain relief around the cord* (Figure 5-130). There are two things to watch out for during this part of the operation: first, that the braid doesn't melt through the insulation to the inner conductor; second, that you let the whole assembly cool down before crimping the strain relief into place around the cord. Otherwise, you might force the braid to melt through the inner conductor insulation, causing a short. Don't crimp the strain relief *too* tightly, but make sure it does hold the cord firmly in place.

6. *Screw the plug cover in place* (Figure 5-131). This photo shows the plug with an insulating cardboard sleeve in place before the cover is screwed on. If your plug doesn't have a cardboard sleeve, then wrap a few turns of electrical tape around the guts of the plug to keep it from shorting against the metal cover. If you're using plugs with plastic covers, you don't have to worry about shorts against the plug guts; but you do have to worry about someone stepping on the cover and cracking it. When finished, the plug should look like Figure 5-132.

7. *Now attach the other plug in place.* First, however, make sure you place the plug cover on the cord (and oriented with the open part facing *away* from the plug you've already installed) before you do any soldering. It's embarrassing to wire a plug in place, only to find out that you have to take it off again in order to screw the cover in place . . . you'll see what I mean the first couple of times you make a cord. Finally, check the continuity of the cord (and check for shorts) using an ohmmeter, as described in Project No. 19.

Don't expect to make a perfect cord the first time out; while the process appears simple, making a sturdy, well-soldered cord takes a bit of practice. You might want to start out your cord-making career by repairing an old cord to get your chops together, and then moving on to the more advanced stuff.

Figure 5-129

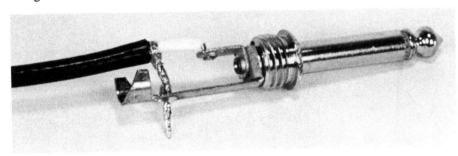

Figure 5-130

Figure 5-131

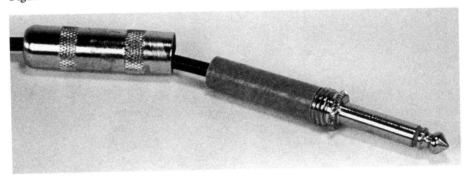

Figure 5-132

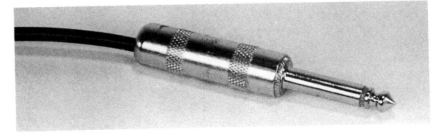

TALK BOX

Definition: Imparts a "talking" quality to the sound of musical instruments; used on many records to give a "talking guitar" or "talking keyboard" sound.

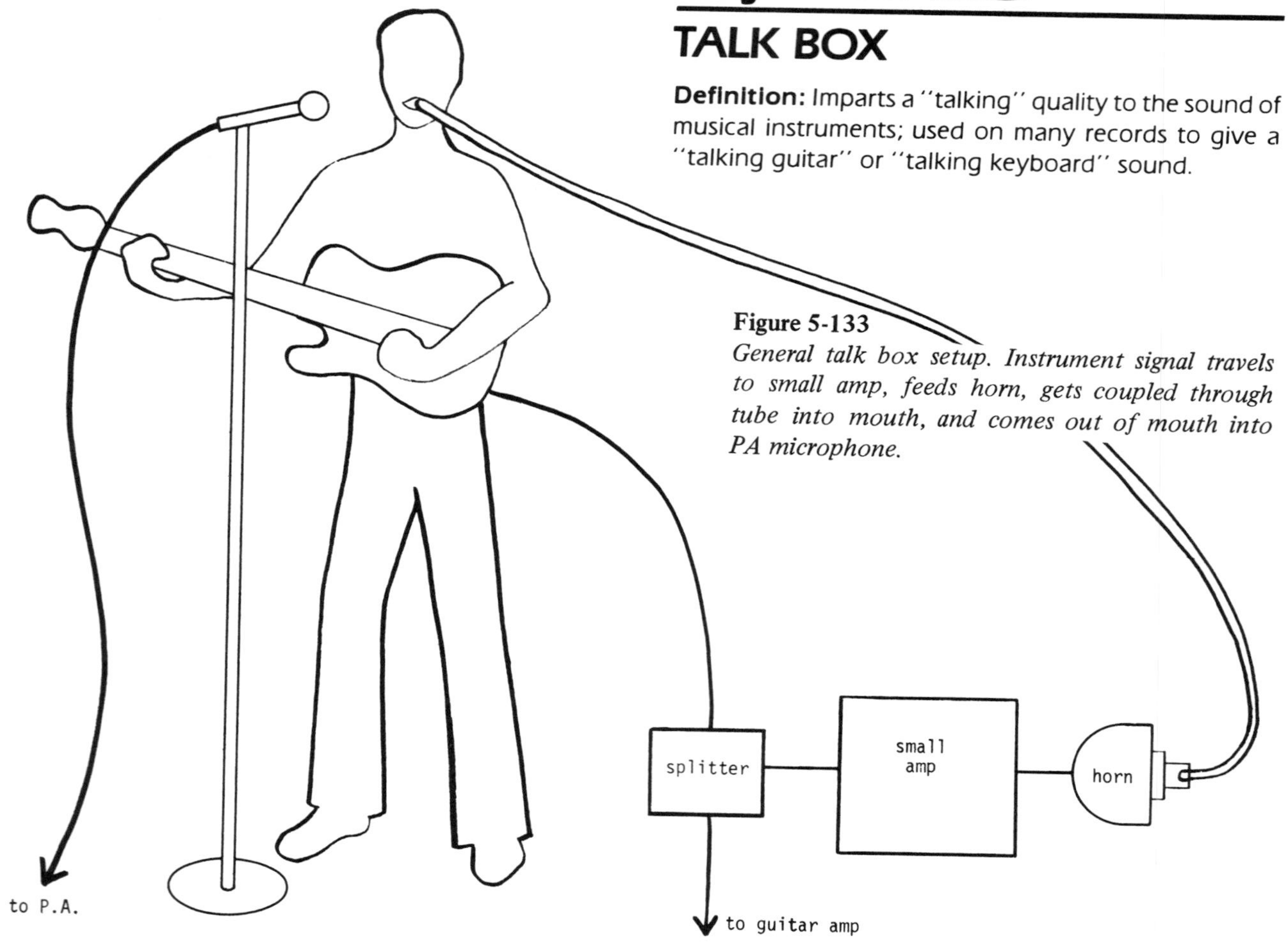

Figure 5-133

General talk box setup. Instrument signal travels to small amp, feeds horn, gets coupled through tube into mouth, and comes out of mouth into PA microphone.

to P.A.

splitter | small amp | horn

to guitar amp

Background

Figure 5-133 shows signal leaving the instrument and splitting through a Y-cord or splitter box into two independent channels. One of these channels goes to the main-stage amp for an unmodified guitar sound, while the other channel feeds a small amp (in the 1 to 10W range). This amp feeds a horn driver type of loudspeaker, but with the horn removed—either by unscrewing it from the driver or by sawing it off. The output of this horn couples acoustically into a flexible plastic tube that carries the sound up to the musicians's mouth. By inserting the tube loosely between your molars and making words with your mouth, the instrument seems to "talk" by taking on the filtering characteristics of your mouth. Biting down on the tube stops the sound from coming into your mouth. By positioning your mouth in front of a microphone, this talking instrument effect then comes out through the PA. Since the signal coming out of your mouth is relatively weak, it's usually necessary to crank up the PA mic level considerably for a good sound.

Features

■ Extremely simple construction.

■ Gives many of the sounds obtainable with a Vocoder at a fraction of the price.

Level of Difficulty: Beginner

Construction Tips

■ Figure 5-134 shows a splitter box that you can build in a small metal case. Pushing the footswitch determines whether your signal feeds the talk box amp or regular amp.

■ Use a low-power amp for the talk box amp (such as Project No. 5). Some people claim that too high a volume level could rattle your teeth around, so play it safe. If you don't get enough volume, turn up the PA mic—don't increase the wattage level of your talk box amp.

■ The horn driver isn't too critical. I used a Radio Shack horn tweeter for my first talk box experiment, and it worked just fine; a midrange horn worked even better by giving a wider frequency response. *Caution:* Most horns include (or recommend that you include) a blocking capacitor to attenuate low frequencies (see Figure 5-135). Since horns are designed to handle mid- and upper-range frequencies, too much bass puts a strain on the driver; the blocking capacitor takes care of this. With really low-power amps (1W or so) the blocking capacitor may not be necessary, since you're not generating enough power—even in the bass range—to cause any damage. If you have any doubts, err on the conservative side and include a blocking cap. A smaller value restricts bass to a greater extent.

■ Finding plastic tubing: Most hardware stores and plastic supply houses carry flexible plastic tubing. Specify the nontoxic variety; after all, you are going to be putting the thing in your mouth. As far as size goes, smaller-diameter tubing is easier to stick in your mouth, but doesn't let through as much sound; larger tubing is louder, but harder to deal with. A 1.5 cm (5/8") outside diameter seems to be the best compromise.

■ Coupling the horn driver to the tubing: If the driver is only a little wider than the tubing, stick the end of the tubing in boiling water to soften it up, then push it over the end of the driver. As it hardens, it will tighten in place. Another approach is to use two or more sections of tubing to give a telescoping mounting (see Figure 5-136). If all else fails, you can always mount the driver in a box, drill a hole in the box, and stick the tubing into the box . . . not a very elegant or airtight solution, but a workable one nonetheless.

Using the Talk Box

Feed your instrument to the talk box amp, and listen to the sound coming out of the end of the tubing. If there is no sound, recheck your setup. If all is well, put the end of the tubing in your mouth and start to get the feel of the talk box.

You'll find that it is not easy to make an instrument "talk"; in fact, it requires a great deal of practice just to make any sounds that are intelligible. It is much easier to start out by doing wa-wa-type sounds, which builds up your technique. Since the letter "s" doesn't come across too well with a talk box, you might want to cheat a bit and make "s" sounds directly into the mic with your mouth to cover up for the lack of response coming out of the tube. You might also find it easier to use the talk box if you add compression (Project No. 8) or fuzz (Project No. 24) to your instrument before going into the talk box. This is especially true for guitar, as the increased sustain gives you more sound to play with at the mouth end of things.

In Case of Difficulty

Very little can go wrong with the talk box. If you don't get any output from the tube, then either the amp isn't working, the driver isn't working, or the splitter isn't working. Test each one individually until you find the source of the problem.

Figure 5-134
Splitter box; the footswitch routes the input to two different outputs. Build it in a small metal enclosure.

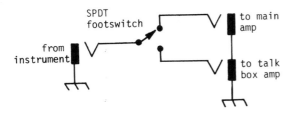

Figure 5-136
I slipped a plastic container over the midrange horn, and cut a hole through one end of the container; the tubing goes into this hole and picks up sound from the driver. You could also slip the tubing inside progressively larger pieces of tubing, until the inside diameter of the tubing was large enough to fit over the horn driver.

Figure 5-135
Adding a blocking capacitor.

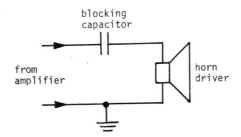

Project No. 24

TUBE SOUND FUZZ

Definition: Recreates the types of distortion normally associated with tubes, but with a solid-state design for low current consumption, compactness, and reliability.

Figure 5-137
The Tube Sound Fuzz mounted in a small box for onstage use.

Background

Musicians in general, and guitarists in particular, prefer the sound of tube amps to the sound of conventional transistor amps. However, tubes have certain disadvantages (fragility, sensitivity to mechanical vibration and shock, need for high-voltage power supplies, high current consumption, and change in sound as they age); therefore, transistor amps are often used where reliable operation is paramount.

Luckily, however, there is a member of the transistor family called the field effect transistor *(FET) that happens to distort in very much the same manner as a tube. This fuzz takes advantage of the FET's distortion characteristics to yield a tube-type distortion sound.*

Features

- Low-level or line-level operation
- Low noise compared with conventional fuzzes
- *Rhythm/lead* switch gives low levels of distortion for playing chords, and high levels of distortion for playing lead lines.

- *Fuzz* control varies intensity of fuzz in the rhythm mode
- Distortion increases smoothly as input level increases (soft clips over a wide range rather than hard clipping at a single overload point)
- "Warm" distortion sound accents even harmonics for a musical fuzz effect
- Only requires a single 9V battery (+15V operation is allowable, but not preferable)

Level of Difficulty: Beginner to intermediate

Contruction Tips

- This project uses CMOS ICs; *be sure to reread* the instructions on handing CMOS ICs included in the "Construction Tips" section of Project No. 15.

- Plug the IC into its socket *after* all wiring is complete but *before* you apply power to the unit.

- Separate input and output leads by at least 1 cm (1/2").

■ Shield the input lead. If the wires connecting to S1 and R5 exceed 7.2 cm (3"), use shielded cable for these also.

■ Even though sections IC1C-IC1F appear to have no influence on the operation of the circuit, be sure to wire them up exactly as shown. Leave the outputs of these sections unconnected.

■ Keep all wiring as short and direct as possible.

Using the Tube Sound Fuzz

This fuzz works best with line levels; however, it will also work very well with low-level inputs. With S1 in the *rhythm* position, R5 compensates for differences in input signal levels.

■ Plug your instrument into J1 and patch J2 to your amp. Although most people associate fuzzes with guitars, this unit also works well with electric pianos and other keyboards.

■ With S1 in the *rhythm* position, vary R5's position. You should obtain more intense fuzz effects as you turn this control clockwise. Try playing some "chunky," R&B types of riffs; adjust R5 until you get that old tube amp type of sound.

■ To increase the fuzz beyond the options offered by R5, change S1 to the *lead* position.

■ By turning R7 up full, you can probably overload the input of your amp and thereby create additional distortion.

■ To increase the intensity of the fuzz still further, patch a compressor (Project No. 8) between your instrument and the fuzz input.

Modifications

■ De-emphasized low-frequency response: Reduce the value of C4 to 0.05μF or even 0.02μF. This gives you nice, biting lead lines for guitar without having the bass strings muddy things up too much when you hit them.

■ De-emphasized high-frequency response: Increase the value of C2. A value of 50pF starts rolling off the high frequencies at approximately 4000Hz.

■ Less intense fuzz effect: Line-level signals may produce too fuzzy a sound for some tastes. In this case, increase R3 to 220k or even 470k.

In Case of Difficulty

■ Excessive current consumption (eats batteries): Some 4049s draw more current than others. If you have a couple fo 4049s around, try plugging in different chips (turn off power while changing chips!!) and reading the current consumption with a meter (see Project No. 19). Choose the chip with the lowest current consumption.

■ Oscillations or squeals: Check lead layout. Check that C6 is correctly polarized. Increase the value of C2 to 20 or 30pF.

Figure 5-138
Artwork for the foil side of the circuit board, shown 1 to 1.

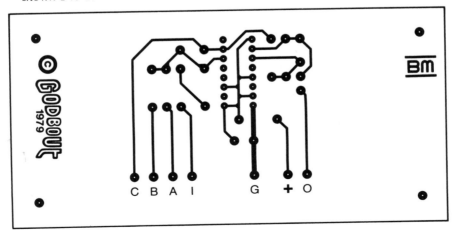

Specifications

Current consumption: +7mA (depends on the individual 4049)

Maximum input before clipping, S1 in *lead* position*: 15mV

Maximum input before clipping, S1 in *rhythm* position, R5=0*: 150mV

*Since this unit doesn't hard clip, these figures represent where distortion starts increasing rapidly. If you observe a sine wave going through the fuzz and slowly turn up the level of the sine wave, it will become increasingly distorted. With very large input levels, the output waveform is a square wave with gently rounded corners.

Figure 5-139
Component layout for the tube sound fuzz.

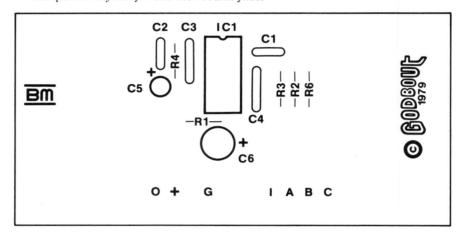

How it Works

IC1 is a 4049 hex CMOS inverter/buffer that was never really intended for audio use. It's a *digital* IC (the type used in computers), and is generally grouped with lots of other digital ICs to implement some type of digital function (microcomputer, industrial control, and so on). But as it so happens, each inverter of the IC may be modified to run as a *linear* (audio) IC, and because these inverters are based on FET circuitry, distorting them gives a tube-type distortion sound.

The input couples through R3 and C4 into the first stage of the fuzz, IC1A. This basically amplifies the input signal a lot, and may or may not add some distortion, depending on the setting of S1/R5. However, even if this stage doesn't add distortion, the greatly amplified signal level will overload the second stage (IC1B) and cause distortion in that stage. C1 and C2 are designed to discourage oscillation in the first and second stages, respectively; C2 also helps cut out some of the superhigh frequencies generated by the fuzz. After leaving the second stage, the output signal couples through C5 into output control R7.

How a musician reacts to a fuzz is highly subjective, perhaps more so than with any other type of effect. Nonetheless, this fuzz has pleased hard-to-please musicians . . . it distorts in a very smooth manner, doesn't sound gritty or harsh, and is very quiet (I measured the noise spec in the *lead* position as -58dB, which is pretty remarkable for a fuzz device!). One prominent manufacturer has even based the design of one of its products around this circuit; I hope you enjoy it as much as other people have, and that you find it as useful as I have.

172

Figure 5-140
Tube sound fuzz schematic.

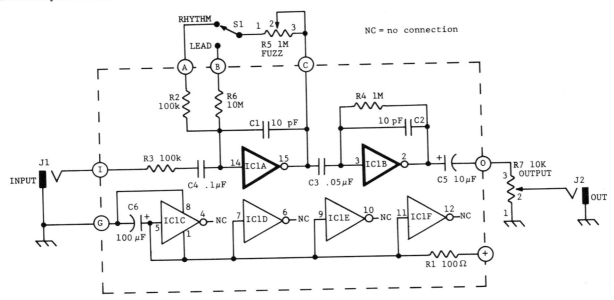

IC = CD4049

Project No. 24 PARTS LIST

Resistors (all are 1/4W, 10% tolerance, except as noted)

R1	100Ω
R2, R3	100k
R4	1M
R5	1M linear taper pot—controls *fuzz intensity* when S1 is in the *rhythm* position
R6	10M
R7	10k audio taper pot—controls *output level*

Capacitors (rated at more than 10V for +9V operation)

C1, C2	10pF, disc ceramic
C3	0.05μF (mylar preferred, disc acceptable)
C4	0.1μF (mylar preferred, disc acceptable)
C5	10μF, electrolytic or tantalum
C6	100μF, electrolytic

Semiconductor

IC1	CD4049 CMOS hex inverter

Mechanical Parts

J1, J2	Open circuit 1/4" mono phone jack
S1	SPDT toggle switch—selects *rhythm/lead*
Misc.	Case, knob, 16-pin IC socket, wire, solder, etc.

Project No. 25

ENVELOPE FOLLOWER

Definition: Accepts an audio signal at its input, but produces a DC voltage at its output that is proportional to the volume level of your playing. When used in conjunction with other projects, the envelope follower synchronizes the effect of that project to the dynamics of your playing. The way the envelope follower accomplishes this synchronization is by listening to the dynamics of your playing. The louder you play, the more voltage it produces; when you play softer, the envelope follower puts out less voltage. By using this voltage to control effects that have been specifically designed to respond to a controlling voltage, you can control that effect with the dynamics of your playing.

Background

First, we need to clarify a common misconception. The first time I saw an envelope follower (EF for short) was on a big Moog modular synthesizer in the '60s, and for all I know the envelope follower predates the particular Moog module I played with. However, the envelope follower is not an effect, but rather a means of controlling an effect. For example, in an amplifier the envelope follower would control the gain; in a filter, the resonant frequency; in a phase shifter, the amount of phase shift; and so on.

One of the most popular applications for the envelope follower is to control a filter (or wa-wa) type of effect. By making the filter responsive to the dynamics of your playing, playing louder is equivalent to pushing down on the pedal normally found on a wa-wa; playing softer is like pulling up on the pedal, thereby giving an automatic wa-wa sound that is synchronized exactly to your playing. There are several commercially available effects boxes that combine an envelope follower and filter together in the same enclosure. Musicians generally call these "envelope followers," although you can perhaps see why that term is misleading . . . a more accurate term would be "envelope-follower-controlled filter," or more simply, "envelope-controlled filter." The reason why I'm being picky with the terminology is that envelope followers are by no means limited to controlling filters, which many musicians erroneously believe is the case.

Features

- Single IC construction
- Operating range (low or line-level) set with two resistors
- On-board dual opto-isolators
- Controls Project No. 17 for automatic wa-wa effect
- Controls Project No. 21 to make the phase shifter respond to the dynamics of your playing instead of to the internal LFO
- Converts the noise gate into a gate that follows the dynamics of your playing (as opposed to being an on-off device)
- Controls the internal oscillator frequency of the ring modulator
- Controls some commercially available effects

Level of Difficulty: Advanced

Construction Tips

- Read the entire project text thoroughly—paying special attention to the modifications section—before you even begin to warm up your soldering iron. There are many important points that need to be considered, and I'm sure you will want to get things right the first time around.

- The wire going to pad I should be shielded.

Figure 5-141

How to control the phase shifter with either its own built-in low-frequency oscillator, or the envelope follower. Connections other than those pertinent to this wiring are not shown for clarity. Notice how power for the envelope follower taps off the power connections to the phase shifter.

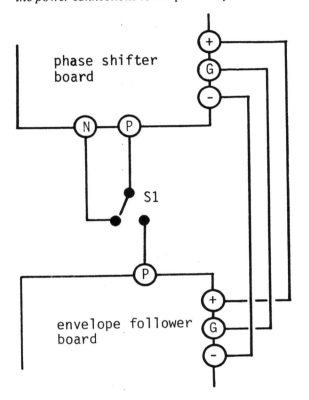

■ Be careful when soldering the CLM6000s; refer to the general instructions at the beginning of this chapter for advice on how to properly handle these parts.

■ D3's polarity is crucial; make sure you get it right, or the envelope follower will not work.

■ Suggestion: Mount the envelope follower inside the same enclosure as the effect it's controlling, since this module really doesn't lend itself to a modular approach. Additionally, you'll no doubt want to use different envelope follower settings for different effects. If you need to conserve panel space or cut down on "knob clutter," consider making R7 a trimpot.

Using the Envelope Follower

Get ready for some detailed reading, 'cause here we go . . . lots of words that will hopefully make everything clear.

Controlling the Phase Shifter

■ Begin by locating the power and ground leads going to the shifter, and tap power for the envelope follower from these leads. NOTE: The EF works best from a ±9V DC supply. Plug your instrument into J1 of the envelope follower, then run another cord from J2 to the input of the phase shifter. Patch the output of the phase shifter into your amp. We're assuming that R7 is wired correctly to the envelope follower and that you've found some place on the phase shifter chassis to mount this pot.

■ Next, locate the jumper that connects pads N and P on the phase shifter; cut this jumper, and wire pad P of the EF to pad P of the phase shifter (ignore pad N on the shifter). By adding switch S1 as shown in Figure 5-141, you may control the phase shifter by the EF or the internal LFO.

■ Now set R11 and R7 fully counterclockwise, and start playing. As you turn R7 clockwise, there should be a brief section of the rotation where nothing happens to the sound; then, at some point, the phase-shift effect will become noticeable. Turning R7 further clockwise will raise the resonant frequency of the phase-shift effect.

■ Return R7 to the point where the phaser effect *just started* to become noticeable. Continue playing and turn up R11. At some point, you will hear the phase-shift effect being controlled by your playing . . . the louder you play, the higher the phase shifter rises. Continue experimenting to get a feel for how R11 works, then experiment with different settings of R7 to get a feel for that control also.
CAUTION: It takes some time to really become a whiz at adjusting the controls. Don't be impatient if you can help it; realize that everyone takes a long time to perfect envelope-follower effects.

Controlling the Super Tone Control

■ Hook up the power connections as described in the phaser modification, plug your instrument into J1 on the envelope follower, plug J2 into the input of the tone control, and patch the output to your amp.

■ Locate the wire that goes from pad D of the super tone control (STC for short) board to R16A, terminal 2; disconnect it at the R16A end, and reconnect this wire to pad D on the EF. Next, take the wire going from pad H of the STC to R16A terminal 3, disconnect it from R16A, and reconnect it to pad E on the EF. Note that a wire should still connect pad H of the STC with terminal 3 of R9, the high-pass level control.

■ Locate the wire going from pad E of the STC to R16B terminal 2; disconnect it from R16B, and reconnect it to pad J on the EF board. Next, take the wire going from pad B of the STC to R16B terminal 3, disconnect it from R16B, and reconnect it to pad K on the EF. Note that a wire should still connect pad B to terminal 3 of R8 and to terminal 3 of R17. You may now remove R16 if required.

■ As in the case of the phaser, start your experiments with R11 and R7 fully counterclockwise. As you turn R7 clockwise, there will again be a dead space where nothing happens, and then the filter frequency will start to rise as R7 is turned more and more clockwise. Now, return this control to the point where the sound first started changing. Turn up R11 and you should hear an automatic wa-wa effect.

- Adjust R11 to match your picking style so that your maximum volume gives the highest filter resonant frequency. If the filter sweeps over too wide a range, you can *raise* the lowest part of the sweep by turning up R7, and *lower* the top excursion of the sweep by turning down R11.

Controlling the Noise Gate

- Remove the CLM6000 from the noise gate board; then, use this part for OI1 on the EF board.

- Run two wires from pads D and E on the EF board to the two holes on the noise gate board where the photocell leads of the CLM6000 (the long, thin ones) are soldered to the board.

- Hook up power to the EF, plug your cords into the various jacks, and you're ready to go. Adjust R7 just below the point where you start hearing your signal, and adjust R11 to suit.

Controlling the Ring Modulator

- Disconnect the wires going to R15 from the ring modulator board, and attach two wires from D and E on the EF board to pads A and B on the ring modulator board (in essence, we're replacing the pot with the photoresistor section of the CLM6000; leave the other connections going to pad A intact).

- Hook up power, plug in cords as described in the previous sections, adjust R7 for the *lowest* desired carrier frequency, then adjust R11 for the *highest* desired carrier frequency when you're playing at maximum volume.

Controlling Commercial Effects

Examine the effect's pot that you want to control with the EF, and determine whether it's hooked up as a two-terminal, or three-terminal, control (see Figure 5-142). If it's a three-wire control, you're out of luck—the modification will not be easy to make. But if it's a two-wire job, run those two wires to pads D and E on the EF board, and you're set for envelope control once you've made all appropriate connections to the EF board.

Figure 5-142

If terminal 2 connects to either terminal 1 or terminal 3, the control may be envelope-controlled by the envelope follower. If the three-pot terminals connect to separate wires, then it cannot be controlled by the envelope follower.

Modifications

- Since the EF responds to your particular style of playing, and since everybody has a different style, it follows that it would be of great advantage to allow us to adapt the EF as closely to our style as possible. If you find that you have the sensitivity control just barely cracked open in order to get the effect you want, then the EF is too sensitive. To adjust, lower the values of R9 and R10—say, to 100k. If, on the other hand, the EF just isn't sensitive enough and you're a soft player, then raise the values of R9 and R10—try 470k for starters, and go higher if necessary. Remember to always change these resistors together as a pair, and to keep both values equal.

- Eliminating J1 and J2: In the previous examples on using the EF, we talked about plugging into the EF and then plugging the EF into the effect. However, if you look carefully at the EF schematic you'll note that J1 and J2 are simply tied together so that the EF can "tap off" your signal. You could just as easily connect lug 3 of R11 directly to the *hot* lead of the *input* jack on the effect you're controlling, thereby eliminating J1 and J2 in the EF section.

- R11 is a 1M control; it presents a minimum of loading on the EF's input signal. Unfortunately, if you use a 741 op amp for IC1, changing R11 will also appear to affect the setting of R7—not much, but enough so that you might find it annoying. To remedy this, use an LF356 or similar FET input op amp for IC1.

- Altering the EF's decay time: As you play the EF, you'll note that it has a pretty rapid attack time (i.e., when you strike a note, the response is pretty fast); but if you suddenly mute your instrument, there is a certain amount of decay time. Increasing C4 increases the decay time, while decreasing its value decreases the decay time. Too fast a response time produces an erratic or buzzing type of sound; too long a decay time makes the EF respond to the dynamics of your playing in a "mushy" kind of way (which in some cases can be pleasing). You might want to include a switch to choose between a couple of different values of C4 if you feel limited by having a single, fixed decay time.

- Other modifications involve money-saving options. When connecting the EF to the phase shifter project, neither OI1 or OI2 is necessary, and may be eliminated from the board along with R2-R4. For controlling Project No. 17, R5 is not required. For controlling the noise gate or ring modulator, OI2 and R3 are not needed. Since opto-isolators are expensive, there is no point in having one sitting on the board unless you really need it in the circuit.

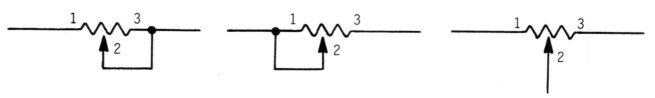

In Case of Difficulty

■ If the EF appears to not work properly, your first step is to *carefully check all control settings.* If R7 or R11 is incorrectly adjusted, problems can range from no output at all to an output that doesn't respond to the dynamics of your playing.

■ Turning up R11 doesn't cause changes, but R7 works properly: Check D3's polarity.

■ Neither R11 nor R7 works properly: Check IC1. Check opto-isolator LED polarity (they must be installed properly). Check power supply connections.

How it Works

IC1 amplifies the audio input signal, then feeds this output to D3. This diode only passes the positive peaks of the signal, thereby turning the audio signal into a DC voltage. Capacitor C4 adds filtering to the signal to smooth the rectified audio into a DC voltage . . . its function is similar to the filter capacitor found on power supplies.

This voltage goes to two different places. One place is pad P, which can connect to the LED inside of a CLM6000 to make the photoresistor change in synchronization to your playing. The EF can drive up to four CLM-6000s with no problem, making it ideal for use with Project No. 21. The envelope-following voltage also goes through R2-R4 into OI1 and OI2. The photoresistor portions of these parts can then be used to replace variable resistors on non-envelope-controlled effects to make them envelope-controlled.

C1 protects against oscillation or excessive high-frequency response, while R7 injects a variable bias voltage into IC1 to allow for biasing the LEDs in the opto-isolators to a "just on" condition. This allows R11 to have the maximum amount of sweep range.

Figure 5-143
Artwork for the foil side of the circuit board, shown 1 to 1.

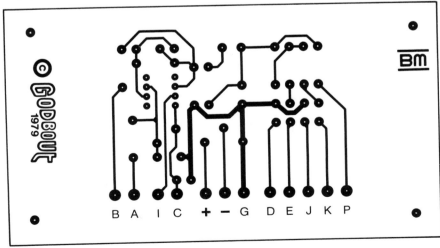

Figure 5-144
Component layout for the Envelope Follower.

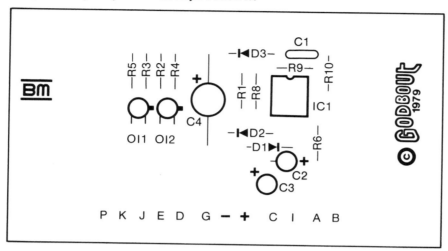

Figure 5-145
Envelope Follower schematic.

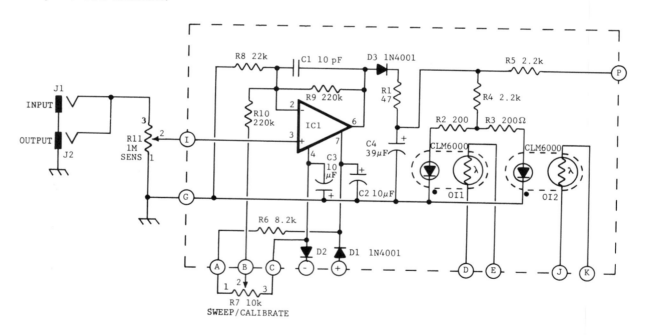

Project No. 25 PARTS LIST

Resistors (all are 1/4W, 10% tolerance, except as noted)

R1	47Ω
R2, R3	200Ω
R4, R5	2.2k
R6	8.2k
R7	10k linear taper pot—controls *sweep/calibrate*
R8	22k
R9, R10	220k (see text)
R11	1M linear or audio taper pot—controls *sensitivity*

Capacitors (rated at more than 10V for +9V operation)

C1	10pF, ceramic disc
C2, C3	10μF, electrolytic or tantalum
C4	39μF, electrolytic or tantalum (see text)

Semiconductors

IC1	LM741 or LF356 (see text)
D1-D3	IN4001 or equivalent silicon diode
OI1	CLM6000 opto-isolator (Clairex)

Mechanical Parts

J1, J2	Open circuit 1/4" mono phone jack
Misc.	Circuit board, 8-pin IC socket, knobs, wire, solder, etc.

Project No. 26

SPLUFFER

Definition: A "spluffer" is a combined dual splitter/active buffer.

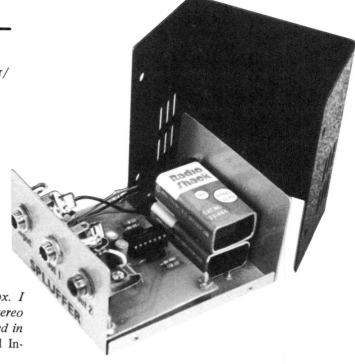

Figure 5-146
The spluffer mounted in a small metal box. I elected to switch power on and off by using stereo jacks for the input and output 1, as described in the beginning of this chapter under General Instructions.

Background

The Spluffer is not a "glamor" project; it doesn't make your axe sound like flying saucers or anything like that. However, its buffering action can clean up the sound of a guitar going through a chain of commercially available effects, and its signal-splitting capabilities can provide numerous utilitarian functions.

Features

- Operates at low or line level
- High-impedance input preserves the fidelity of instruments with high-impedance outputs
- Dual independent low-impedance outputs provide lots of drive capacity for driving effects or chains of effects
- Configurable as pedal-controlled panpot
- Low noise and distortion
- Operates from ±5 to ±18V DC
- Optional control for the two signal splits

Level of Difficulty: Beginner

Construction Tips

■ "Cx" is a 5pF ceramic disc capacitor, or a homemade "gimmick" capacitor (see Figure 5-147). To make this part yourself, cut two pieces of solid (not stranded) no. 22 or no. 20 gauge wire about 2.5 cm (1") long; then cut about 60 mm (1/4") of insulation off *one* end of *each* piece. Twist the *unstripped* ends of the two wires together tightly, and keep twisting until you reach the two stripped ends; then solder the two stripped ends into the circuit board, just like a normal capacitor.

■ Keep any cords going between your instrument and J1 as short as possible with a high-impedance-output instrument (such as guitar). All cords have a certain tendency to diminish the high-frequency response of a guitar's signal (some more than others); using the shortest possible length minimizes this problem.

■ The way you hook up pads A-F will vary, depending upon which spluffer function you wish to implement. Read the next section over carefully *before* starting construction to get an idea of the various possibilities.

Figure 5-147

Here's what the gimmick capacitor should look like. This part must comprise two separate pieces of wire, and these two pieces should not be shorted out at any point along their length.

Using the Spluffer

■ As a buffer for guitar: See Figure 5-148. Some amplifier or effects inputs can load down the output of the guitar, reducing the output level and degrading the frequency response. A buffer such as this circuit places a very light load on the guitar, while simultaneously providing a more powerful drive capability than a standard guitar pickup to subsequent boxes. Note that buffering does not necessarily provide more volume; rather, it's designed to provide better fidelity.

Figure 5-148

The Spluffer as buffer. Power supply and ground connections are omitted for clarity; ignore pads A, B, D, E, and F.

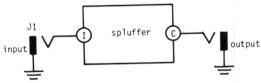

■ As an active splitter to feed two amps, two tape channels, or two whatevers from your instrument; Add another output jack to pad F as shown in Figure 5-149. Both outputs are completely independent of each other. You can think of this configuration as a "super Y cord" where plugging something into the output splits the signal into two different paths; for example, one splitter output could feed an amp, while the other output provides a direct feed to a recording studio console or PA mixer. With bass, an excellent splitter application is to feed one output through a chain of effects with the other split going directly into an amp (see Figure 5-150). This way the bass player can add effects to the bass sound without losing any of the essential bass "bottom" sound. Varying the gain of the amp channels varies the balance between these two sounds, or with a single channel amp you could blend both outputs into a mixer (Project No. 18) and then feed the mixer output to the amp.

Figure 5-149

The Spluffer transformed into an active splitter. Power and ground connections are omitted for clarity; ignore pads A, B, E, and D.

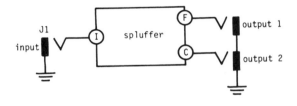

Figure 5-150

In this application, a bass feeds the spluffer; one output goes through a line of effects, the other directly to the amp. Varying the amp's channel level controls varies the balance between the two channels.

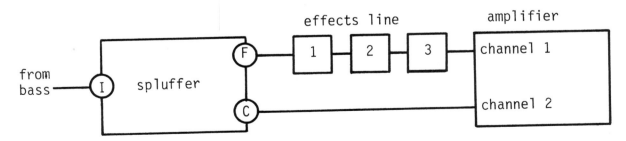

Figure 5-151

Footswitch selecting the spluffer outputs. S1 and S2 mount in a remote footswitch box; the ground lead that works back to pad G on the board should connect to the footswitch box, thereby shielding the switch cases. The input and power connections are omitted for clarity.

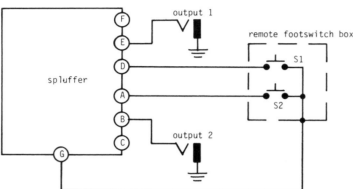

Specifications

Current consumption: ±7mA
Maximum available output: 10V pk-pk
Maximum input before clipping: 10V pk-pk
Frequency response: ±0.5dB, 40Hz-20kHz
Signal-to-noise ratio (worst case):
    -75dB below 0dB
    -90dB below maximum output

■ As a footswitch-controlled signal splitter: Make the changes shown in Figure 5-151; this time, pads F and C go unused. Note, however, that the wires going from pads A and D to the switches *must* be shielded cable or you will probably pick up hum. One footswitch controls one channel, while the other footswitch controls the other channel. This is useful for those of you with two-channel amps, as you can set up one channel for one type of sound and the other channel for a completely different sound. You can then use the footswitches to select one, the other, or both channels.

■ As a panpot: Follow the connection diagram shown in Figure 5-152. Use a 10k dual-ganged *linear* taper pot. Resistors R3 and R4 change the pot's taper to optimize the panning effect. If you mount the 10k pot in a footpedal you can have pedal-controlled panning, but as with the footswitch-controlled setup mentioned above, the wires going to this pot must be shielded or you'll pick up hum.

Figure 5-152

How to configure the Spluffer as a panpot. Note that the dual-ganged pot terminals are wired in reverse, so that when one is up full, the other is all the way down. Remember that the various ground leads end up connecting to pad G on the circuit board (or that all ground leads, including pad G, connect to a common ground lug that bolts to whatever metal enclosure houses the spluffer). Input, ground, and power supply connections are omitted for clarity and hook up as shown in the schematic.

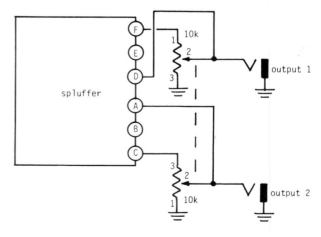

Modifications

■ If you intend to use the spluffer with guitar only, you may lower the noise level even further by replacing C1 with a wire jumper.

■ Cx provides protection against radio interference. It may be eliminated for better high-frequency response, however, this makes no *audible* difference.

182

Figure 5-153
Artwork for the foil side of the circuit board,
shown 1 to 1.

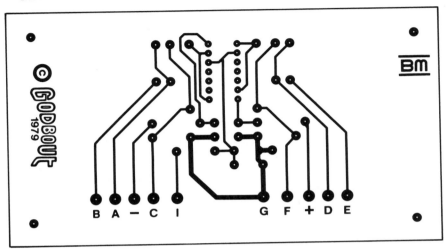

How it Works

IC1A and IC1B are set up as unity-gain buffer stages (unity gain means they neither amplify nor attenuate the signal). Each output goes through a coupling cap and tie-down resistor (R5 and R6) to minimize "popping" when plugging into the spluffer or when doing footswitching. Diodes D1 and D2 add polarity reversal protection; C4 and C5 add decoupling.

Figure 5-154
Component layout for the spluffer.

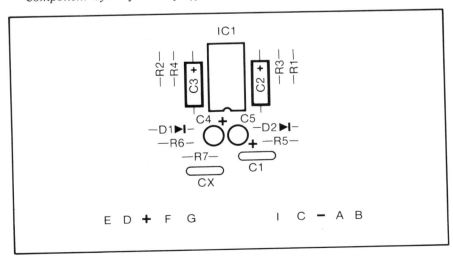

Figure 5-155
Spluffer schematic.

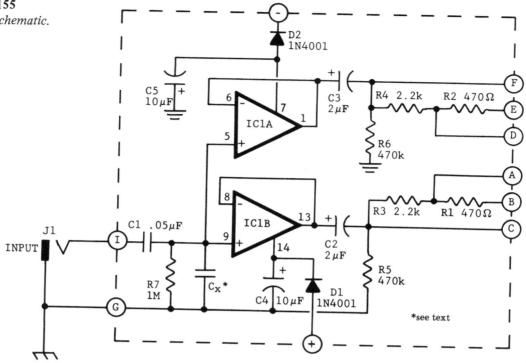

Project No. 26 PARTS LIST

Resistors (all are 1/4W, 10% tolerance, except as noted)

R1, R2	470Ω
R3, R4	2.2k
R5, R6	470k
R7	1M

Capacitors (rated at more than 10V for ±9V, more than 15V for ±15V)

Cx	5pF, ceramic disc or "gimmick" capacitor (see text)
C1	0.05μF (mylar preferred, disc acceptable)
C2, C3	2μF, electrolytic or tantalum
C4, C5	10μF, electrolytic or tantalum

Semiconductors

IC1	RC4739 or XR4739 dual low-noise op amp
D1, D2	IN4001 or equivalent silicon diode

Mechanical Parts

J1	Open circuit 1/4" mono phone jack
Misc.	Circuit board, 14-pin IC socket, solder, wire, etc.

Optional Parts (depend on application; see text)

10k dual-ganged linear taper pot—controls *panning*
(2) SPST footswitches—control *channel in/out switching*
(2) Open circuit 1/4" mono phone jacks for dual outputs

Figure 5-156
The noise gate mounted in a Vector-Pak module.

NOISE GATE

Definition: Whenever a musical signal goes through an effect, it tends to mask any system noise; the noise becomes noticeable only when the musician is <u>not</u> playing. A noise gate squelches the audio line whenever there is no musical signal present, thereby eliminating residual noise.

Figure 5-157
Block diagram of the noise gate.

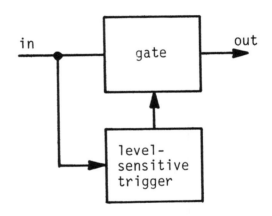

Figure 5-158
The left drawing shows the input to the noise gate; note that the noise gate threshold is set just above the noise level. The drawing on the right shows the noise gate output; anything below the threshold is deleted, including the noise.

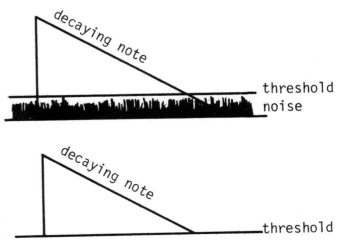

Background

A noise gate can—and cannot—do certain things. The noise gate is not a panacea for noise problems, and is not a noise reduction system like the dbx or Dolby systems. Paradoxically, it is most effective with signals that don't contain a lot of noise; in other words, a noise gate is excellent for making a reasonably quiet signal into a noiseless signal, but it cannot take an extremely *noisy signal and clean it up without also altering the sound you want to hear along with the noise.*

Basically, the noise gate is an audio "gate" controlled by level-sensitive trigger circuitry (see Figure 5-157). This gate has two states: on *and* off. *Normally, the gate is* off *or* closed. *This means that any noise contributed by previous stages is simply cut off from the audio signal, as if there was a disconnected switch in the signal path right where the noise gate resides. However, whenever a signal occurs at the input of the gate that exceeds the level specified by the threshold control, then the gate opens and lets the signal through.*

Figure 5-158 shows how the noise gate processes a signal, such as a decaying guitar or piano note, that also includes a certain amount of noise. By setting the threshold level just above *the noise level, then the gate only opens when the input signal (plus noise) exceeds this level. So, when you're* not *playing, the noise remains below the threshold level and keeps the gate closed. This prevents the noise from making it through the noise gate, and gives us a mercifully quiet sound.*

However, there are some limitations. The more noise a signal contains, the higher you'll have to set the threshold control—and the more signal you'll remove along with the noise. Another problem is that not all instruments have a nice, smooth, predictable decay curve. As a result, towards the end of a note the signal level may dip below the threshold (closing the gate), then rise above the threshold again (opening the gate), and finally fall back below the threshold again. This produces a "chattering" effect that is not very pleasant or musical. As I said at the beginning, the noise gate is not a panacea; but it can be tremendously helpful . . . which you'll find out for yourself should you build one.

Features

- Works with line-level signals and some low-level signals
- Operates from ±9 to ±15V DC
- Variable reduction
- External triggering option for special effects and synchronization
- Fast attack, slow decay
- Variable sensitivity
- Excellent noise and distortion characteristics

Level of Difficulty: Advanced

Construction Tips

- This is another project that uses the CLM6000 opto-isolator, so make sure you read the cautions at the beginning of this chapter on how to handle the part properly.

- The transistors are heat sensitive (solder quickly), and must be oriented correctly for the project to work. Identify the letters "E," "B," and "C" embossed or printed on the transistor's case, and match them up with the letters shown on the parts layout designation.

- Shield the wires going to pad M, J2, pad T, and pad K.

- Capacitor Cx is a gimmick capacitor, fabricated in exactly the same manner as the gimmick capacitor described in Project No. 26. If you don't want to use a gimmick capacitor, then use a standard 5pF disc ceramic as a substitute. The only difference will be a slight lack of sensitivity of the noise gate trigger at high frequencies (i.e., 10-20kHz). For all practical purposes this lack of sensitivity may be ignored, since very few sounds contain a lot of energy in the 10 to 20kHz range.

Using the Noise Gate

As usual, plug in your inputs and outputs. I wouldn't advise plugging a low-level instrument directly into the noise gate; that's not really what it's intended for. In most applications, the noise gate should be preceded by another effect, tape recorder output, echo unit output, or the like.

- Start off with S3 (the reduction switch) in position 1, R16 fully counterclockwise, and S1 on *internal*. With the controls set in this manner, you should hear your signal as if the noise gate wasn't in the circuit at all.

- Change S3 to position 5 while *not* playing your instrument. One of two things will happen: Either the noise will drop out, which means that the noise is less than the minimum possible threshold R16 is capable of resolving. More likely, the signal will still sound as if the noise gate is not affecting the circuit. If you still hear the noise, slowly advance R16 until the noise *just* drops out.

- Next, play a note on your instrument. When you play, the gate should open and let your instrument's sound through; when you stop playing, the noise should drop out. If the noise doesn't drop out when you stop playing, advance R16 just a little bit further.

- S3 determines how much the noise is reduced compared to the signal. Position 6 gives the maximum amount of reduction; with this setting, the noise gate acts almost like an on-off switch. In position 5, the noise is reduced by a smaller amount; each successive switch position gives a little less reduction, until position 1 bypasses the effect of the noise gate. The reason for varying the amount of reduction is that the act of gating a signal on and off imparts a certain degree of unnaturalness to the sound. By giving the option to gate the signal from on to "slightly" off or "mostly" off, the gating action sounds less severe.

- S1 allows the noise gate to be used for special effects, and the results can be quite dramatic. By switching S1 to the *external* position, the gating action is no longer controlled by the input signal, but by whatever input is plugged into J2. Here's a patch that demonstrates an application of this switch: Plug the output of an automatic electronic rhythm machine (electronic drum set) into J2. Now, plug an instrument (guitar, piano, whatever) into J1 and fool around with R16. At some setting of this control, you'll find that the gate opens and closes in precise synchronization with the drum unit. With S3 in position 6, the instrument will come through only when the drum unit hits a "drum." Lesser amounts of reduction will allow the instrument sound to leak through between drumbeats.

- Another special effect, this time *not* using the external triggering capability, again involves the use of percussive instruments (like drums). When miking drums, you can pass the drum output through a noise gate and intentionally set the threshold to an unrealistically high level. This will remove much of the drum's decay, giving a "clipped" sound that will also have no apparent leakage from any of the other drums. Setting a very high threshold level with guitar will turn the guitar into a much more percussive instrument by cutting the sustain short; in fact, just about any instrument can be made more percussive through proper application of the noise gate.

Modifications

■ Since the noise gate may end up being used with commercially available effects, some of which may need to feed a device with a high input impedance, I've deliberately made the input impedance of the noise gate rather high. If you're going to be gating the output of one of the effects presented in the book, you can change R15 to 10k and C1 to 2µF for *slightly* lower noise.

■ If the idea of a noise reduction switch seems too complex, you can replace it with a noise reduction control as shown in Figure 5-159. I'd recommend using a pot with an on-off switch so that you can disconnect the pot from the circuit when the absolute maximum amount of reduction is desired.

■ For details on turning the noise gate into a pseudo voltage-controlled amplifier, refer to Project No. 25.

Figure 5-159
Replacing S3 with a 500k pot. The switch can mount on the back of the pot, so that turning off the switch gives the maximum amount of reduction. Ignore pads C - F when implementing this modification.

In Case of Difficulty

■ If the noise gate doesn't function properly, first check that all the controls are properly set.

■ If the noise gate neither opens nor closes correctly, look for troubles with IC2, Q1, Q2, and the CLM6000.

Specifications

Current consumption: ±10mA
Frequency response: ±0.5dB, 40Hz - 20kHz
Maximum input before clipping: 10V pk-pk
Threshold sensitivity, R16 at minimum:
   1kHz: 12mV pk-pk
   10kHz: 40mV pk-pk
   20kHz: 60mV pk-pk
Threshold sensitivity, R16 at maximum:
   3V pk-pk at any frequency

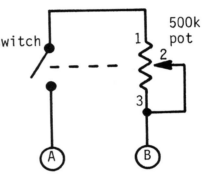

How it Works

IC1A buffers the input, and the output of this buffer splits into two paths. One path passes through the CLM6000, which is the actual element used to "gate" the signal. When the gate is open, the signal ends up appearing at the output of IC1B, and passing through to the output via C5.

The circuitry that controls the CLM6000 is rather involved, but also rather interesting. The second signal split coming from the buffer we referred to above goes to comparator IC2, which is hooked up in a manner similar to the ultra-fuzz (Project No. 6). When the threshold set by R16 is exceeded, IC2 turns whatever signal appears at its input into square waves. Q1 generates a replica of the comparator output square wave at its emitter, while the collector produces the same signal—but reversed in phase by 180 degrees. Both square waves are then coupled through C2 and C3, and have their negative portions cut off by diodes D3 and D4. These positive square waves are then summed via R10 and R11, and turn on Q2. This pulls current through the CLM6000, thus closing the gate.

When the signal appearing at the comparator drops below the threshold level set by R16, the output of the comparator reverts to a steady-state DC voltage instead of a square wave. Under these conditions, C2 and C3 block any DC voltage from reaching Q2, which turns off the transistor and therefore closes the gate. Figure 5-160 shows the waveforms at various points throughout the circuit to help you visualize how this triggering method works.

Figure 5-160
Waveforms at various points of the noise gate.

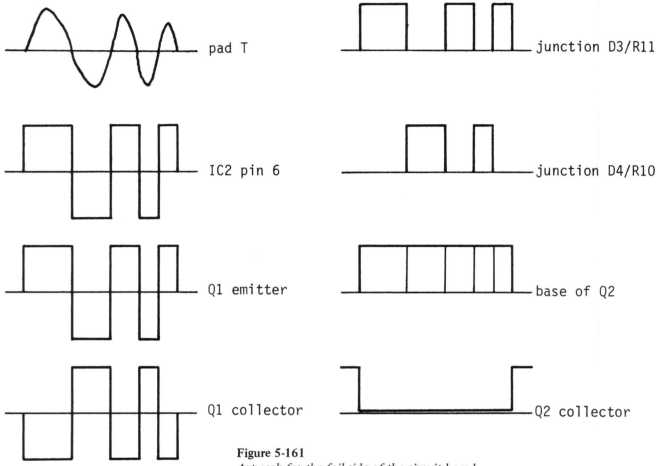

pad T

IC2 pin 6

Q1 emitter

Q1 collector

junction D3/R11

junction D4/R10

base of Q2

Q2 collector

Figure 5-161
*Artwork for the foil side of the circuit board,
shown 1 to 1.*

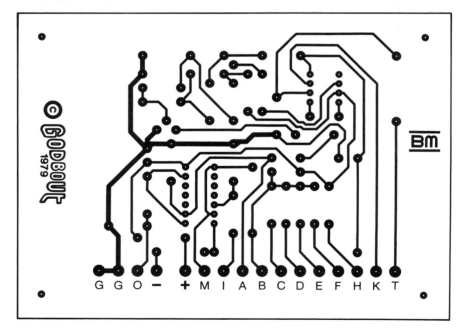

Figure 5-162
Component layout for the noise gate.

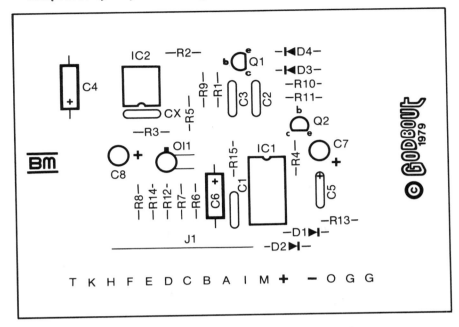

Figure 5-163
Noise gate schematic.

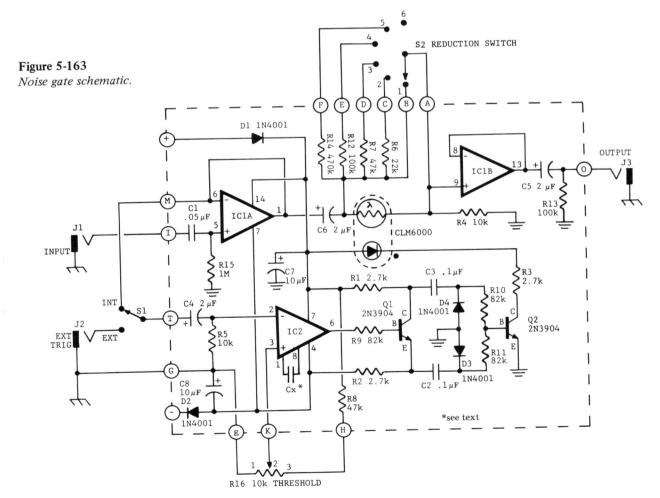

Project No. 27 PARTS LIST

Resistors (all are 1/4W, 10% tolerance, except as noted)

R1-R3	2.7k
R4, R5	10k
R6	22k
R7, R8	47k
R9-R11	82k
R12, R13	100k
R14	470k
R15	1M
R16	10k linear taper pot—controls *threshold*

Capacitors (rated at more than 10V for ±9V, more than 15V for ±15)

C1	0.05μF (mylar preferred, disc acceptable)
C2, C3	0.1μF (mylar preferred, disc acceptable)
C4-C6	2μF, electrolytic or tantalum
C7, C8	10μF, electrolytic or tantalum
Cx	"Gimmick" capacitor (see text)

Semiconductors

D1-D4	IN4001 or equivalent silicon diode
IC1	RC4739 or XR4739 dual low-noise op amp
IC2	LM301, LM201, or LM748 op amp
OI1	CLM6000 opto-isolator (Clairex)
Q1, Q2	2N3904 or equivalent general-purpose NPN transistor

Mechanical Parts

J1-J3	Open circuit 1/4" mono phone jack
S1	SPDT toggle switch—selects *internal* or *external* triggering
S2	SP6T rotary switch—selects *reduction* (see text)
Misc.	Circuit board, 14-pin IC socket, 8-pin socket, wire, solder, knobs, enclosure, etc.

Chapter Six

Now that you've built all these goodies, here's how to use them to maximum advantage.

Introduction

When effects were first introduced, most musicians had only one or two boxes—usually a fuzz box of some kind and a wa-wa pedal. Times have certainly changed; you now see stage setups that have literally dozens of effects. However, expanding the number of effects in a system has not occurred without some problems—noise, frequent battery replacement, loss of sound when many effects are used, and the like.

As a result, the most logical way to treat effects is to package them into a well-integrated, flexible packaging scheme which is often referred to as a "pedalboard" (whether or not foot pedals are actually present). This means that effects can be run from a common power supply, saving batteries; long patch cords can be eliminated, improving the sound; and different switching or convenience features can be added to suit the needs of individual musicians.

Again, though, there is a snag. As of this writing, no standardization exists for signal-processing devices. Some work on low levels, some on line levels; there are many different power supply voltages in use; some devices load down instruments such as guitar; and so on. As a result, many pedalboard setups still don't perform as well as hoped.

But, help is on the way: All of the signal-processing devices in this book have been specifically designed to work together in a harmonious and compatible way—without creating noise, loss, or similar problems. This makes them eminently suited for multiple effects systems, as well as for stand-alone use. Since many readers will doubtless want to put together effects systems, this chapter presents information on different ways of combining effects, technical and packaging considerations, and some typical applications.

The Different Ways of Connecting Effects

Figure 6-1 shows a typical *series* connection of effects.

Figure 6-1

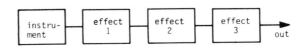

Note that the instrument plugs into the input of effect 1; effect 1's output plugs into effect 2's input; effect 2's output plugs into effect 3's input; and effect 3's output goes to an amplifier. You could easily expand the number of effects so that you had, say, 9 or 10 effects in a series.

Most pedalboards use series connections of effects. However, you may also connect effects in *parallel* (see Figure 6-2). Here we split the instrument signal three

Figure 6-2

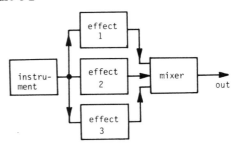

different ways—into the inputs of effects 1, 2, and 3. We then mix the outputs of the three effects together, giving us the paralleled sound of the three effects. This connection is a little more complex than series connections, because we need an additional output mixer. Nonetheless, adding the mixer is a small price to pay for the increase in sonic flexibility.

Another way to connect effects together is in *series/parallel*. Figure 6-3 shows one example, where we have several series chains of effects connected in parallel with each other. Figure 6-4 shows a more complex arrangement, but one which is still a variation on basic series and parallel connections. A series effect splits into a number of parellel effects, whose outputs are mixed together; the mixer output then goes through another series effect.

As you can imagine, these various combinational possibilities represent an almost unlimited way of connecting effects together for a customized sound. In fact, maybe the number of possibilities is just too great, because people are often confused about how to hook up their effects for best results. Should a compressor go before, after, or in parallel with a fuzz? Should a filter follow a phase shifter? Where does an envelope follower fit in the system? And so on.

Actually, there is no ideal answer. Different combinations of different units make different sounds, some of which you might like, some of which you might not like . . . and what's more, some people may not like the sounds you like, and vice-versa. So really, in the final analysis the "right" way to connect effects is purely a matter of personal preference. Experiment around; that's why these things have jacks and patch cords . . . so that you can check out different sounds. Rest assured that it's virtually impossible to damage any of these devices by plugging something in the "wrong way"; there *is* no wrong way, just ways that give less pleasing sounds to your ears.

Packaging Multiple Effects Systems

There are many possible ways to package these boxes together. You can wire two or three projects together in one box, and eliminate the input and output jacks by connecting the output of one effect directly into the input of another effect. For example, consider the fuzz super module for guitarists shown in Figure 6-5.

Figure 6-3

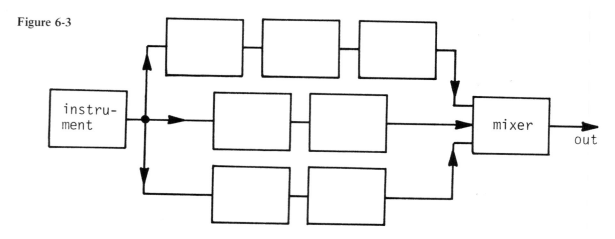

Figure 6-4

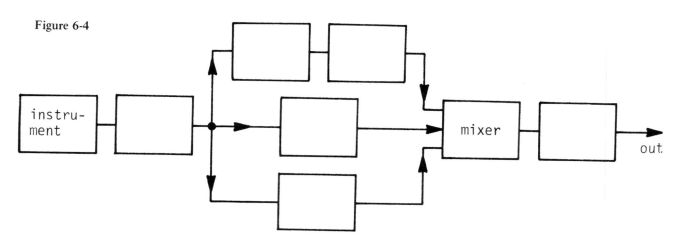

Figure 6-5

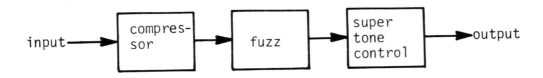

The reason for placing these effects in this particular order is as follows. The compressor increases the sustain of the instrument, which presents a more uniform signal to the fuzz, thereby creating a smoother fuzz sound. The super tone control then tailors the overall timbre. The important point is that these are no longer three separate effects; they are three stages or submodules of a single effect, which resembles a conventional fuzz but gives you much more control over the sound.

However, once you create a module like this, you eliminate the chance to experiment with the different submodules. For example, preceding the fuzz with the tone control can also give some interesting results; if you filter out the bass before going into the fuzz, then the treble strings will be fuzzed more than the bass strings.

If you want to go for maximum versatility, your best choice is to construct a *modular* system of effects. With a modular system, you have several effects with their individual input and output jacks brought out to a front panel, rear panel, or separate patch bay. Then, you assemble the sound you want by patching the various modules together with patch cords—just like putting together something with building blocks, except you're playing with audio building blocks.

If we had wired the fuzz super module we described a few sentences ago with separate input and output jacks for each module, and we wanted the order of effects to be compressor-fuzz-tone control, we'd patch the instrument into the input of the compressor, the output of the compressor to the input of the fuzz, and the output of the fuzz to the input of the tone control. Want to try putting the tone control before the fuzz? Sure . . . just change the patch cords around so that the output of the compressor feeds the input of the tone control, and the output of the tone control feeds the fuzz.

The arguments against a modular system are basically two fold: 1) You have to make patch cords, and 2) it takes time when playing live to set up different patches. In response to the first argument, I'd say that the extra versatility you gain with a modular system more than pays you back for any effort invested in making patch cords. Also, the way these effects are designed, adding patch cords does not degrade the sound unless those

patch cords are REALLY long (like 30 feet or so)—and it is highly unlikely you'd have an effects system that big!

The second argument has its merits, but really, there's no reason why you can't patch things together in a configuration specifically designed for live use. In the studio, you always have the option to rearrange the patches. We'll cover an effects system that fulfills this function towards the end of this chapter.

Of all the methods of packaging discussed in Chapter 4, I think the Vector-Pak module is probably the most rugged and versatile way to create multiple effects systems. While some compromises have to be made, I feel the benefits of using the Vector-Pak system outweigh any disadvantages. The benefits are:

1. Modules are easily removable for servicing, modification, calibration, and so on.
2. The front panel is ideally suited for placement of controls, whereas the back panel is perfect for installing patch points and power connectors.
3. The printed circuit boards are held firmly in place by card guides, and all circuitry is completely shielded.
4. Modules are standardized in terms of size and interchangeable. For example, if you come up with a better fuzz module, you can pull out the old one and try out the new one in a matter of seconds.
5. The module cage is professional-looking and rack-mountable.

The disadvantages that I've found are:

1. Cost. To package 10 modules in a Vector-Pak enclosure costs $160 as of this writing—not cheap by any standards. However, if you put each effect in a little $7 or $8 chassis you'd still be out $80, without the benefits of modular construction, card guides, rack mounting, etc. I figure the cost of the Vector-Pak box can be justified by the savings you derive by building the effects in the first place (at least, that was a good enough reason for me!).

2. Lack of panel space. Once you commit yourself to building your modules in a particular size Vector-Pak, then commit yourself to a common front panel size. I should add that other Vector-Paks are available where you can use modules with varying front panel widths, but these more flexible enclosures are also more expensive. As a result of working with fixed panel space, devices having seven knobs are expected to take up the same panel space as devices using only one or two controls. I did have some trouble trying to fit certain devices like the super tone control and phase shifter in the given panel space, but worked out a way of dealing with it (described later).

This is by no means the only way of creating an effects system; the other packaging methods described in Chapter 4 for effects are certainly applicable. But I've found that overall, the Vector-Pak is rugged, easy to use, and very flexible; at that price, it should be. Figure 6-6 shows a completed effects system mounted in a Vector-Pak module.

Figure 6-6

Distributing Power to the Modules

Using batteries with an effects system can prove to be pretty cumbersome; an AC adapter (Project No. 13) is really the only way to go.

We've already discussed how to distribute power to a number of separate effects, using stereo plugs and jacks, in the text for Project No. 13. However, with the Vector-Pak enclosure I use a somewhat different (and less expensive) way to hook up power.

First, I brought three power leads out of the back of each module (of which one connects to the circuit board's [+] pad, another to the board's [-] pad, and a third that connects to the common ground point of the effect), and soldered them to a three-wire male connector made by Molex. Incidentally, if the electronics store in your area only has four- or five-wire connectors, then just use three of the connectors and leave the other ones unused.

I then made up a power cord with multiple female connectors; the process is serialized in Figure 6-7. The (+) line from the power supply connects to the top pin of each connector, the ground connects to the middle

pin, and the (-) line connects to the bottom pin. Plugging the male connector from any module into the "power grid" connects it directly to the power supply.

Figure 6-7a
Two wire ends are twisted together, and soldered to the connector male pin.

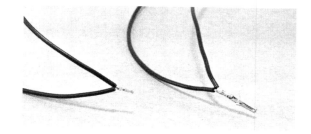

Figure 6-7b
Push the pin into the connector until it clicks firmly into place.

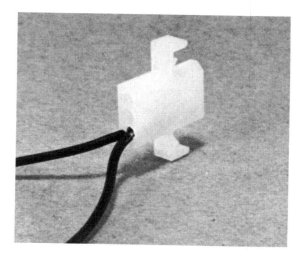

Figure 6-7c
A connector with all three power wires set in place.

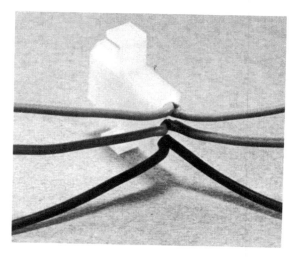

Figure 6-7d
The power grid connector mating with a module connector.

Figure 6-7e
This photo shows the back of the Vector-Pak module, with the power grid connected to all the modules. Note the extra slack in the wire to allow for easy removal and servicing of individual modules.

The easiest way to wire up this power grid is to twist two stripped wire ends together and solder them to a female pin, then insert that pin into the nylon female connector shell. Next, twist the end of one of these wires together with another wire, solder the combined wires into another female pin, and insert that pin into the next female connector shell. Continue on in this fashion until you've wired up all the connectors required by your system. Incidentally, I'd strongly advise using three different wire colors for the three different supply lines to avoid confusion.

Another three-wire connector (or stereo plug) plugs directly into the power supply. I would not advise build-ing the power supply inside the Vector-Pak enclosure; rather, build it in a separate box. If a power supply dies, all your effects are out of commission . . . so always carry a back up supply, and make it as easy to replace as possible. (Of course, according to Murphy's Law, a power supply will only go bad on you if you *don't* have a replacement handy!).

That basically takes care of getting power to the various modules. Leave some extra wire in between connectors when soldering up the power grid line so that you can pull a module out far enough to work on it, without having to unplug any of the other power connectors from the other modules.

Impedance Matching

A lot of people complain that their pedalboards don't work right because they're having impedance matching problems with their effects, i.e., one box isn't strong enough to drive another box, or one box loads a previous effect and degrades the sound, or some similar problem.

Luckily for us, though, with any effects system based on the modules in this book you don't have to think about impedance problems at all. The output of any effect can drive the inputs of *at least* 5 (and usually 10) effects. Also, all of the effects are high impedance in/low impedance out for optimum signal transfer (you don't have to know what that means technically; in terms of performance it means that you can feed the output of any effect into the input of any other effect and everything will work out just right). Also, because you're using the total bypass switching system talked about in Project No. 11 (or the electronic version in Project No. 15), you won't notice any signal loss when all the effects are switched out. So, combine effects in any order you like —series, parallel, or series/parallel—and don't worry about a thing.

A Typical Effects System

We're now going to discuss one possible effects system in depth rather than gloss over a bunch of different versions. Hopefully by digging in as deeply as possible into one specific way of connecting effects, you'll learn enough to carry on successfully with your own experiments.

Effects Format

Figure 6-8 shows the block diagram of a multiple effects system designed more or less for guitar. I made several design decisions based on this format . . . for example, note that there are a few cases where we want to have *one* output feeding several inputs (such as the compressor output feeding both the ring modulator and mixer, or the fuzz feeding three effect inputs). This implies that each module should have a number of output jacks, all connected in parallel (see Figure 6-9), for feeding different effect inputs if desired. Since each Vector-Pak module has room for four jacks (five if you mount them closely together), there is usually room for an input jack and at least a couple of output jacks. Having these additional outputs comes in handy when experimenting with parallel connections. You could also mount three parallel jacks together in a metal box to make a *splitter* or *multiple box*.

As to the reasoning behind placing effects in this particular order, my first consideration was to have a line level system not only to keep noise to a minimum, but to also make it compatible with recording gear and synthesizers. This meant that early in the signal chain I needed something that would bring a low-level instrument (such as guitar) up to line level. As a result, the first effect is the preamp (Project No. 1) for bringing a low-level signal up to line level without changing the sound. The second effect is the compressor (Project No. 8), set to work with *low-level* signals; this effect can bring a low-level signal up to a compressed line level signal.

You might ask why not set the compressor to accept line level signals, and always leave the preamp in the signal path to drive it. Well, remember that a compressor brings up the noise of any effect preceding it. So, when I

Figure 6-8

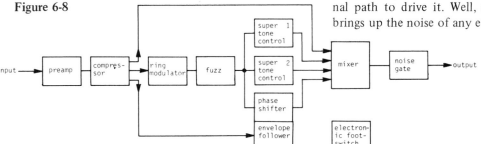

Figure 6-9   from module output

196

want a line level compressed sound, I punch in the compressor; when I want a line level unprocessed sound, I punch in the preamp . . . but I don't punch them both in at the same time except on rare occasions.

After these first two effects, all the remaining boxes are designed for line level operation. I placed the ring modulator before the fuzz because the ring modulator generates a very complex sound that makes for unusual fuzz effects when both effects are used together.

The fuzz output splits into three signal paths, two of which lead to separate tone controls (Project No. 17), while the remaining split goes to an envelope-controlled phase shifter (Projects No. 21 and No. 25). Since I generally prefer envelope control to low-frequency-oscillator control, I built the envelope follower in the same module as the phase shifter. The outputs of the three parallel effects patch into the mixer along with a straight feed from the output of the compressor. This particular combination of effects allows you a lot of control over timbre; for example, you can punch in the fuzz, use one super tone control to mix in some midrange using the bandpass level control, and use the other tone control to mix in some additional bass using the low-pass level control.

A noise gate follows the mixer to get rid of any residual noise. As it turns out, though, the noise isn't really too noticeable . . . I seldom feel the need to use the noise gate as a noise gate, but do use the external trigger feature a lot.

The final module in the system is the electronic footswitch (Project No. 15). Since I designed this system for studio use, I built the electronic footswitch into a sepa-rate module so that I could use it anywhere I wanted in the signal chain. I usually use it to control the fuzz, or to shut off one of the parallel effects lines. Had I wanted to design this system for live use, I would have included many more electronic footswitches, and built them into the modules they were controlling (there is enough room in most of the modules for two, and sometimes three, circuit boards).

Modifications to the Basic System

One of the best aspects of building your own equipment is that you can modify it to suit your exact needs (hopefully, the section on modifications included with each project will get you started in the right direction). Following is a description of the various modifications I made to make the system more suited to my particular needs, both in terms of performance and packaging.

Preamp. First, I left off the VU meter because this system almost always terminates in a tape recorder . . . . so the recorder's meter is just fine for setting levels. I also added a bypass switch between the input jack and noninverting output jack to quickly cut the preamp out of the signal path if desired. As far as patch points go, I put the input jack on the front for easy access. The back panel includes two output jacks (inverting output and noninverting output), the meter amp output, and the meter amp input (just in case I need to use the meter amp).

Compressor. The compressor is essentially unmodified. There is an input jack, along with three paralleled output jacks, on the back panel. I might add another switch to change the operation from low level to line level, just to cover all possible situations.

Tube/Ultra-Fuzz. Since I figured I wouldn't be using two fuzzes at the same time, the tube fuzz and ultra-fuzz are mounted in the same module, with a switch to select between one or the other fuzz. Figure 6-10 shows the switching schematic; the output control controls the output for both fuzzes. The bypass switch cuts whichever fuzz is selected in or out of circuit.

Figure 6-10
How to switch between the ultra-fuzz and tube sound fuzz. S1 is the bypass switch for cutting the fuzz out of the signal path; S2 selects either the tube fuzz or ultra-fuzz. Note that the two fuzzes now share a common output control.

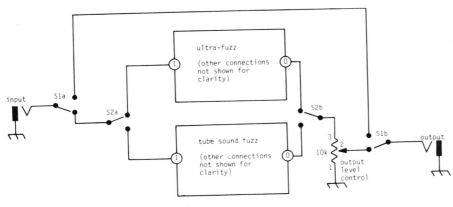

Ring modulator. The ring modulator is unmodified, with one exception: I left out the effects loop jacks to make room for three paralleled output jacks and one input jack.

Super tone control. Here's where I ran into a real problem: The Vector-Pak enclosure I chose [with 13-cm-high (5¼") panels] only has room for four knobs, but the super tone control has five controls, a switch, and in some situations a bypass switch. Here are the tradeoffs I made.

First to be eliminated was the bypass switch. Since the super tone controls are paralleled with the unprocessed signal, to hear the unprocessed signal I don't bypass the tone controls, but turn down their associated mixer input controls and turn up the straight signal's mixer control.

Next, I decided that I had to keep the three level controls and frequency control as front panel controls, so that meant the resonance control had to go. As it so happens I'm not a really big fan of high-resonance settings anyway; however, I didn't want to be limited to a single resonance setting either. So, I selected a volume control for R9 with a push-on/pull-off SPST switch mounted on the back of the pot. In one position, pad B connects directly to pad C—this gives a low-resonance sound. Adding a 47k resistor in between these points introduces a moderate amount of resonance (see Figure 6-11). For additional resonance options, you could also replace R7 and R8 with pots that have integral SPST switching and switch three different resistors in and out. Although having two resonance positions satisfies my present needs, I generally use filters for equalization (control of tone) rather than as an effect; those who like to get unusual sounds out of their filters would probably miss having a resonance control much more than I do.

On the back panel, each tone control has one input jack and three output jacks.

Figure 6-11

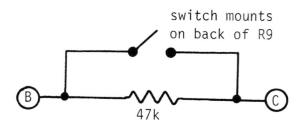

switch mounts
on back of R9

47k

Mixer. Again, an essentially unmodified module, but with only four of the eight possible inputs connected up to the mixer board. The back panel includes input jacks for the four channels plus a jack for the noninverting output.

Envelope-controlled phase shifter. This is another module that required extensive modifications to fit in the Vector-Pak enclosure. First, I didn't need the frequency of offset controls associated with the LFO, since I wasn't including the LFO. Also, I didn't need the vibrato/phase switch, since the vibrato mode is not very effective with envelope control. However, I kept the add/subtract switch and resonance controls.

I ended up mounting the sensitivity and sweep controls for the envelope follower, along with the resonance control from the phase shifter, on the module's front panel; however, there was not enough room for the phase shifter's intensity or output controls. I decided to compromise and turn these controls into trimpots, mounted inside the module itself. I set the intensity control for the most intense setting, and trimmed the output for unity gain when I toggled the bypass switch back and forth. In practice, I haven't really missed these two controls all that much; they're useful, but not mandatory in a systems context.

The rear panel has one input jack, two paralleled output jacks, and an input jack for the envelope follower. I usually patch the envelope follower input to one of the paralleled output jacks of the compressor; when the compressor is punched in, then the envelope control signal is also compressed. When the compressor is punched out of circuit and the preamp is in the signal line, then the envelope control signal is not compressed. In theory, a compressed signal feeding the envelope follower doesn't give as much control range—and this theory holds up in practice. However, since I'm not inclined towards using massive amounts of compression, the difference between the two types of envelope control is not that great, and can actually be used to advantage in some circumstances. This goes to show once more that practice is not always predictable from theory; you must check it out yourself by experimentation to know for sure.

Electronic Footswitch. This module was modified in a few ways. For one, I added a panel bypass switch in parallel with the footswitch to allow for panel or foot control of the module. I also added a parallel set of jacks on the back panel for the input, effect input, output, and effect output jacks. When using the electronic footswitch with some other module in the effects system, I do all my patching on the back panel. When using the electronic footswitch with outboard modules, or to control something that's separate from this particular effects system. I generally patch into the front set of jacks because it's more convenient.

Noise gate. Unmodified from the text. The back panel includes an input jack, two paralleled output jacks, and the external trigger jack.

198

The point of mentioning these various modifications is not so that you can precisely duplicate my particular effects system (although of course you're invited to do so if it fits your needs); rather, the point is that adding a few simple modifications can help create a personalized and unique setup.

Additional Effects Systems

Now that we've covered one system for guitar in detail, here are some other possible ways to connect effects together for a variety of instruments. Again, remember these are merely suggestions and *not* rules; for example, although one system description notes that phase shifters connected in series sound good with string synthesizers, the same patch also sounds just great with guitars. So why didn't I include two phase shifters in the guitar system? Well, at some point you've got to draw the line . . . but that's the beauty of a modular system: when I do need another phase shifter, I can patch it into the effects system on a temporary basis. I can't emphasize enough that only *you* can create a system that's perfect for you, and that only occurs through a process of experimentation and through careful analysis of your needs.

Effects System for Microphones (Figure 6-12). This system is designed specifically for sophisticated tone con-

trol. A preamp brings the mic output up to line level; the compressor smooths out loud volume peaks and produces a more consistent sound. The compressor output splits into two super tone controls and an envelope-controlled phase shifter. For the least gimmicky results, use subtle envelope control on the phase shifter and mix it in lower than the the outputs of the two filters. An additional feed from the compressor output could also terminate in the mixer so that you can mix in unprocessed line-level sound, along with the various processed sounds. Finally, a noise gate mutes the microphone when you're not singing to give a cleaner sound.

Effects System for Miked Drums or Electronic Drum Sets (Figure 6-13). In many cases you'll need a preamp to boost the microphone or electronic drum output up to line level. The preamp output splits into the ring modulator (this module adds complex harmonics that sound particularly good with drums), an envelope-follower-controlled super tone control (adds nice filtering effects that are synchronized to the drums), and a straight path for feeding unprocessed sound into the mixer. The mixer feeds an envelope-controlled phase shifter; the envelope follower input taps off the preamp output. The phase shifter can also sound good when added in parallel with the ring modulator and super tone control.

Figure 6-12

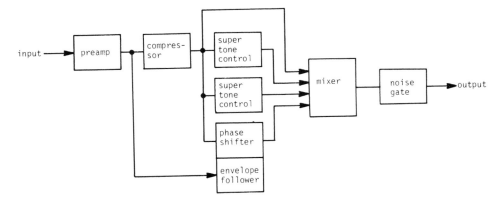

Figure 6-13

Low-Level Effects System for Guitar (Figure 6-14). Remember to modify the compressor, tube fuzz, and phase shifter for low-level operation if you want to use this set-up. The compressor adds sustain to the guitar; the fuzz adds a raunchy, distorted sound; the phase shifter adds ambiance effects; and the super tone control allows precise timbral adjustments.

Two Effects Systems for Combo Organ/String Synthesizer (Figure 6-15 and 6-16). In the first system, a preamp brings the instrument up to line level if necessary, and feeds two series/parallel chains; the two paralleled tone controls allow you to adjust the tone with great precision, and the two paralleled phase shifters give a more "diffused" phasing effect than a single phase shifter.

The second system is similar, but mixes the outputs of the super tone controls together. We also have a straight (unprocessed) line going into the mixer. The mixer feeds two phase shifters connected in series, which gives a particularly nice sound—phase shifters seem to like series and parallel connections. Since we've put a few noisy effects in this system, an optional noise gate can help keep things quiet when you aren't playing.

Effects System for Electric Pianos (Figure 6-17). Again, a preamp brings the piano output up to line level; it may not be required with some of the newer electronic pianos that deliver line-level outputs. The preamp feeds a ring modulator, which adds unusual overtones to the piano sound. Due to the percussive nature of an electronic piano, envelope control is a very appropriate way to control any subsequent effects; in this case, we've shown an envelope-follower-controlled super tone control. The phase shifter can be either envelope controlled, or synchronized to its own built-in low-frequency oscillator. Adding an additional phase shifter, again either LFO or envelope controlled, after the first phase shifter creates a more complex sound that is very pleasing.

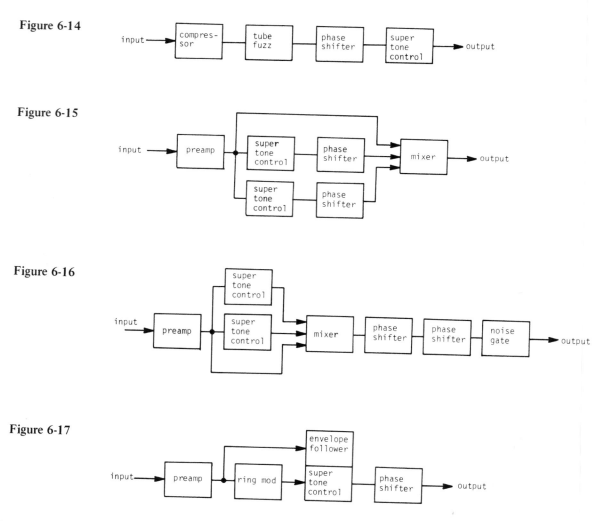

Figure 6-14

Figure 6-15

Figure 6-16

Figure 6-17

Chapter Seven

At some point, something you build isn't going to work right. This chapter is designed to help you get it working.

At some point, something that you assemble won't work. Although this may seem like a problem (and it is), in finding the solution your knowledge of electronics will grow considerably. Don't get discouraged; perseverance furthers, as they say.

Troubleshooting is a combination of logic, intuition, and the process of elimination. You go from the most probable cause of difficulty to the least probable, and if you're inexperienced, this can take a while. Experience is the key to fast repairs, but using your knowledge is the key to the solution. Two ground rules I should mention: First, go over things with a friend, if possible. Not only are two heads better than one, but frequently you can acquire a mental block about an error that someone not intimately involved with the project can immediately recognize. Second, if you're getting tired or frustrated, *stop*. Coming back with a refreshed outlook may solve a problem in minutes, whereas hours of frustration actually leads you further away from the answer. Take it from me—don't work on something if the vibes aren't right. Go into it like the educational puzzle it really is.

Luckily, there are a batch of tools to help with the job, from voltmeters to complex oscilloscopes which actually allow you to "see" the circuit action, like a TV screen. But the most useful tools are your brain and your senses.

Your eyes come first. The initial step in troubleshooting occurs *before* you try anything out, by making a thorough visual examination of the completed project. Trace all the wiring against the schematic, checking the solder connections as you go along. Make sure you didn't leave any wires out, or have any unaccounted for. On circuit boards, check for solder bridges between traces, cracks in the circuit board, or poor solder connections.

Remember, electrons aren't very big, and just a little sliver of metal in the wrong place can be a short circuit.

Check the parts, too. Are the polarized parts oriented properly? Are the values correct? One hint to keep in mind: you may have misread the resistor color code, mistaking orange for red, or white for gray. So if you have any doubt, check the resistor before wiring it into the circuit (you'll find out how later on). Have you wired the jack terminals up correctly? When you put the complete circuit board in its case, does anything short out to the chassis?

By far, the most common cause of error is human error and poor soldering techniques. Rarely can you trace a nonfunctioning circuit to a bad part. What's worse, sometimes, by overlooking a simple error, you can think there's something really wrong with a circuit and start testing the daylights out of it. Testing can cause problems, too. If a test probe from your voltmeter slips and you short something together accidentally, you have two headaches: the original one, and the malfunction you just caused trying to fix the first problem.

Watch your test procedures. Don't probe around sloppily; don't apply power more than you have to with a nonfunctioning circuit; and if you start to see smoke, a part overheating, or some other symptom of gross failure, shut the thing down immediately and scan the wiring.

Sometimes, though, even sharp eyes and a keen mind won't find the error, human or otherwise. I don't know why, but people tend to make the same mistake over and over again, and not see the mistake. Test equipment can help show up that mistake in a very obvious and readable manner, as well as give you a better understanding of the circuit's action.

The most basic piece of test equipment is the VOM,

which we discussed at length in Project No. 19. In addition to that information, there are several books on the market that explain VOM applications. For those who want to get involved with more sophisticated test equipment, the oscilloscope is the answer. You can sometimes find one used or surplus for under $50, although the multi-thousand-dollar types are a beauty to behold. The scope is the king of test equipment, and allows you to measure voltage and frequency and actually "see" the waveforms of various instruments and signals . . . as well as how a particular circuit processes these waveforms. Unfortunately, a complete explanation on the workings and applications of the oscilloscope is beyond the scope of this book; but as is the case with the VOM, there are many fine books available that give a clear idea of how to best use this instrument.

Back to test procedure. You've already checked the project over thoroughly, and applied the power, but nothing happened. Check it over again, more carefully this time. I cannot emphasize enough that baffling problems are often caused by the most obvious mistakes. Believe me, I know.

But suppose nothing obvious seems wrong. Hook up the power again, and check for abnormal warmth, or other dramatic symptoms. Nothing? Well, that's good. If there's smoke, shut things down. Now, analyze what's happening. Maybe you don't have the controls set right. For example, you may have wired up the volume control in reverse, and what you think is full volume is actually no volume. Change the controls a bit and see if that improves matters. If you hear something—anything—it means that there's a good chance it's a minor problem, like a misplaced part, or perhaps an incorrectly wired jack. If absolutely nothing happens, then the problem is major and obvious—a dead battery, a short, something big. Paradoxically, these are the easiest to fix. It's the little aberrations that drive you crazy.

If the circuit board is still nonfunctional, it's time to get out the VOM. Scrutinize the schematic. Trace IC pins back until they meet other components. Measure their voltages, and use all the logical powers you have to isolate the problem. If something seems to connect to a battery, why is it not reading? Is a short shunting the voltage to ground? Is there a component that's missing? Try to see the logic and flow of the circuit, and why there might be a problem associated with a particular pin of the IC or component.

After your measurements, you may come to the conclusion that the problem is a component. Proper procedure is to isolate the most probable cause of failure, and substitute a part *known to be good,* while checking the removed part for any abnormalities. If you pull out a capacitor and it crumbles in your hand, put a new one in and that should do it. Certain parts require specific testing procedures with a VOM, which are outlined below.

Semiconductors. This is the type of part voted "most likely to fail." Check by pulling the questionable part out of its socket and putting in one known to be good.

Resistors. These seldom, if ever, fail; and when they do, it will usually be something obvious such as the body of the resistor being cracked during insertion, or perhaps a lead being pulled out of the body. However, there have been cases where the color code on the resistor has been smeared or the colors have changed, and for these instances you'll need to check the resistance value with a VOM. Make sure you check the resistor in question *before* you solder it into the circuit, as other parts may influence its value when the resistor is soldered in place. When measuring ohms with a VOM, first switch to the desired range, then short the probes together and adjust the *zero ohms* control until the meter reads exactly 0. Then, attach probes to the resistor in question. By the way, soldering a resistor will temporarily change its value until the body of the resistor cools back to room temperature.

Disc Capacitors. Again, these need to be checked out-of-circuit. First, short out the capacitor by touching a piece of wire to both leads at the same time (this removes any charge already present in the capacitor). Next, connect the VOM leads to the cap; the meter may read nothing at all (infinite ohms), or there may be a momentary deflection. If the meter reads a low value of ohms, the capacitor is leaky; if it reads 0Ω, the capacitor is shot and should be thrown out. After any initial deflection, a capacitor should read like an open circuit.

Electrolytic Capacitors. Again, short out the capacitor first. Since big capacitors can give quite a spark when shorted, it's best to use a 100Ω resistor from the plus end to the minus end of the capacitor as a discharge path. This is also better for the capacitor. Then, touch the ohmmeter probes to the capacitor leads; the meter should swing over to the low-ohms area, then slowly work its way back to a higher and higher value.

Batteries and Power Supply Voltages. We've already covered how to test batteries in Project No. 19; and it goes without saying that if your power supply isn't working correctly, then there's no way the project is going to work properly. So before you check anything, check out the power supply voltages. By the way, if you buy a quantity of batteries, stick them in the refrigerator—it helps keep them fresh.

Diodes and LEDs. Touch one probe to one end of

the diode or LED, then reverse the probes. One of the readings should have been close to inifinite ohms, and the other one should have been relatively low (say, under 10k). If both readings are the same, the diode is no good. Figure 1-20 in Chapter 1 shows an alternate LED tester, which helps to determine which of the LED leads goes to positive and which goes to ground.

Jacks. When I first got into electronics, I had a terrible time figuring out how to identify the terminals on stereo jacks, or which solder tabs went with which contacts. A VOM solves that. Touch one probe to the solder tab, and check the two contacts with the other probe (meter set on the ohms scale). When you get a 0Ω reading (indicating *continuity*), that's the one. Look at Figure 7-1. This same technique also works for stereo plugs, which can also be confusing. Checking for continuity can also tell you which terminals of a switch connect together for different switch positions (when the switch mechanism is inside a monolithic black body, this can be good to know).

Another topic that comes under repair techniques is contact cleaner, a chemical spray that often can cure the problem of a scratchy pot. Just spray the contact cleaner in the back of the pot so it gets to the resistance element, then work the pot back and forth to spread the contact cleaner around.

One thing I didn't emphasize before is that it is possible to destroy semiconductor devices. People call this "blowing them up," but the phrase is meant metaphorically. (Once, however, I had a light dimmer hooked up incorrectly across the AC line, and the SCR [another electronic component] inside it actually split down the middle, sending both halves flying around the room with great force.) Chances are that none of the stuff in here is going to put on much of a light show if you blow it, but be careful especially with projects involving house current.

Final Comments _____

Much time and effort has been spent developing these projects, and if you build them using the indicated parts and construction techniques, you will be rewarded with a well-working unit. Probably the biggest enemy working against the successful completion of a project is not a defective part, but a human error—I can't emphasize that enough. Impatience in particular has probably sabotaged more projects than any other factor; if you rush through the wiring, don't take time to solder properly, or fail to familiarize yourself with the unit before trying to use it on stage, you are jeopardizing your odds for success. One of my fears concerning this book is that someone will build a project carelessly, and rather than not work at all, it will work in an inferior fashion—and the builder will therefore think that I don't know what I'm doing or, worse yet, lose confidence in his or her own abilities. Suffice it to say that these projects should give performance equal to, and in some cases better than, what's available commercially. So if something doesn't sound like it does on the soundsheet, check over what you've done, and reread some of the introductory material in case you've missed a possibly crucial point. There should never be a case where "the project doesn't work." Maybe an IC doesn't work, or maybe a solder connection is bad, or maybe there's a small break in a connecting wire; but the project *will work* if properly assembled. Try not to become discouraged by the process of troubleshooting, and never get down on yourself if you discover the source of the problem was some stupid mistake . . . everybody makes them.

Figure 7-1
Touch one VOM probe to A, and the other probe to terminals B and C. When the meter reads zero ohms, you've shown the continuity between the two tabs.

Chapter Eight

Ways to learn more about musical electronics.

One of the most common questions I'm asked is, "Where can I learn more about this stuff?" Unfortunately, the answer is not simple. Most of my learning came together in a haphazard way over a number of years by combining articles I read, suggestions from other electronics people, and trial and error. You'll have to follow a less than optimum path in order to get further along in the world of musical electronics; the field is new, and there isn't a lot available on the subject. Electronic music books (about synthesizers, tape manipulations, and the like) are starting to come into their own, but few books recognize the validity of combining electronic processors with traditional instruments.

This may sound like a discouraging situation, but if you take a closer look, things aren't quite as bad as they seem. For one thing, there is much material available on general electronics; it's a small step from learning about electronics to figuring out how to apply circuits to musical ends. Next, there is more literature available every day on synthesizer technology. Some of it isn't useful if you're a traditional musician, but much of it is applicable.

Finally, there will probably be a snowballing effect in regard to electronics and music. As more and more musicians find out that it's not difficult to learn the basic of electronic theory and construction, there will be more communications on the subject. Musicians will swap schematics as well as licks. By getting involved now, at the ground floor, you'll be that much ahead when it comes to making musical sense out of radically changing technology. And, more and more musicians are finding out that electronics is more accessible than they thought.

In my own experience of learning about musical electronics, I've relied on five major sources of information: people, magazines, books, libraries, and semicon-ductor manufacturers. But before we look at these sources in depth, let's consider some ways that *aren't* that great for learning how to apply electronic knowledge to music.

Don't expect to learn about musical electronics in college engineering courses. Except for a few forward-thinking schools, engineering and art courses (such as music) are segregated. To obtain a specific degree (which seems to be the reason why many people go to college), you generally undertake a fixed and formulated set of courses that lead towards that degree; unfortunately, this doesn't always contribute to a well-rounded education. I don't mean for this to sound like a general indictment against colleges; it's just that many of the skills involved in creating electronic music devices are not the skills traditionally associated with engineering. For example, when trying to decide what type of tone control *sounds* best, having a good ear will help you more than, say, knowing calculus. It has been my experience that a musician with a minimal amount of electronic knowledge can often create more useful (and musically valid) devices than someone with a Ph.D. in physics; on the other hand, the musician is probably a complete klutz when it comes to applying infrared spectrometry! While as an engineering student you may become proficient in designing hydroelectric dams, instrumentation amps, power supplies, and other circuits, little (if any) of your experience will involve hands-on, hardware-oriented practical knowledge concerning music and electronics. But interestingly, many colleges are now using this book in their music courses; so, perhaps times are changing for the better.

Also don't expect to learn musical electronics from mail-order sources. These are generally job- and career-oriented and deal with subjects like getting an FCC license, becoming a TV repairman, and fixing CB transmitters. Although some basic electricity correspondence courses may be helpful, you'll usually be better off learning from other sources.

What Does Work?

The first thing you have to recognize is that the responsibility for your education falls totally on your shoulders. There are few books and fewer authorities, and in any event we still know very little about the nature of sound and how it affects the human body and psyche. So, your education is going to have to be a do-it-yourself proposition. If you really want to learn, you need motivation, tenacity, interest, curiosity, and patience; there are no magic short cuts or formulas. It has taken me over twenty years to get where I am now, and I *still* feel that I'm just starting to get a handle on this whole subject.

Once you decide to undertake your education, you'll find that there are a number of options you can pursue. These include . . .

People

Nothing increases knowledge as fast, or inspires as thoroughly, as mutual brainpicking with similarly inclined musicians. The problem, of course, is how to find these people. One method that works is to take out a classified ad in one of the smaller electronic music publications and ask if there are any like-minded musical electronics enthusiasts in your area. Another place to find people is in schools and colleges with experimental music departments. Put your name up on a bulletin board or hang around the music classrooms. Another advantage of music schools is that their libraries often contain books and magazines about electronic music and synthesizers.

Yet another way to meet people is at conventions and trade shows. If you live near a large city, there are exhibits of hi-fi equipment from time to time, and sometimes there are audio conventions which cover audio and related fields like electronic music. One of the best ones I know about is the Audio Engineering Society (AES) convention. There you can see the latest in studio equipment, sound synthesis technology, and the like. There is an admission charge for these kinds of affairs, but it's well worth it.

There is one warning about learning from other people, though. Sometimes, you'll find that a little knowledge is a dangerous thing—and someone who really doesn't know that much about musical electronics will feel qualified to expound on it just because he or she knows how to fix toasters. Therefore, unless someone really knows their stuff, look for answers independently or get a consensus. Advice can be helpful; however, I have seen some kits that had nothing wrong with them except for a bad solder joint until an "expert" tried to troubleshoot it and made matters far worse. But if you know someone who can be a partner in learning, then you've got it made. I owe a lot to the people who were, and are, kind enough to share what they know with me.

Magazines

Virtually all industrial countries have magazines devoted to electronics hobbyists, such as *Elektor* for the United Kingdom, *Haut-Parleur* in France, and *Electronics Australia*. Many of these publications recognize that a substantial portion of their audience is interested in music, and publish musical or music-related stories and projects; you can get quite an education in electronics just by subscribing to a few of the various available periodicals. If you can't afford subscriptions, many libraries take a number of publications devoted to electronics, and some even subscribe to more esoteric journals such as *Electronotes*.

Another reason to read magazines is that they keep you posted on what's happening. For example, if some company comes up with a faster way to make printed circuit boards in the home, chances are you'll see it first in a magazine ad. By reading the ads, you can find what's available, from whom, and for how much.

Below are some of the magazines which I would recommend. A possible problem is that many of these magazines assume that you know something about electronics; as technology becomes more sophisticated, less and less editorial space is devoted to the beginner. But even if the words aren't all that clear, keep reading and they soon will be. Like learning a foreign language, the only way to learn about electronics is to immerse yourself in it.

Write to the addresses below for subscription rates, as these change often due to fluctuating paper and printing costs, and to postal rates. Final note about magazines: if you want to see more articles on electronic music and processing in the various publications, *write them* and make your wishes known. Editors do read letters and act on them. Just a few letters of approval actually stand for thousands of happy readers.

(Note: An asterisk next to the title indicates that I contribute articles on a regular or semiregular basis to the magazine.)

The Audio Amateur (P.O. Box 576, Peterborough, NH 03458). This is a magazine for the hard-core audio enthusiasts of this world. Audio people and musicians are constantly running into each other, and this is one of the meeting grounds; learn about big amps, transistors, unusual speakers, how to ground things properly, and other interesting subjects. They also have a parts company on the side which provides hard-to-find hi-fi parts. Not really for beginners, but highly recommended, and generally fun to read.

Contemporary Keyboard* (20605 Lanzaneo, Cupertino, CA 95014). *CK* is to keyboards what *Guitar Player* (see below) is to guitars; in fact, they are both published by the same company. *CK* includes a column on synthesizer technique, and occasional feature articles of interest to electronic musicians.

DB–The Sound Engineering Magazine (1120 Old Country Road, Plainview, NY 11803). Just what the title says it is. Concerns itself with mixers, studios, electronic music, microphones, and the like. A little more technical than something like *Modern Recording*, but it's aiming for a more technical audience.

Elektor (Elektor House, 10 Longport St., Cantebury CT1 1PE, Kent, United Kingdom). This magazine isn't widely distributed in the United States, which is a shame–this classy little magazine is almost all construction, and usually includes an article per issue involving musical electronics. If you're really interested in electronic construction–including "paranormal" electronic devices and games–write them and see what you can do about getting a subscription.

Elementary Electronics (380 Lexington Avenue, New York, NY 10017). A general magazine for beginner and intermediate level hobbyists. A typical issue includes articles on computers, CB, hi-fi, basic theory, and occasionally, a music project. Most of the projects are inexpensive and don't assume great amounts of prior knowledge.

Guitar Player* (20605 Lanzaneo, Cupertino, CA 95014). The People at *GP* recognize that electronics is just as much a part of music these days as strings and picks; they act accordingly by publishing feature articles on effects boxes, guitar cords, do-it-yourself projects, and the like, as well as my column on guitar-oriented electronics.

Modern Recording* (14 Vanderventer, Port Washington, NY 11050). Contains interviews, construction articles, equipment reviews, record reviews, and general information that applies to recording and music. This publication is very responsive to its readership, and manages to make some pretty complex concepts understandable to people who don't have extensive technical backgrounds.

Popular Electronics* (1 Park Avenue, New York, NY 10016). This is the world's largest circulation electronics magazine. It features a mix of construction projects, columns, and ads. It's a great place to window shop, check out prices, get addresses for catalogues, and find out what's new and what's available. There's a representative amount of musical construction projects, and occasionally you'll find feature articles on musical equipment and hi-fi. You can often get a subscription through magazine subscription clearing houses, but it's also available at newsstands and is carried by most libraries.

Radio-Electronics* (200 Park Avenue South, New York, NY 10003). This is another large circulation magazine that has been active for many years. While catering a bit more to technicians and service people, it nonetheless has published many articles oriented towards musical electronics. Again, this is an excellent place to window shop, read ads, and find parts sources. *Radio-Electronics, Popular Electronics,* and many other magazines have a reader service number plan, whereby you can circle an appropriate number on a card in the back of the magazine to receive free literature about new products.

Recording Engineer/Producer (Box 2287, Hollywood, CA 90028). This is a controlied-circulation trade magazine, meaning that it's sent free to qualified recording engineers and producers–all others pay. Although it's a specialized magazine, it does contain many articles of interest to musicians who work in recording studios. It also strikes a balance between the technical and musical side of things, a quality often lacking in publications that deal with music and technology.

73 Magazine (Peterborough, NH 03458). This is a magazine primarily for ham radio operators, who are a breed apart. However, each issue is loaded with construction articles, as well as occasional pieces on theory that are written specifically for beginner and intermediate level readers. Of course, if you're into musical technology and were to subscribe to only one magazine, this wouldn't be it; but should you want to branch out into other electronic worlds, this is a good place to look.

The following two publications are devoted *exclusively* to musical electronics. They sometimes don't come out according to schedule, and are more labors of love than moneymakers for their publishers. Nonetheless, they continue to survive and remain on the leading edge of musical technology.

Electronotes* (1 Pheasant Lane, Ithaca, NY 14850). This is the longest-running publication devoted to electronic music; many synthesizer modules that are commonplace today were first presented in the pages of this modest, but highly respected, subscriber-supported newsletter. While not totally for beginners (proficiency in math and electronics is assumed for many articles), it contains a wealth of information for the electronic music enthusiast—especially those into keyboard synthesizers.

Polyphony* (P.O. Box 20305, Oklahoma City, OK 73156). This was the first publication to treat computer-controlled synthesis in practical, understandable terms; it also runs a lot of material on home recording. The rest of the magazine covers new products and construction, and includes reviews, letters, occasional theory articles, and interviews. As the editor of *Polyphony,* I often find it possible to include articles concerning modifications to projects from this book.

Books

Books are another valuable reference source. There aren't that many books available on both music and electronics, but there are many excellent books available on the subject of general electronics. They range from beginner level to advanced, from simple project books to complete programmed-learning theory texts. Perhaps the most useful type of book is the *cookbook*, so called because it contains lots of schematics and practical information with a minimum of math and jargon. While it's impossible to list all books of interest, here are some of the "greatest hits":

IC Op Amp Cookbook (by Walter Jung; published by Howard W. Sams & Co., 4300 West 62nd St., Indianapolis, IN 46268). Everything you ever wanted to know about op amps, in a surprisingly nonintimidating format. There's also a spinoff from this book entitled *Audio Op Amp Applications,* which is a smaller version of the *Op Amp Cookbook* and contains only material pertinent to audio applications.

Active Filter Cookbook (by Don Lancaster; published by Howard W. Sams). Explains how to design active filters (with a minimum of math) using op amps. While somewhat specialized, those of you who need to learn about filters will find this book useful and interesting.

Don has also written the *CMOS Cookbook* to familiarize people with CMOS logic circuits and how to use them, as well as the *TTL Cookbook,* which performs the same function for TTL logic circuits.

Audio Cyclopedia (by Howard Tremaine; published by Howard W. Sams). Contains over 1700 pages of question-and-answer-type material on almost anything involving audio. While dated in some ways, this is nonetheless the recognized reference book for audio. The answer to anything you want is probably in here, but finding it can be quite an operation. It's good to have around and fun to browse through—if you can afford it.

Electric Guitar Amplifier Handbook (by Jack Darr; published by Howard W. Sams). While mostly oriented towards the servicing of musical instrument amplifiers, this book contains schematics of a number of guitar amps and info on the basics of amplified music systems.

Home Recording for Musicians (by Craig Anderton; published by Music Sales, 33 West 60th Street, New York, NY 10023). This book is intended to demystify the art of recording high-quality tapes at home, and is written in a style similar to that of this book (I think of it as a companion volume). The introductory sections on audio basics should be of great help to readers of this book who want to delve further into dBs, sound, and the like. There is also information on how to build an inexpensive, high-performance mixing board.

The Byte Book of Computer Music (Byte Publicatons, 70 Main Street, Peterborough, NH 03458). If you're into music and computers, this book combines selected articles from past issues of *Byte* magazine along with new material written specifically for inclusion in this book.

Radio Shack carries a number of well-written books that teach basic electronic principles. These include the *Semiconductor Applications Handbook, Understanding Solid-State Electronics, Understanding Microprocessors, Practical Electronics* (volumes 1 and 2), and several others.

For more technically minded people, Rider Books (a division of Hayden Book Co., 50 Essex St., Rochelle Park, N.J. 07662), Prentice-Hall, Inc. (Englewood Cliffs, N.J. 07632). and McGraw-Hill (1221 Avenue of the Americas, New York, NY 10020) all publish engineer-level books on various phases of electronics. By now you should be getting an idea of what's available; again, look in the ads in electronic magazines for information on what's new, and check out the library and technical book stores to find more books that will add to your knowledge.

Libraries

I can't understand why so many people overlook libraries as a source of knowledge; but now that you've been warned, you won't have to make that mistake. I can't tell you how many hours I've spent in engineering libraries located in schools I've never even attended . . . but that's another story. Anyway, libraries not only have books but magazines and a listing of periodicals, so that you can find out what's going on in the great, wide world out there. One suggestion: Suppose you and a couple of friends want to subscribe to a magazine like *Guitar Player,* but don't have the bucks. Well, if each of you contributes one-third of the subscription price and then donate that subscription to the library, not only will it arrive every month for you and your friends to look at, but it will also be there for the use of others in your community . . . and you'll be doing a good deed at the same time.

Semiconductor Manufacturers' Data Books

These are books published by semiconductor manufacturers, available both from mail-order suppliers and stores. Data books list the characteristics of different parts—how much voltage you can give them before they blow up, some representative circuits using the device, test rigs for determining optimum performance, and other data of use to engineers. These books help when you want to get into designing circuits and need to know just how much gain something can put out when running full blast, or how much power you can draw from a miniamp before it turns into charcoal.

While we're on the subject of semiconductor manufacturers, I should mention that if you have a hard time finding some of the parts in this book, you can always write to a manufacturer and ask where the nearest distributor is. For example, I specify a lot of Raytheon parts because in my opinion they're good parts, and they're readily available where I am. If you have a hard time locating a Raytheon distributor, write them and ask where you can get their parts. This applies to all manufacturers; I only chose Raytheon as an example. Below are some of the addresses of semiconductor manufacturers.

Fairchild Semiconductor, 313 Fairchild Drive, Mountain View, CA 94040
Motorola Semiconductor, Box 20912, Phoenix, AZ 85036

National Semiconductor, 2900 Semiconductor Drive, Santa Clara, CA 95051
Raytheon Semiconductor, 350 Ellis Street, Mountain View, CA 94040
RCA Solid State, Box 3200, Somerville, NJ 08876
Signetics, 811 E. Arques Avenue, Sunnyvale, CA 94086

"Hands-on" Ways to Learn Electronics

Book learning isn't all there is to knowledge; there's also the need for practical experience to which you can relate this theory. Towards this end, check out the "100-in-1" lab kits. Electronic stores such as Radio Shack often carry miniature electronic "labs" which allow you to perform around a hundred or so electronic experiments —you know, little amplifiers, wireless microphones, light bulb switches, tone makers, that sort of thing. These are aimed at high school science fair types, but are eminently suitable for anyone wanting to learn basic electronics. They cost around $20 to $50, which really isn't too bad; I learned a lot from one of these . . . it taught me more in four weeks than I learned in one year of college.

Another possibility is the "solderless breadboard," made by a number of manufacturers and available both from stores and via mail order. By getting one of these and a number of parts, you can build up circuits without soldering—thus, you can use the same parts over and over again. These solderless breadboards (also called prototype boards) have a grid of holes that connect together electrically; thus, plugging a lead from a capacitor and a lead from a resistor into adjacently connected holes hooks them together electrically to make a completed circuit. In many ways, this is the grown-up extension of the 100-in-1-type kit mentioned above. Get yourself a fistful of ICs, resistors, capacitors, a couple of batteries and jacks, some wire, and you are ready to go.

Prototype boards aren't cheap (anywhere from $5 to $80 and up), but they're worth every penny, both in terms of knowledge gained and in parts that aren't destroyed. For my personal setup, I have a couple of these prototype boards bolted on to a metal chassis, along with some extras, like a couple of power supplies, a headphone amp, signal generator, and a batch of pots and switches. I can breadboard just about anything that uses 15 ICs or less, which gives a lot of latitude. The total cost came to under $100.

Kits

If you would like a relatively painless introduction to electronics, you might want to check out some of the offerings of various kit manufacturers. There are three major kit makers: Southwest Technical Products Corporation (219 W. Rhapsody, San Antonio, TX 78216), PAIA Electronics (Box 14359, Oklahoma City, OK 73114), and Heathkit (Benton Harbor, MI 49022). SWTPC offers some musical kits, such as amplifiers, reverb units, and mixers. Their speciality is hi-fi equipment at fair prices. Though the kits aren't made for novices, if you have read this book and successfully built a project or two, you probably won't run into any problems. PAIA is a company that is highly music-oriented. They have a complete line of synthesizer module kits, many of which are applicable to guitar and other electrified instruments. Their kits are inexpensive, but still give a good amount of performance for the low price. They now offer complete instruments as well. Finally, Heathkit is the giant of the kit manufacturers. They have color TV sets, test equipment, some ultra-sophisticated projects, and some really simple stuff. One advantage to building a Heathkit is that the instructions assume you are a total beginner, and guide you every step of the way (i.e. hold this end of the soldering iron). As a result, if you want an introduction to electronics and have no one to help you, their instructions are about as complete as you're going to get. However, they don't have that many musical kits: their music line comprises organs, guitar amps, a mixer, and some accessories.

Correspondence

One subject I'd like to mention in closing is the subject of correspondence. When I write an article, I frequently get letters from people (it works, it doesn't work, design me a mixer, and so on). This is a part of the writing process that I enjoy—a chance to close the feedback loop with the people for whom these articles were intended. However, while in the past I have answered every letter that included a self-addressed, stamped envelope, my present volume of mail is making it difficult to continue this practice. So that we can keep this operation going, you're going to have to follow the rules below in order to get a response.

1. Almost half my mail asks questions already answered elsewhere in the book. Needless to say, answering these is really quite unproductive because I end up referring the writer of the letter back to the book anyway. Don't ask me where to find an RC4739 or a CLM 6000—that's what Chapter 2 is all about. Write only if you're sure the material hasn't already been covered in the book.

2. Include a *self-addressed, stamped envelope*. No exceptions. People in countries outside the U.S. who don't have access to U.S. stamps can purchase an International Reply Coupon at their local post office, providing that their country is a member of the Universal Postal Union (just about every country is).

3. Keep your questions short and to the point, and preferably typewritten for legibility. You can feel free to make comments, ramble on about yourself, your views of the world, or music—just don't let the questions pile up too high, or I won't be able to answer any of them.

4. Do not ask for custom designs, schematics, reprints of past articles I've written, how to modify or repair commercially available equipment (write the company directly), or recommendations concerning equipment. It is not possible for me to answer these types of questions.

Finally, writing me a letter is somewhat like playing a game of chance, since you never know when the payoff will occur. I've answered some letters in two days, while others have taken nine months. I try my best to be prompt in answering, but if a letter is difficult to answer or exceptionally lengthy, I throw it in a big pile of similar letters . . . eventually I get around to answering them all in a more or less random order. Those letters that are easy to deal with generally get dealt with the fastest.

I debated whether to include a section on how to correspond with me in this edition, since I'm getting a lot of mail and it does take my time away from playing music, or playing in the lab for that matter. But the fact remains that you people out there are a constant source of inspiration, ideas, suggestions, and encouragement; and I don't want to give up the process of knowing you, even if it is only through the mail. I listen very carefully to what you have to say (your letters were what told me what should be included in this updated edition, for example), and I deeply appreciate comments both pro and con. Write me c/o Music Sales, 33 West 60th Street, New York, NY 10023.

Chapter Nine   Questions and answers.

Over the years since the first edition of this book was printed, I've received many letters asking questions about the projects, about finding parts, about electronics in general, about how to find a career in musical electronics, and so on; here are answers to some of the most-asked queries.

Q. *I have a 9V battery eliminator sold by a local electronics store to power my projects. Although it works with most effects, with some of them I get really bad hum problems. What should I do?*

A. Add some additional filtering, as shown in Figure 9-1. This should reduce the hum. More capacitance will reduce the hum further, as will more resistance; but adding more resistance decreases the available voltage.

Figure 9-1

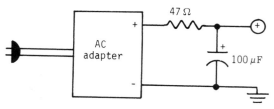

Q. *Store-bought effects cost so much more than your projects. Aren't we being ripped off?*

A. In the vast majority of cases, no. First, the manufacturer must pay labor, cover defective parts, testing, servicing, the distributor's cut, payroll taxes, advertising, business taxes, social security payments, and probably an accountant to figure out just how to pay those taxes . . . plus an occasional attorney's fee. Then the stores must add on a certain amount to cover insurance, burglar alarm systems, employees, taxes, repairs, fixtures,

and more; and if they don't make a profit in all this mess, the store will never be able to expand or buy new toys to keep up with the competition. This means that the store will eventually go down the tubes. I'm not saying this setup is good or bad; but that's the way it is. Most companies and stores are too busy worrying about survival and the competition to cook up elaborate schemes on how to rip off musicians. Besides, many of these businesses are run by musicians themselves; I think compassion is often more appropriate than criticism.

Q. *I know you've been writing about musical electronics for a number of years, but I have just gotten into the field recently and would like to find copies of some of your older articles. What should I do?*

A. Magazines often have limited numbers of back issues available; other than that, the library is an excellent source of information . . . they may even have a copying machine available.

Q. *I'm using a product that uses lots of 741s, which I notice you don't use because they tend to be noisier than some other parts. I'd like to upgrade the performance somewhat; can you recommend a replacement op amp?*

A. The TL071 from Texas Instruments is billed as a low-noise (18nV/root Hz), low-distortion (0.01% harmonic), high-slew-rate, plug-in-compensated replacement for the 741. It draws about the same or less current than a 741, so no power supply modifications should be necessary. The LF351 and LF356 from National Semiconductor are also suitable. Note, however, that in some circuits the improvement in performance will not be all that noticeable.

210

Q. *Why don't you include more noise specs for your projects? Also, I'd like to know how your stuff stacks up against professional equipment. Do your projects result in professional-quality units?*

A. You've really asked two questions, so we'll cover both. Why no noise specs, with a few exceptions? For one thing, I really don't have sophisticated enough test equipment to make definitive noise and distortion measurements; but perhaps more importantly, there is no standardized way of deriving specs for musical equipment, which makes comparisons between products produced by different manufacturers virtually meaningless. (How many times have you seen a S/N spec given as something like "-86 dB"? What is that supposed to mean . . . -86dB below the maximum available output? Or below a nominal 0-dB level? Or maybe -86 dB below the noise level produced at Grand Central Station at 5:15 P.M. on a Friday? You tell me.) So, until there is some standardized way to take measurements, I can either play the same specsmanship games as some other companies to make my stuff look great, or give what I feel are more honest specs, which, compared with some of the overinflated specs on the market, would *appear* to indicate a unit that's not all that good. At the moment, neither alternative really seems satisfactory; but I will say that I am very sensitive to even little bits of noise, and all the projects pass my personal standards for truly low noise operation.

Are these projects professional quality? In a word, yes. Many studios and musicians who could choose any available effect often opt for mine; then there are the readers who replace their commercially available equipment with my units. That should be saying something right there.

Finally, to tie the two questions together . . . specs don't guarantee a professional unit, performance does. Every project in this book has been tested and used in the studio, and hopefully represents the best compromise between high quality and reasonable cost (and available parts). At the very least, you get more than your money's worth; at the very best, you get something that's unique and offers exceptional performance. I don't write something up unless I'm satisfied with it, and as many people will tell you, I'm not easily satisfied!

Q. *How can I measure the input impedance of an effect?*

A. Here's a method that gives reasonably accurate results. You will need an oscilloscope, a signal generator with a low output impedance, a VOM or DVM, and some variable resistors (pots). Set the generator for 1kHz, and feed it into the effect while observing the output of the effect on the scope. Turn up the signal genera-

tor so that you get a readable signal amplitude, say 1V peak-to-peak. Make sure that while you're doing this you aren't overloading the effect with too strong a signal, or it may throw off your readings. Next, insert a pot (hooked up like a rheostat) between the signal generator output and effect input. Adjust the pot until the output signal is exactly *one-half* the peak-to-peak voltage of the reading taken *without* the potentiometer in circuit. Remove the pot, and measure its value with the VOM. The resistance of the pot is approximately equal to the input impedance of the device at 1kHz. At other frequencies, the reading might vary somewhat.

Q. *I'd like to mount the preamp (Project No. 1) in my guitar. How do you recommend going about this?*

A. First of all, I suggest you consult Project No. 1's section on modifications and remove any parts not pertinent to your needs. This will allow you to fit the preamp into the smallest possible space. You will also have to figure out how to put two batteries inside your guitar, and how to switch them on and off. Radio Shack carries a 1/4" phone jack (stock #274-277) with two *independent* built-in switches that close whenever you insert a plug—this is ideal for switching two batteries on and off. If space limits you to a single battery (see next question), you will have to use a pot with a switch on the back, or a separate on-off switch, in order to interrupt the battery's (+) or (-) line.

While I have installed electronic devices inside the guitars and basses of various friends, I prefer not to use active electronics in my own guitars and basses. First of all, any electronic device generates noise, so attempting to use a compressor after a guitar with a built-in preamp will produce more noise than simply compressing the original signal, and *then* amplifying it to a greater level. Since I tend to use quite a few effects and noise is cumulative, any way to gain a couple more dB of signal-to-noise ratio is welcome . . . and that rules out active guitar electronics. Additionally, the science of electronics is constantly evolving, but a good guitar is forever. As a result, I wouldn't want to commit a favorite guitar to using a particular circuit, as I will no doubt want to upgrade that circuit in the future. Finally, I don't like to replace batteries; and running power to the guitar up through the guitar cord usually requires some kind of special cord or connector, which I don't feel is a suitable alternative.

On the plus side, for players who don't use a lot of effects. a built-in preamp can provide the punch necessary to drive professional power amps, or overload regular guitar amps for a sustained, fuzzy, rock 'n' roll kind of sound. On-board preamps can also give improved fidelity, as they usually buffer the guitar from subsequent stages that can degrade the overall sound; under these conditions, the guitar will feel more responsive and sound "crisper." So while active preamps and the like can definitely be put to good use by some players, for others the best approach is a separate modular system that can be easily modified or upgraded.

Q. *Most of your projects use two batteries, but I'd like to power them from only one battery. What should I do?*

A. First, you should understand that without exception using the power supply recommended for each project will give the best results. A project powered from a single battery, for example, will not be able to give adequate *headroom* (the ability to withstand strong signals without distorting) with line-level signals; this lack of headroom also means a lowering of the signal-to-noise ratio throughout a system.

However, if you're only powering one or two effects and need to mount them in your guitar, or even if you're using one or two floor boxes and don't want to go through the hassle of building an AC adapter, there are two simple ways to derive a bipolar supply from a single 9V battery. The drawing in Figure 9-2a shows the simplest method; you should try it first, because nine times out of ten it will do the job just fine. Make sure the resistors are fairly well matched; 5% units are preferable to 10% types. Also, since each project includes on-board power supply line bypass capacitors, the capacitors shown will probably not be necessary . . . although it never hurts to add them. Figure 9-2b shows an alternate method suited to projects drawing up to about ± 10mA of current or so. Again, the resistors should be added to the circuit regardless of whether or not the individual projects have bypass capacitors. The op amp can be a simple 741 type, or half of a 4739 if you have a spare op amp section available.

I would *not* recommend trying to power the phase shifter, envelope follower, or any other unit that draws a fair amount of current with a single battery. And if you do use a single battery for powering a project, you'll need to include a separate on-off switch, since the stereo jack power "switch" (described in the first part of Chapter 5) will not work with single-battery configurations.

Q. *I'd like to build some of your projects, and sell them to friends to help finance my parts buying. Would you object to this?*

A. Well, all projects presented in this book are intended for private, noncommercial use; and while I believe that they are all original and free from patent infringement, I cannot guarantee that making these for profit might not infringe on somebody's patent somewhere of which I am unaware. While building a couple of projects on the side for friends certainly wouldn't bother me, it could bother any person who claims to own a patent on which you might be infringing. But, remember I'm no lawyer, so if you want additional information beyond the above, consult an attorney.

Q. *How many projects will the power supply handle?*

A. Lots! As stated in the specs, the supply will provide up to about ±200mA (actually, that's quite a bit on the conservative side). To determine whether you're pushing the power supply, look up the current consumption figure for each project and total them together. For example, if one project draws ±4mA, another ±10mA, and another ±20mA, then you're drawing ±34mA total from the supply—which, when subtracted from ±200mA, leaves you with ±166mA of reserve capacity.

Figure 9-2a

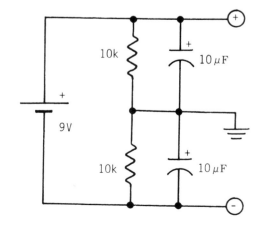

Figure 9-2b

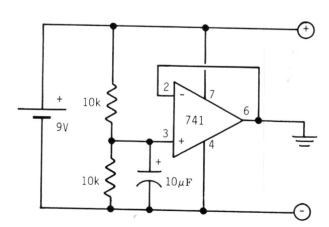

Q. *I can't find the parts used in your projects anywhere!*

A. I keep getting letters like this, but if you follow the advice presented in Chapter 2 and resign yourself to the fact that not all parts will be available locally (you may have to order some by mail), you can locate any part used in this book. I've gone out of my way not to use unusual, expensive, or limited-supply parts in any of these projects.

Q. *I'm fascinated with musical electronics, and would like to turn it into a career. However, talking with a few instructors at my school makes it sound like my chances are slim to none . . . they say I have to go to audio school, have a superb ear, gain plenty of experience, and even have good connections. Any answers?*

A. Of course, there are no universal answers; but perhaps the following four points will be helpful.

1. Decide what you want to do. It can be a list that includes 91 different things, but evolve a plan.

2. Educate yourself. Read, learn, and use real equipment in real situations. If you're serious about being a recording engineer, you'd better at least have a four-track studio in your home to try out new techniques and develop your "chops." This requires money; it is the capital required to start your business. Work two jobs, figure out a supplemental gig, take out a loan, whatever it takes as long as it's ethical—but no matter how you look at it, you're going to need some bucks to gather together the tools you're going to be working with. Really want to get into circuit design? Buy data books, parts, some breadboards, an old scope . . . and do it. Don't depend solely on academicians to educate you in a totally satisfactory manner; colleges often run on different rules from those in the real world. If you have a unique talent to offer or if you can do somebody some good, they aren't going to complain because you don't have a certain piece of paper.

3. Start at the bottom if necessary, but start. Want to be a recording engineer? Offer to work part time at ridiculously low wages as a setup, cleanup, and "gofor" person at the studio. Go out and get the coffee, or the pizza; but when you're not, observe everything like a hawk. Learn how to align the machine, how to clean it, how to be a diplomat should the musicians start arguing with each other, all that stuff. Learn about good microphone placement by watching a pro. At some point you'll become a tape operator, and then perhaps collaborate on a mix or two when your talents are needed. And then one day the regular engineer will get sick, or get offered a better paying job somewhere else, and the studio will need an engineer . . . and you're on. If they like what you do, you'll do the next session; and if

you've been observing, and educating yourself, they *will* like what you do.

Want to do design work? Start off as a product tester or quality control person. Find out what things go wrong, what doesn't work, and what does. Move your way up, and what you learn during the course of your advancement will come in handy more than once during your trip.

4. Perseverance is the key. You can't give up, even if you make mistakes, even during the year where you make $2500 and it's only your mate's part-time job that allows both of you to eat. The fates have a strange way of working, but at the least expected moment someone will call up with a job, or someone will have heard about you from someone else . . . you get the idea. .

In many respects, your teachers are right. You have to be educated, but you can educate yourself; you have to have a good ear, but good ears are made as well as born; and experience and connections don't hurt. But, *you* are the one who gathers experience by *your* actions, and those actions create connections. Have faith in yourself, be honest in your dealings with people, and rely on yourself—no one is going to do your work for you. Oh yes, and expect things to really start happening for you about ten years after you start your career in earnest. If you can't wait that long, I'd advise looking for something more secure.

Q. *Are you aware that your metric equivalence calculations aren't too accurate?*

A. Yes, but that's on purpose. Let's say you want to strip off a certain amount of insulation from a piece of wire; in fact, you decide that about a half inch is right. To convert a half inch to metric, you remember that there are 2.54 centimeters to the inch, and therefore the amount of insulation you need to remove is 1.27 cm. But in reality, there's no need to be that precise about something as trivial as removing a bit of insulation; so, I've elected to usually round things off—in this case, 1.27 cm rounds off to 1 cm.

Q. *You mention designing the various effects to a consistent set of standards. What are these standards?*

A. While I don't claim that any of these standards is perfect, I do feel that adopting the various points mentioned below insure a greater compatibility between different effects. This results in quieter operation, as well as the ability to connect the effects in numerous ways (see Chapter 6).

Operating levels. As mentioned earlier, all effects are optimized to work with line-level signals. The main reason for doing this is that there are many line-level signal sources used in music, from tape recorder inputs/outputs, to synthesizers, to pro-level mixers, to guitars with on-board electronic preamps. Besides, it is a simple matter to add a preamp or buffer stage after a stock, low-level guitar to change it into a line-level output instrument. Line levels also help to increase the signal-to-noise ratio through a system, which is a *very* important consideration. However, recognizing that many users of low-level instruments will still not want to add a preamp to their system, whenever possible I made each device easily modified for low-level operation (this generally involves changing one or two resistors).

Phase response. It is vital that the signal coming out of an effects box is *noninverted* compared to the input; otherwise, putting effects boxes in parallel can cause annoying response cancellation.

Input impedance. This required a compromise. As a general rule, high input impedances (like 1M) give the minimum loading on an instrument, but gives higher noise levels than lower input impedances (such as 10k or so). So, I settled on an input impedance of 100k or greater—not as light loading as 1M, not as quiet as 10k, but an acceptable compromise between the two extremes. Some of the projects have higher input impedances (such as the spluffer and preamp, which should generally present the minimum possible amount of loading).

Gain through the effect. I specified all devices as being able to put out more signal than is put in by at least a factor of two, with some kind of output control available to trim back to unity gain. There are times when you want a volume boost when switching an effect into the signal path; a gain of two is generally enough. Devices which convert low-level signals into high-level sig-

nals (compressors, etc.) have the capability of putting out much more signal than is put in.

Output impedance. Less than 10k (preferably 1k, or as low as possible) seemed like the best way to go. That way, with a 100k standard input impedance the output of one effect could drive the inputs of *at least* five effects paralleled together.

Q. *How did you derive the specs?*

A. I don't have the most sophisticated test bench in the world, so I tend to give very conservative specs that the various units can easily meet. For example, many effects have their maximum available output listed as 10V peak-to-peak—but in reality, it's more like 12 or 13V. Also, all specs are taken at +9V unless some other supply is indicated; with +15V, some of the specs are much better, and conversely, +5V operation degrades the performance to a certain extent. Input signals are assumed to come from a device with an output impedance of essentially 0 Ω, and output signals are assumed to feed into a device that offers essentially no loading (although in practice, output levels will remain constant even if the load is as low as a few thousand ohms).

Q. *Do you plan on putting out a book with more advanced projects like flangers, analog delay lines, and synthesizer modules?*

A. I hope to continue writing books for as long as there are people to read them and publishers to publish them; an "advanced" *Electronic Projects for Musicians* is something I'd like to do very much, as well as books on synthesizers and guitar hot-rodding.

Appendixes

About the Soundsheet

The soundsheet is a vital part of this book: it demonstrates the sounds of most of the projects so that you can decide which ones you'd like to build, and also provides a point of reference so that you can determine whether the effect you've built is functioning properly. Unfortunately, due to the time limitations of the soundsheet, I could only show a fraction of each project's capabilities; and some projects had to be left entirely. Maybe next book, we'll include an LP. . .

In any event, if you have a tape recorder I strongly suggest that you tape the soundsheet. While soundsheets are fairly sturdy, they are not as long-lasting as a conventional record; making a tape allows you to go over certain sections repeatedly if you want to catch the subtleties of a particular sound.

For best results, place a conventional 12" LP on your turntable first and then place the soundsheet on top of the LP. If the soundsheet slips as you play it, place a penny near the center of the record spindle. Usually this adds enough weight to prevent slippage; if it doesn't, add a nickel instead.

How the Soundsheet Was Recorded

In order to present the sounds of the effects as accurately as possible, all projects except No. 23 were recorded direct (no intervening microphones or amplifiers) on to tracks 1 and 3 of a TEAC A-3340S four track recorder. Tracks 2 and 4 were used for narration and synchronization purposes while recording, and were later erased. The basic studio setup is identical to the one profiled in Chapter 9 of *Home Recording for Musicians*.

To show the variety of sounds available from an effect, in many cases I repeated a rhythmic figure over and over again, with the first few bars showing one effect setting, the next few bars another effect setting, and so on. This required lots of punching in and punching out, which is impossible to do while playing. In order to overcome this problem, I developed a remote footswitch especially for this application that allowed for "no-hands" punch-ins and punch-outs. (There's an article on how to build this remote footswitch in the July 1980 issue of *Modern Recording* magazine.)

The final tape turned out to be way too long, so I got busy with a splicing block and splicing tape. Eventually the tape got whittled down to under 6 minutes; after leadering, I ended up with a 1st generation master from which the soundsheet was duplicated.

There is no narration on the tape other than an announcement of the project number before each demonstration. Following is additional information on the various sounds presented in the soundsheet.

1 **(Preamp)** The first four measures show the clean sound of the preamp; the next two measures illustrate the dirty sound of the preamp with the gain control up about halfway; and the last two measures show the dirty sound of the preamp with maximum gain.

3 **(Passive Tone Control)** Each strummed chord shows a different setting of S1. The first five sounds have S2 in the full coil setting, while the last two use the 1/2 coil setting.

6 **(Ultra Fuzz)** As mentioned in the text, this triggered fuzz fades out in a somewhat unusual way: when the signal drops below a certain point, the fuzz effect

cuts out completely. So, as you listen to this cut, pay particular attention to the way in which the fuzz decays at the end of the last note.

7 (**Bass Fuzz**) The intensity control is set about halfway, and the tone control is off.

8 (**Compressor**) This cut shows how the compressor evens out dynamic range, and was all done in "real-time" with no punching or splicing.

The first guitar figure is without compression; I then cut in the compressor using project No. 15 and played the same figure. Note that the compressor output control has been adjusted to match exactly the levels between the compressed and non-compressed sounds. Next, I switched the compressor back out again and played some harmonics. I then cut the compressor in once more, and played the same harmonics in the exact same way. Note how much louder the compressed harmonics are than the preceding non-compressed ones—this illustrates how low-level signals are brought up to maintain a uniform dynamic range. After playing the harmonics, I then strummed a chord as hard as I could. As you can hear, there is very little difference in level between the harmonics and the strummed chord. By being careful not to overcompress, the noise performance is still excellent.

9 (**Ring Modulator**) The first lead line is ring modulated sound only, while the second lead line has some straight signal mixed in with the ring modulated sound.

10 (**Dual Tone Filter**) This cut first uses the "Organtua" organ as a signal source, then segues into guitar. The first two chord figures show the unmodified organ sound. Figures 3-6 show different filtered sounds. Figure 7 adds overdrive to the filtering. The music then punches into guitar, which demonstrates three different "fuzzed" sounds using the unit's overdrive and filtering capabilities.

12 (**Guitar Rewiring**) The first two tonic-flatted 7th progressions use the bass and treble pickups in a standard parallel configuration. The next two progressions have the treble pickup out of phase; note how the sound has a more pronounced midrange and less overall level. The next two progressions have the two pickups in series. This gives a boomier sound and a great increase in level (no attempt was made to compensate for level changes while recording to give the most accurate indication of relative levels). The next two progressions also have the pickups in series, but with the treble pickup out of phase. The cut finally closes out with the same parallel pickup sound used at the beginning, in order to provide

a standard of comparison at both the beginning and end of this segment.

14 (**Treble Booster**) First you hear straight guitar, then treble boosted guitar. I used the footswitching techniques described in project No. 11 to switch the booster in and out.

17 (**Super Tone Control**) In order to show the different effects of the filter controls, I used the "Organtua" organ again as a signal source since it produces a complex signal with lots of harmonics.

This cut starts off by sweeping the frequency control from low to high in the lowpass mode with no resonance. This is followed by an identical sweep in the bandpass mode, then a sweep in the highpass mode, a sweep in the notch mode, and finally a sweep in the lowpass mode with a moderate amount of resonance. Note that there are no spaces between the sweeps, so listen carefully for the point at which each upward sweep begins.

After the organ section there are a number of different guitar sounds. These use various mixes of the lowpass, bandpass, and highpass controls; the frequency control is set to a different frequency for each sound.

21 (**Phase Shifter**) In the first four measures, the speed control is set for the slowest speed and there is no resonance. The next four measures have the same settings, but with greatly increased resonance. The next two measures show the fastest possible speed (with some resonance), while the next two measures have the same settings but with S2 in the "subtract" mode for the first time. The final strummed chord that closes out the cut shows the vibrato capability of this project.

After demonstrating various phased guitar sounds, this section closes with a brief example of phase shifted "Stringz and Thingz" string synthesizer (set for no internal modulation or flanging).

23 (**Talk Box**) I used a tiny 1W amplifier to drive the speaker, and patched a fuzz in front of the amp to give a raunchier sound.

24 (**Tube Sound Fuzz**) The first part shows how the fuzz sounds with rhythm guitar. Note that as the guitar chords are hit more and more forcefully, the distortion increases smoothly in intensity. This gives a sense of dynamics missing from most fuzzes. The second part shows how the fuzz sounds in the "lead" position; note how the plucked harmonics come out sounding sharp and defined.

25 **(Envelope Follower)** Most people know what an envelope followed filter sounds like, since there are many commercial products (Mutron III et al) using this particular effects combination. Envelope followed phase shifters are more rare, so I used the envelope follower in conjunction with project no. 21. The phasing effect follows the dynamics of the signal quite closely, and adds "motion" to the sound—especially during the rhythmically chorded part.

26 **(Spluffer)** The cut begins with the sound of a guitar being loaded down by a 10k input impedance; as you can hear, the sound is muddy and lacks any kind of presence. By cutting in the spluffer, note how the sound becomes bright and sparkling. Incidentally, the record levels were not boosted when the spluffer was added . . . it really does make that much difference! If the guitar is loaded down by a 47k or 100k input impedance, the spluffer still makes a difference although it is not quite as noticeable.

27 **(Noise Gate)** Since the sound of a noise gate gating out noise is not very interesting, I elected to show the external triggering function instead. In this instance, a "Dr. Rhythm" electronic drum set drives the external input, thereby imparting a rhythmic quality to the guitar part being fed through the noise gate circuitry.

That's it for the soundsheet; I hope you enjoy listening to it.

Glossary of Terms

Understanding Specifications

AC Volts, peak-to-peak (abbreviated V pk-pk): Expresses the strength of an audio signal. This is usually measured by observing the signal on a calibrated oscilloscope scale, and measuring the voltage difference between the most-positive and most-negative signal peaks.

AC Volts, RMS: An alternate method of measuring the strength of audio signals, particularly sine waves.

Clipping: A form of distortion where a signal cannot increase beyond a certain level, and is therefore clipped at that level.

Current consumption: Indicates the amount of energy consumed by an effect, and is expressed in either amperes or watts (or smaller units, such as milliamperes or milliwatts).

DeciBel (abbreviated dB): A unit of ratio measurement applied to the ratio of two audio signals. When referenced to AC peak-to-peak voltages, 6 dB represents a 2:1 ratio. Therefore, if a signal is 6dB *louder* than another signal, it has *twice* the peak-to-peak voltage. If it is 6dB *softer,* it has *half* the peak-to-peak voltage. If it is 12dB louder, it has four times the peak-to-peak voltage . . . 18dB, eight times the peak-to-peak voltage. 20dB represents a 10:1 change, 40dB a 100:1 change, 60dB a 1000:1 change, and 80dB a 10,000:1 change.

Frequency response: Expresses how a device responds to different audio frequencies, and the deviation that one might expect within a given range. For example, a frequency response specification of "100Hz to 20kHz, ±3dB" means that in the range of 100Hz to 20kHz, the response will deviate no more than 3dB in either direction from the mean.

Headroom: The dynamic range of a given device. A unit with 5V of headroom can handle up to a 5V pk-pk signal without adding distortion.

Impedance matching: Traditionally, for optimum power transfer the output impedance of one effect should be matched to (equal to) the input impedance of the next effect. However, with most modern circuitry voltage transfer is more important than power transfer. An industry rule of thumb is that the output impedance of a given device should be 1/10th the value of the input impedance of the device that it is feeding.

Input impedance: All effects have a certain amount of resistance from the effect input to ground. When this resistance applies to an audio signal, it is referred to as impedance; since it connects to ground, it shunts some of the audio signal away from the effect input to ground. A low input impedance shunts more signal to ground than a high input impedance, and, therefore presents more of a load to preceding stages than a high input impedance. However, high input impedances tend to be more prone to noise and hum pickup, so most audio systems only use high impedance stages where absolutely necessary. For guitarists, it is very important that the guitar feed a high impedance stage before feeding any low impedance stages, since guitar pickups are very susceptible to loading from low impedance stages.

Maximum available output: The greatest amount of signal level that a device can produce at its output, assuming that it is not being loaded by a subsequent input. Light or moderate loading will not affect the maximum available output in most cases.

Maximum input before clipping: The maximum amount of signal that can be applied to a unit before distortion occurs.

Output impedance: All effects have a finite but measurable amount of resistance in series with their outputs. A device with a low output impedance has greater drive capability than one with a high output impedance; for example, a device with a low output impedance can easily drive a subsequent device with a high input impedance, whereas a device with a high output impedance has difficulty driving a subsequent device with a low input impedance.

Phase: A non-inverting effect with respect to phase is one where a positive input signal gives a positive output signal; an inverting effect gives a negative output signal for a positive input signal.

Signal-to-noise ratio (abbreviated S/N): Expressed in dB, this measurement specifies the ratio of a signal to a given amount of noise. If the signal pk-pk voltage is 1000 times greater than the noise (a 1000:1 ratio), the signal-to-noise ratio is 60dB.

About the Illustrator

Vesta Copestakes' interest in visual art began when she was a child, and in 1970, when she met Craig Anderton, her talents turned to electronic illustrations and photography. She is currently the head of CAVE Grafix, a California ad agency, and enjoys playing the saxophone and restoring Volkswagens.